POLITICAL CRIME IN THE UNITED STATES

Analyzing Crime by and against Government

Julian B. Roebuck
Stanley C. Weeber

PRAEGER PUBLISHERS
Praeger Special Studies

New York • London • Sydney • Toronto

Library of Congress Cataloging in Publication Data

Roebuck, Julian B
    Political crime in the United States.

    Bibliography: p.
    1. Political crimes and offenses--United States.
2. Income distribution--United States. 3. Equality.
I. Weeber, Stanley C., joint author. II. Title.
HV6304.R63   364.1'3'0973   78-19463

ISBN 0-03-044241-9

PRAEGER PUBLISHERS
PRAEGER SPECIAL STUDIES
383 Madison Avenue, New York, N.Y. 10017, U.S.A.

Published in the United States of America in 1978
by Praeger Publishers,
A Division of Holt, Rinehart and Winston, CBS, Inc.

89   038   987654321

Printed in the United States of America

To our parents:
Henry Llewelyn Roebuck and Mary Elizabeth Wynn Roebuck;
Woodrow Weeber and Elizabeth Weeber.

PREFACE

In this work we divide political crime into two major categories: crimes by government against the people and crimes by the people against the government. Political crime is endemic to all modern national states and occurs whenever and wherever governments violate the law by omission or commission either to sanction those who threaten or appear to threaten the establishment (that is, the existing government and supporting economic system), or in order to maintain and enhance the existing political and economic systems. Crimes against the government by the people comprise violations designed to protest, change, or bring down the existing establishment. These crimes are regarded by political authorities as detrimental to the state, whether they violate special laws passed to suppress expressions of political dissidence, or conventional codes enforced for political reasons (Clinard and Quinney 1973, p. 154).

Unlike other criminologists (for example, Clinard and Quinney 1973; Ermann and Lundman 1978) who deal with political crime and white-collar crime, we do not separate crimes by government from crimes by corporations. Taking a critical theoretical stance, we consider government crime and corporate crime to comprise one unit of political criminal behavior because we see the government as an extension and instrument of the economic system—a system dominated by the corporate structure. Though all political crimes have an economic base, throughout this work we refer to crimes committed by government agents, capitalist agents, or by a combination of these agents as political crimes for heuristic and illustrative purposes.

Our focus is on the criminal acts of persons or groups of persons, committed during the normal course of their activities as employees or members of formal organizations, that are intended to achieve organizational goals. Persons or groups within these organizations may simultaneously enhance their personal fortunes or organizational careers through these violations, but one objective must be organizational benefit.* We focus on criminal organizational patterns rather than on individual criminality. Each type of political crime is analyzed along four interactional dimensions: action patterns, goal of the offender, legal status of the offense, and nature of the offense.

Because codified legal categories do not cover some organizational "transgressions" that we consider criminal, our definition of political crime encompasses a wider range of behaviors than that found in statute law and therefore requires special terminology. Violations of legal codes are obviously deemed to be illegal. They are "surrogate-illegal" if criminalized by the state for political reasons, and "para-legal" if defined as socially injurious acts. This extension of

---

*See Neil Shover's (1978, p. 39) definition of organizational crime.

iv

legal definitions will undoubtedly offend many, but we emphasize the point that the operational definitions of offenses and offenders used herein are not meant to impugn anyone or to replace the existing code of law. In any event, most violations defined as political crimes in the study are unlawful.

Our typology of political crime is based on a critical theoretical approach (that is, one assuming class conflict in an advanced capitalist society). The typology outlines our study of political crime by and against the government of the United States from 1960 to 1978. Our sources are as follows: the criminological literature; government documents; media accounts; autobiographical accounts; law reviews; criminal statutes; regulatory agency and commission rules; regulations and adjudications; court documents; and legal, political, and economic commentaries. Seven major types of political crime are delineated: domestic intervention by government, foreign intervention by government, intervention against government, domestic surveillance, domestic confrontation, evasion and collusion by government, and evasion and collusion against government.

We do not claim that this typology is inclusive of all forms of political crime or that it can or should be applied as a policy mechnism. All typologies are somewhat arbitrary and necessarily reflect the *a priori* views of the typologist. We do maintain that this schema incorporates the most significant organizational forms of political crime in the United States and supports the critical theory approach. Since Edwin H. Sutherland, few sociologists have been concerned with "upperworld" organizational crime (Wheeler 1976), though many have studied the "underworld" (Inciardi 1975). This book about political crime as a form of upperworld organizational crime is written as collateral reading material for criminology, deviance, and social problems courses at all academic levels. Students of political science, economics, social stratification, and history, as well as laymen interested in political economy, will find it provocative and useful.

We wish to thank Richard Quinney, Professor of Sociology at Brown University, for his seminal suggestions and early encouragement.

CONTENTS

INTRODUCTION

SELECTED REVIEW OF THE LITERATURE

This book presents a constructed typology of political crime in the United States from 1960 to 1978. Lawyers, journalists, historians, and sociologists have produced a vast literature about political crime during this period, but they offer a welter of conflicting accounts and perspectives. Moreover, the extant scholarly body of criminology literature on political crime is not ordered for systematic analysis. Criminological studies of political crimes and criminals may be roughly classified into a descending order of theoretical abstraction.

Crime in a Political Perspective.

Writers adopting this perspective claim that all crimes are a direct consequence of the structure of social, economic, and political institutions. Crime is a social injury, a violation of human rights, which exposes the contradictions in our major institutions that create in this country a "crimogenic" social structure (Quinney and Wildeman 1977; Galliher and McCartney 1977; Reasons 1974). Criminal behavior is conceptualized not simply as behavior which violates a legal norm, but as institutional behavior that results in a social injury, such as the denial of the right to racial, sexual, and economic equality. These writers call for a new criminology, a critical criminology, severed from service to the power elite. Following the Marxian conception of the state and legal system, they envision the criminal law as a creation and tool of the dominant capitalist class.

These writers, by encompassing all crime as political crime, leave little room or justification for the delineation of various units of political criminal behavior, that is, a typology. Though they focus on social injuries (such as violations of human rights, racism, sexism, and institutionalized violence) resulting from a class-dominated society, their supporting data are limited, lacking in specificity, and not well ordered.

1

Conceptual Definitions of Political Criminals and Political Crime

Writers in this vein hold that political criminals are "true believers" who define their ideologies and illegal acts as necessary incursions on the spurious established social order (Schafer 1974). Political crime is defined as politically-motivated lawbreaking behavior by altruistic individuals (Minor 1975). Austin Turk (1975) defines political criminals as individuals who have been identified by the authorities as current or potential political threats because their ideologies or acts are seen to challenge the system. Such persons become targets of political policing, and the offenses attributed to them are political crimes. Turk de-emphasizes the importance of legal nomenclature in delineating political crime, and notes that legal norms defining political offenses are exceptionally vague. Virtually any law can be used by the authorities as a basis for taking action against what is viewed as intolerable opposition. Authorities may interpret conventional crimes as political ones, and then claim that they are defending the people as a whole from persons endangering the regime (for example, arson or vandalism may be labeled sabotage). The implementation of political crime laws has one overriding objective: to neutralize or destroy intolerable opposition, and thereby to prevent any radical transformation of the structure of power. Turk suggests that criminologists should focus on the labeling and neutralizing process of political policing, rather than on attempts to classify political crimes and political criminals according to legal or objective criteria. The only common attribute of political criminals is that they are targets of political policing against whom any legal norm or agency of government may be used as a weapon.

Stephen Schafer, W. William Minor, and Turk, along with other scholars attempting to develop conceptual definitions of political criminals and political crime, have made some preliminary progress in this direction. Schafer and Minor offer objective conceptions, whereas Turk has developed a subjective process model that can be combined with a more structured paradigm for research purposes. Unfortunately, these conceptualizations are limited to crimes committed by the people against the government.

Jethro Lieberman has attempted to explain why many people find it difficult to accept the idea that those in government can violate the criminal law. He claims that lawbreaking by the government is often excused or overlooked because of a widespread view that a government cannot be expected to obey laws that are inconvenient or unsuited to the needs of the times. For instrumental reasons, government must exercise its power in the maintenance of law and order, even if certain laws are broken in the process. According to Lieberman, executive officials, prosecutors, judges, congressmen, police, and other high officials may break the law without incurring strong societal reaction. Many people interpret government officials' known criminal behaviors more leniently than the criminal behaviors of conventional offenders, such as robbery, rape, and murder (Lieberman 1972, pp. 19-23). Unfortunately, too many criminologists appear to have adopted this view of the state, and therefore they have restricted their studies to conventional crime and criminals. One notable exception to this restricted position is found in Gresham M. Sykes' text, *Criminology* (1978), which includes a chapter on political crime. Sykes offers a conceptual definition of political crime and criminals that encompasses crimes by and against government, but he fails to consider the organizational nature of crime by the people against the goverment.

Cross-Cultural Studies

This criminological literature includes comparative legal studies of political crime and political criminals. Some nations provide for these two categories in their legal codes, whereas others, like the United States, do not. Scholars have tried to explain why some nations (for example, Japan) prescribe light and honorable punishments for political offenders, while other countries (for example, the United States) do not. Throughout its history, the United States has treated "political offenders" as common criminals (Ingraham and Tokoro 1969).

This cross-cultural research has been based upon historical studies of refinements in the legal definition of political crime (Schroeder 1919; Ferrari 1920; Kirchheimer 1961). These works trace the development of political crime laws in Western Europe from the seventeenth century to the present. Cross-cultural studies are valuable for their focus upon the political offender and his treatment in different cultures. However, they avoid the issue of government crimes, and analyze political criminals and political crime in strictly legal terms.

Social Movement Studies

Writers employing this perspective hold that political crime in the United States evolves from contemporaneous social movements. Collectivized violence, anti-poverty marches, civil rights demonstrations, and antibusing demonstrations have violated a plethora of conventional criminal statutes. In the past decade, these political actions have encompassed conduct that violated health and fire ordinances, and laws proscribing assault, trespass, theft, trashing, destruction of government property, disturbing the peace, parading without a permit, vagrancy, and unlawful assembly. Many of these violations involved actions of well-organized and well-articulated social movements such as the civil rights, women's rights, gay rights, radical students' rights, antiwar, and anti-poverty movements. Recently, militant factions within some of these movements have engaged in violent activities and wholesale thefts that symbolically point out inequities in the existing political and economic order. The bombings by the Weather Underground are a case in point. Some criminologists have labeled violent conventional crimes motivated by political ideology as "social movement crimes" (Hancock and Gibbons 1975; Sykes 1972, 1974).

The concept "social movement crime" enables us to separate for study a body of political crimes and criminals heretofore treated as conventional crimes and criminals. Social movement studies also provide a target area for an analysis of organizational crimes commited against the government. On the other hand, the concept of social movement crime lacks specificity and does not cover crimes by government.

Trans-historical Analysis of Political Crime and Criminals

Historically, the process of political organization everywhere has entailed the creation of laws aimed explicitly at intolerable challengers and resisters to authority. The modern nation state has been particularly preoccupied with the deterrence, control, and punishment of individuals whose ideologies or acts challenge constituted authority. Historically, the state has treated those who appear to challenge the existing political system as political criminals. Whatever ideologies, acts, or implied acts are manifested by these challengers constitute political crime (Turk 1975).

Historical studies document the fact that political crime and criminals are not confined to the recent scene. These works deal primarily with enemies of the state who violate, threaten to violate, or appear to violate criminal laws in an attempt to change or modify the existing structure of political power. Virginia Engquist and Frances S. Coles (1970), for example, present excerpts from the prison writings of Kate Richards, Holley Cantine, and Dachine Rainer, who were pacifists jailed during World War I and World War II. Marshall B. Clinard and Richard Quinney (1973, pp. 175–177), using historical materials on political radicalism in the United States, document the brutal treatment, arrest, and incarceration of members of the Industrial Workers of the World, anarchists, and other radicals in the late 19th and early 20th centuries. Other writers have noted the prevalence of political crime and political offenders in many nations throughout history. Michael Waldman (1973), for example, reports the circumstances surrounding the arrests of the Paris communards following the 1871 revolution.

Schafer underscored the ubiquity of this kind of offense in his assertion that "political crime is perhaps the oldest of all crime types. It is virtually impossible to find a history of any society which does not record political criminals" (1971, p. 380). He has buttressed this claim with analyses of political crimes committed by a variety of historical figures, such as Jesus, Joan of Arc, Charles I, Louis XVI, and others (Schafer 1971, 1974). Nevertheless, historical studies (with the exception of Clinard and Quinney's work) have not delineated crimes by the government against the people. Historical accounts, furthermore, have neither designated and analyzed various types of political crime occurring within specified time periods, nor examined the organizational nature of political crime.

Case Studies of Political Crime

Some writers have preferred to describe and analyze concrete case studies within the broader area of political crime. These investigations have been concerned with both crimes by government and crimes against government. An example of the latter is Richard Moran's article on Daniel M'Naughton (1977), which gives a concrete analysis of M'Naughton's assassination of the secretary to the English Prime Minister in 1843. Moran concludes that M'Naughton's crime was induced by the political and economic disequilibrium in England at the time. M'Naughton was appalled by the economic gap between the rich and poor, and hoped that the assassination of a key English leader would topple the Tory government. Another example in this genre is Willard Gaylin's book on imprisoned war resisters (1970). He interviewed six resisters and gathered information about the personality, family, and institutional influences upon their decisions to resist the draft.

Joseph C. Mouledoux (1967) conducted a case study of crimes by government. He reported and analyzed the criminal misconduct of government officials in Mississippi during the civil rights struggles of the early 1960s, and concluded that the south was then dangerously close to becoming a closed authoritarian society—a society in which government crimes were basic to the functioning of the social system. M. David Ermann and Richard J. Lundman have edited the most significant political crime case study reader to date, *Corporate and Government Deviance: Problems of Organizational Behavior in Contemporary Society* (1978). Unlike previous case studies found in the literature, Ermann and Lundman's work analyzes several types of corporate and government offenses within a clear-cut theoretical frame of reference, organizational crime. Although these case studies were drawn from diverse sources and written by a variety of authors with differing political ideologies, the theoretical framework appears applicable to the cases at hand. However, in our view, the authors erred in separating corporate and government deviance for purposes of analysis, because corporate and government organizations frequently work as teams in the commission of similar (and sometimes the same) crimes. Nevertheless, their substantive materials and analyses are the most significant to date.

Case studies are certainly needed in the study of political crime and criminals, because they provide data blocs that may be analyzed systematically within a theoretical frame of reference. Such works also provide concrete and current information on the political and economic scene—the social context in which crime occurs. Finally, case studies offer new insights and perceptions of political crime. Most extant case studies, however, provide fragmented and isolated accounts of political crime and criminals that are not theoretically guided by frames of reference anchored in societal structural conditions.

Studies of Corrupt and Violent Police Conduct

The official misconduct of police organizations increasingly has been considered a form of political crime. Ellwyn Stoddard (1967) was among the first to deal with police corruption as an organizational form of deviant and criminal behavior. Later, William J. Chambliss (1971) showed how police organizations function to manage social vices rather than to eradicate them, and how this function involves corruption which is lucrative to the officer and to other public officials. Many recent studies of police corruption have been stimulated by newspaper accounts. The most publicized investigation of police corruption in the last decade, conducted in New York City in the late 1960s, found widespread corruption throughout the police department, particularly in the vice squad (Commission to Investigate Alleged Police Corruption 1971). Thomas Barker and Julian B. Roebuck conducted an organizational study of police corruption and crime in a large southern city in the late 1960s and early 1970s, entitled *An Empirical Typology of Police Corruption: A Study in Organizational Deviance* (1973).

William A. Westley's study (1970) of urban police violence in the early 1950s found that the occupational role of the police officer encouraged violence in the arrest process. Faced by an often hostile public that demanded both social order and fairness (due process), police officers often opted for the former and bound themselves to a code of secrecy. The code insured that police violations of department rules and criminal laws would not be revealed. Secrecy insulated the police from the variegated demands of defense attorneys, judges, civil libertarians, and people calling for "law and order" in their neighborhoods. Violence against criminal suspects tended to be justified by police officers as a private, quick, and direct method to evoke respect for the police—a respect lacking in the public domain.

The 1960s brought a great deal of overt police violence, such as the encounter between police and antiwar demonstrators at the 1968 Democratic National Convention. Rodney Stark's analysis of several episodes of police violence (including those at Berkeley, San Francisco, and Chicago), based upon data gathered by the President's Commission on the Causes and Prevention of Violence, attributes the rioting of demonstrators and police to the behavior of the police themselves. The policy initiated violent acts, including assault and battery, murder, and violations of civil rights, and thereby violated criminal laws.

The studies of police corruption and violence are limited because they rarely scrutinize the linkages between police criminality and that of other government officials and bodies. The police do not formulate public policy, but instead take orders from higher government officials who determine what the police shall and shall not do to maintain law and order. During the Watergate hearings it was disclosed that the illegal infiltration of radical groups in the 1960s was part of a grand strategy to monitor, disrupt, coerce, and intimidate all political dissenters. Some dissenters were provoked to commit violence. The Nixon administration, the FBI, and Mayor Daley of Chicago, among others, ordered the police to commit these illegal acts.

TYPOLOGICAL ASSUMPTIONS

The literature review disclosed a broad spectrum of study topics relevant to political crime, ranging from institutional to individual criminality. Scholarly writings on political crime reflect a morass of competing and often conflicting frames of reference that purport to explain the occurrence of political crime or the behavior of political criminals. Fortunately, a few criminologists have begun to systematize our knowledge in this area. For example, Clinard and Quinney (1973, pp. 154-84) set aside political crime as a separate field of analytical concern. They uniformly compared political crime with several other types of crime (violent personal criminal behavior, public order criminal behavior, occasional property criminal behavior, conventional criminal behavior, occupational criminal behavior, corporate criminal behavior, organized criminal behavior, and professional criminal behavior) along a number of relevant dimensions. Roebuck and Barker (1974) studied one form of government crime, police corruption, and delineated eight types of corrupt practices, many of which were violations of the criminal law. Nevertheless, no attempt has been made to develop a typology of political crime based upon a well-delineated set of theoretical dimensions.

The typology of political crime in this book is based (primarily) upon the action patterns of offenses committed by persons or groups of persons during the normal course of their activities as employees or members of formal organizations; that is, organizational crime. Persons or groups within such organizations may simultaneously enhance their personal fortunes or organizational careers through these violations, but one objective must be organizational benefit. The offense patterns must be engendered and supported by the internal operating norms of the organization, and peer groups within the organization must accept and implement violations based upon these norms (Ermann and Lundman 1978, pp. 7-9). We are concerned here with the units of behavior that comprise political crime, and the interactional settings where such behavior occurs. The focus is upon two kinds of political crime: crimes by government against people and crimes by the people against the government. We assert that organizational crimes by and against government in the United States must be understood in the context of the political economy of advanced capitalism (Anderson 1974).

But can a typology ascertain what is "political" about political crime (Reasons 1974, p. 6)? It could be argued that unless it is linked to the political and economic structure of society, a typology based upon action patterns may not be able to specify why certain categories of behaviors (and offenses) are "political" in nature. Two features of our typology that characterize its political orientation are that it deals with organizational crime, and it distinguishes the action patterns of government and capitalist agents (as members of formal organizations) acting against the people from those of persons and groups (as members of formal organizations) acting against the government. In the past, criminologists have dealt primarily with political criminals as individuals, "natural persons," rather than as "juristic persons" (corporate actors) who work as employees or agents of a formal organization (such as a government or corporation). Our typology views individuals as corporate actors (Coleman 1974).

Criminologists, for the most part, have concentrated on crimes by the people against the government, to the neglect of crimes by the government against the people. Political criminals, acting alone as "natural persons," have been studied as nonconformists rather than aberrant deviants, because they announce their intentions publicly, challenge the very legitimacy of the laws and their applications in specific situations, aim to change the norms they are denying, do not have personal gain as a goal, and appeal to a higher morality by pointing out the void between professed beliefs and actual practices (Merton and Nisbet 1971, pp. 829-32). These offenders have a moral commitment to a "higher social order" than presently exists (Cavan 1964, p. 239; Clinard and Quinney 1973, p. 161).

Unfortunately, this assessment is limited to offenders against the state such as traitors, antiwar demonstrators, and draft resisters. Should one desire to study government lawlessness (for example, that displayed by the CIA, the White House, and the federal regulatory agencies), these assumptions would hardly apply. These government offenders were organizational offenders who wrapped their true intentions in a cloak of secrecy, upheld their legitimacy as agents of the government, aimed to maintain in public the very norms they privately violated, may or may not have sought personal gain, and extolled their moral virtues while deceptively broadening the gap between their professed beliefs and their actual practices. As Clinard and Quinney (1973, p. 154) have suggested, such political offenders are committed to the preservation of the particular social and political order of which they are a part. Our treatment of crime by government, like Clinard and Quinney's (1973), extends the boundaries of the traditional analysis of political crime within a typological format, and includes illustrative examples of organizational crimes such as violations of international law, violations of regulatory agency rules and statutes, pollution of the environment, manufacture of evidence, repression of legal dissent, entrapment, illegal domestic intelligence operations, illegal awards of state and federal contracts and leases, bribery to influence the political process, unlawful police acts, military war crimes, illegal arms sales, and illegal abuse of prisoners.

A third feature of our typology that renders it political is that it is based upon a number of assumptions rooted in political historiography, social class studies, and political theory that allow us to interpret the interactions between government crimes and crimes against government. A few criminologists have begun to explore this interaction. Charles Reasons (1974, p. 101) has called for a perspective on political crime that emphasizes power, conflict, and interest group politics. Quinney and Wildeman (1977) have asserted that all crimes should be viewed as resulting from the structure of social, economic, and political institutions.

Another proponent of a conflict approach to criminology (Chambliss 1974) demonstrates that the process involved in becoming defined as criminal involves two components: rule creation and rule enforcement. Though our typology deals mostly with rule enforcement, rule creation is a necessary aspect of our forthcoming analysis because the designation of political criminals or political crime begins with the creation of criminal law. Laws that define behavior as criminal or delinquent originate with the legislative enactment of a statute, or a decision by a court or an administrative agency, that prescribes penal or administrative sanctions for the commission or omission of an act. The process of defining a criminal act begins at this point; but it ends with implementation of the law, and thus includes the discretionary acts of criminal courts, civil courts, regulatory agencies, police, and intelligence agencies. The police, as well as other enforcement and regulatory bodies, apply existing laws to some persons and entities but not to others. For example, prosecutors make decisions to prosecute certain cases but not others (as do administrative agency officials). Courts, prison officials and parole boards interpret and enforce the laws in certain ways (Chambliss 1974, p. 7).

William J. Chambliss (1974, p. 8) has noted that theories of the origin of criminal law fall into two major divisions: those that see the state as being controlled by and reflecting the interests of particular social classes, and those that view the state as responding to the views of the general public. He supports the first paradigm with historical évidence from the United States and England, and suggests that it is the one most compatible with the facts—that it recognizes the critical role played by social conflict in the generation of the criminal law. Chambliss argues that conflicts may be manifested in violent confrontations between social classes or by institutionalized dispute-settling procedures. Regardless of the form the conflict takes, the existence of structurally-induced conflicts between groups in society finally determines the form and content of the criminal law (Chambliss 1974, p. 8). He concludes that the class or group that controls the economic resources will influence the shape of the criminal law more profoundly and more permanently than will any other group or class, although he recognizes some limits to the power of a ruling class in determining the content of the laws (1974, p. 8).

The assumptions that follow are based on a class conflict model and draw from the ideas and findings of Reasons, Chambliss, Quinney, and John Wildeman, among others. These assumptions provide a guide to understanding the organizational goals and behaviors of political offenders and how these relate to economic and political power, institutional structures, and criminal and regulatory law. We suggest that the structure of income, wealth, and political power shapes the political offenders' goals and acts, and that these organizational goals and acts are economic in nature.* The assumptions are as follows:

---

*Ferdinand (1966, p. 48), in criticizing empirical typologies, states that social scientists employing this approach generally have done so with an implicit theory of human nature in mind. Consequently the resultant typology usually reflects certain ill-defined assumptions regarding the causes of human behavior. This bias means that the researcher will be attentive to certain trends in his data but blind to others. In this work we overcome this bias by presenting our assumptions about political crime prior to presenting the typology.

The social structure of the United States is characterized by an extreme disribu-tion of personal income and wealth. A small group of individuals and families hold an unusually large proportion of the total income and wealth in the United States. The top one-fifth of income earners gets nearly 50 percent of the total income each year (Kolko 1962, p. 14). Even more important is the fact that 1 percent of the total population, dominated by about 2,000 family fortunes, owns and controls high concentrations of property (including real estate, corporate stock and bonds, family trusts, capital goods, unrealized capital gains, and inheritances). Property is the foundation of wealth, much more so than is income. Property changes hands in order to produce profits, while incomes (mostly wages and salaries) are usually applied to the satisfaction of basic human needs such as food, clothing, and housing. Thirty percent of the nation's private wealth is held by 1.6 percent of the adult population (Lampman 1962, p. 23). One percent of the population holds 80 percent of the total corporate stock, and the top 5 percent of this 1 percent (.000t percent of all adults) holds 40 percent of the total (Anderson 1974, p. 144). This concentration is due largely to the fusion of industrial and banking assets and finance capital. Through family trust funds, banks have reached out singly or in combination to gain controlling interests in almost 30 percent of the top 500 industrial corporations (Patman Committee 1972, p. 74).

Stock ownership is concentrated in the hands of corporations (that own other corporations) rather than in the hands of individual stockholders. This monopolistic tendency continues today, as witnessed by the rise and prolifera-tion of multinational corporations (Barnet and Muller 1974). Additionally, the distribution of wealth is upheld by the structure of the tax system, which draws revenue mainly from income and salaries rather than from wealth. Because wealth is central to the fortunes of the upper class, it is seen to that the holdings are not properly taxed (Thurow 1976; Turner and Starnes 1976; Brown 1977). Legislation purporting to lighten the tax burden on the middle and lower classes has been weak and systematically evaded by the wealthy (Kolko 1962, p. 14).

For the majority of Americans, on the other hand, income and wealth are widely diffused. Eighty percent of the population owns only 24 percent of the nation's wealth (Turner and Starnes 1976, p. 23), while 86 percent of the popu-lation is propertyless by virtue of owning no stock whatsoever (University of Michigan 1960, p. 474). Based upon a detailed review of government documents concerning property distribution, Ferdinand Lundberg (1968, p. 23) claims that 70 percent of Americans are poor. Gabriel Kolko (1962, p. 101) claims that half the households in the United States have incomes inadequate for the maintenance of minimal standards of comfort and well-being. Recent research by Turner and Starnes (1976, p. 22) shows that 56.9 percent of families make up only 6.6 percent of the total net worth when the worth of all families is tabulated.

The United States, then, is a class society wherein the system of produc-tion is owned by one segment of the society to the exclusion of another

(Quinney 1977, p. 36). The capitalists own and control the means of production. This highly-concentrated ownership demands that the remainder of the population (the non-owners) be dominated and exploited. The capitalists are wealthy because they have expropriated the labor of the working population, and the working class, in turn, is relatively impoverished because it must sell its labor power to the capitalist owners. Each of the two classes depends upon the other for its symbiotic existence (Quinney 1977, p. 37).

Political power stems from economic power and upholds structural inequality. Power is realized when the ruling class uses political means to enhance and maintain its economic advantage. The ruling class, possessing economic resources garnered from the exploitation of the working class, has captured the political state. As political historians like Eric Foner (1977) have noted, the law and its interpretation are a direct expression of corporate interests. Legal precepts in the nineteenth century developed steadily toward the protection of monopoly capitalist enterprises, while simultaneously disregarding the interests of small businessmen, family farmers, and the self-employed.

Some agents of government have come to play a leading role in the collusion between the economically powerful and the political system. Executive branch officials, the courts, the police, government lawyers, senior congressmen, and heads of regulatory agencies occupy positions which allow them to appropriate, distribute or protect large sums of capital. For example, the regulatory agencies that monitor and regulate corporate financial transactions do little to stop the concentration of finance capital. Understandably, the ruling class is interested in cultivating contacts among government agents, and this is easily accomplished because some agents of government are themselves members of the ruling class. Collusion then benefits groups that are already partially amalgamated.

Large corporations contribute heavily to the presidential campaigns of national office-seekers (Green et al. 1975, pp. 6-18; Mintz and Cohen 1971, pp. 151-78; M. Jensen 1976a, 1976b, 1976c; J. Anderson 1976a; Alexander 1976). Contributions to presidential campaigns have been especially important. Once in office, the president has broad powers to appoint persons to the administrative agencies charged with regulating corporate behavior. Because corporate money is a large factor in the presidential elections, presidents are not inclined to appoint stern watchdogs to head the agencies. Congressmen and senators, also recipients of corporate contributions, are likely to rubber-stamp the presidential appointees. Favoritism to corporations is extended further as legislators and regulators consult corporation officials in the writing of laws and regulations (Domhoff 1970, pp. 156-250; Graham 1976).

At another level, corporate officials are invited to serve on advisory boards and government commissions (Domhoff 1970, pp. 134-37; Shearer 1976; Quinney 1974, pp. 60-75). They occupy positions in policy-planning organizations such as the Business Council, the Council on Foreign Relations, and the Council on Economic Development—each having impact upon government policy (Domhoff 1974, pp. 93-103). These policy-planning organizations provide a setting where bankers, businessmen, and lawyers from throughout the United States join to discuss common problems, settle differences, groom new leaders and spokesmen, listen to the advice of hired experts from universities and think-tanks, and develop policies and programs in keeping with the changing political and economic situation.

These policy-planning groups are connected to the major U.S. corporations through a common leadership, and they link up with government by a web of channels. Group members are frequently appointed to important government positions and to special presidential commissions that suggest new government policies. They and their employees often testify before Congress or serve as consultants to executive branch agencies. Policy-planning organizations publish pamphlets, journals, books, and position papers that government officials and their staffs widely read, and organization members often initiate ad hoc interest groups to influence government and public opinion on specific issues of concern to them (Domhoff 1978, pp. 156-57). The consultation process is strengthened by the rapid movement of corporate executives in and out of government positions (Kolko 1969, p. 17; Sherrill 1974, pp. 214-17). As a supplement to this web of relationships, corporations may bribe politicians or form secret business lobbies, such as the Business Roundtable (Hager 1977), to solicit the enactment of self-serving legislation.

The political influence bought with corporate money or contributions allows the possessors of wealth to proliferate their capital. Certain laws stand in the way of capital expansion, and corporations cannot pursue profits unless the government fails to enforce these laws. The failure of the government to enforce the antitrust laws has permitted businesses to merge into global conglomerates (Barnet and Muller 1974). These mergers proceeded despite the manifold antitrust violations involved in the process (Barber 1971; Sampson 1975, pp. 121-26). Such nonenforcement of the law occurs because government bureaucracies are controlled by those who own society's economic resources (Chambliss 1974, p. 27).

Another very important institution controlled by the wealthy is the criminal justice system. The criminal law, as Quinney (1974) has shown, is formulated, administered, and enforced in the interests of large capitalists. The criminal law process is organized on the basis of the views of those classes that control the economic resources of the nation. A number of historical, cross-cultural, and contemporary studies of criminal law creation have shown how criminal laws are consciously and explicitly enacted to serve those who command economic resources. Wealthy persons are more likely to have their interests represented by the state through the criminal law than are any and all other social groups. Economic elites are directly or indirectly involved in the rule creation process, and they protect their interests by directly influencing legislation. Because of their position, the elites are able to mobilize the forces that oversee the rule-making process (Chambliss 1974, p. 16). For example, such statutes as the Sherman Antitrust Act and the pure food and drug laws are enactments which on the surface appear to limit the power of the economic elite, but in fact were formulated and promoted by the elite as a way of adding to and improving their control over the means of production. The state is not a value-free referee, but rather an agent of the owners and the means of production and distribution. "The criminal law is then first and foremost a reflection of the interests and ideologies of the governing class—whether that class is private industry or state bureaucracy" (Chambliss 1974, p. 37). Only in a secondary respect does the criminal law reflect value consensus, the public interest, or the competition of groups.

An explication of upper class control of the criminal justice system is found in "the entire matrix of recruitment, socialization, and structural pressures upon those who formulate the law" (Chambliss 1974, p. 21). Legislators, appellate court judges, and committee members are predominantly drawn from the upper class. Legal advice comes disproportionately from law firms whose principal clients are the major industrial and financial corporations of the country. Interest groups are organized to define problems and influence lawmakers in the interests of those who have the resources to finance and support the existence of specialists in the rule-creation process. Furthermore, key actors in the criminal justice system (judges, procecutors, and police chiefs) are either men of wealth or those possessing enough wealth to understand the life circumstances of the ruling class. Recruitment to their positions is often predicated upon key contacts with the elite and an understanding of that group's inner workings and goals. Job security depends upon satisfying the elite. Given these pressures, the justice system is no more than the tool of the elite and serves the privileged group's interests. At the same time, the interests of the great majority of Americans are neglected in great part.

The elite also controls the law enforcement and administrative bureaucracies, and determines which laws and rules will be enforced. It is not surprising, then, that the police and other law enforcement officials are more likely to enforce the laws broken by the working class (such crimes as rape, arson, or murder) than those broken by the upper class (involving bureaucratic crime, embezzlement, or consumer fraud). The lower classes are more likely to be labeled criminal because the bourgeoisie's control of the state protects that group from such stigmatization (Chambliss 1975, p. 63). The working class, consequently, is arrested more often and punished more severely than is the affluent (Wald 1967; Goldfarb 1974). Furthermore, correctional systems keep many people out of the labor market and attach a stigma to them which obstructs future access to economic opportunities (Gordon 1976, p. 207). Concurrently, law enforcement personnel frequently neglect crimes by the rich corporate class, such as antitrust violations, consumer fraud and the built-in corporate violence of contaminated medicines, unsafe jobs conditions, and pollution. Capitalists' corporate crimes are usually adjudicated in civil courts or administrative agencies, where offenders escape conviction and the odium of the criminal label.

The United States Congress has institutionalized a special set of rules to govern the socially-injurious activities of the upper class (that is, the capitalist class) through the establishment of regulatory commissions and agencies. These commissions provide administrative and civil hearings and sanctions for corporate offenders, rather than criminal trials and sanctions. The implementation and sanction of regulatory commission rules are weak. Even when the criminal law is invoked against corporations or corporate actors, corporate structures themselves are rarely brought to trial, because the U.S. legal system is based upon a theory that holds that the individual is ultimately to blame, that is, he has *mens rea* (criminal intent). Therefore, corporate crime enjoys low visibility, and corporate actors (juristic persons) escape a criminal label. Conversely, ordinary citizens who break the law are generally tried in criminal courts as natural persons. The American legal system in actuality reflects a system of double-entry moral bookkeeping. Avowedly the U.S. government is a two-party system (Republican and Democrat); but there is only one political party in the United States, the Property Party. Boys in the Club, both Democrat and Republican, are aware of this reality, which enables the large corporations to use the government and its money for their own ends (Vidal 1972).

A more subtle way in which the capitalist class maintains its power is by selling its ideology to the public. Ideological hegemony is a non-violent but repressive means of control that is gained through capturing the state. The state is supposed to regulate the media, including newspapers, magazines, radio, television, and motion pictures. However, due to its failure to regulate the media in the manner required by laws insuring competition, the capitalist class is able to hold a monopoly over the information that is dispensed to the public. A few major networks monopolize the television industry (ABC, NBC, CBS), and they are organized on the basis of capitalist principles. Controversial political and economic issues are rarely dealt with on stations other than educational networks (McKee and Robertson 1975, p. 142). And even then, the issues are always discussed within a capitalistic frame of reference. The ultimate in capitalist control according to Alan Wolfe, ". . . would not be a police state but the complete opposite, one in which there were no police because there was nothing to police, everyone having accepted the legitimacy of that society and all its daily consequences" (in Quinney 1977, p. 47).

The ruling class is the social manifestation of these tendencies. According to William Domhoff, the ruling class comprises about 0.5 to 1.0 percent of the U.S. population, owns about a quarter of all privately held wealth, receives a disproportionate share of the annual national income, and owns and controls the major banks and corporations. This class develops "economic and political programs through a number of policy networks and dominates—at the very least, the federal government in Washington D.C." (Domhoff 1978, p. 175). Domhoff maintains that this national upper class takes the form of interlocking social circles which perceive each other as equals, belong to the same clubs, interact, and intermarry (1974, pp. 82-91).

According to Paul Sweezy, the ruling class comprises the executive officers of the nation's largest corporations—wealthy men with few exceptions, who own substantial amounts of stock in their own and other corporations. Far from being separated from ownership and management, they are simply the most active echelon of what C. Wright Mills called the corporate rich—those who own a large part of the country's wealth. The real managers (the owners) are in fact capitalists in the fullest sense of the term. Many capitalist apologists, like Kenneth Galbraith, have claimed that a managerial class of non-owners exercises real corporate power. This is a myth; the so-called managerial class is in reality an underclass. In any event the "managerial class" shares the capitalists' goals of making as much profit as possible for the capitalists and enhancing the growth of corporate enterprise. These goals suffuse the entire ideology and value system of the business world. Personnel (the technostructure) are hired accordingly, and anyone who chooses to pursue some other aim is promptly fired. Real power in the enterprise is held by those who have the power to hire and fire, and it is precisely this power which inheres in ownership and management. In exercising power, managerial agents act as capitalists and on behalf of capitalists (Sweezy 1973, pp. 3-5).

Beneath the corporate rich is a stratum that is economically, politically, and socially related to the group of large capitalists. This stratum consists of the owners and managers of small and medium-size corporations in manufacturing and trade, locally-based construction firms, large farms and ranches, radio and television stations, local banks, and professionals (especially doctors and lawyers). Many of these people are wealthy in their own right, with incomes and capital assets well above those of the people they employ or of corporate employees. They are interwoven in many ways (for example, through stock ownership) with the corporate rich. Socially, they subscribe to the same life style, the same values, the same ideology. Politically, they dominate communities and electoral districts, often up to the state level. Together with the large capitalists, they constitute, in number and geographic spread, the largest part of a relatively homogeneous class that derives its enormous wealth and privileges from the economic status quo. The higher reaches of the government bureaucracies and the judiciary are overwhelmingly staffed by members of the dominant economic class or people dependent on them. The political party organizations are controlled at every level by the vested interests who stand to gain most from the protection and favors that the local, state and federal government are in a position to hand out. These are facts confirmed by innumerable empirical studies of cities, towns, and political institutions (Sweezy 1973, pp. 5-6).

In response to disclosures about the ruling class and its activities, the propertyless mass of Americans appears to form a separate and self-conscious class based upon their marginal economic and social status (Anderson 1974, p. 137). Powerlessness and feelings of alienation are increasing among such diverse groups as the unemployed poor, auto workers, bank workers, civic employees, federal and state prisoners, and white-collar office, sales, and clerical employees

(Davis 1971; Anderson 1974, pp. 138-39; Leinsdorf and Etra 1973, pp. 12-18; Seeman 1975, p. 97; Quinney 1977, pp. 73-74). White-collar workers and corporate middle-level managers are increasingly becoming proletarianized, that is, sharing the characteristics of the industrial proletariat (Quinney 1977, pp. 73-74).

The ruling class, therefore, controls the political process that determines who gets the greatest share of economic rewards. Conflict ensues between those possessing political power and those seeking access to it. Government and corporate agents want to maintain the status quo, or the existing relations of power, so that they may remain in their positions of economic and political power for profit. The powerless (the economically and politically dispossessed) seek a "higher order," contingent upon drastic structural changes, that will allow them and others to participate in political decision making. In protecting the existing capitalist system, the ruling class commits crimes that are necessary to secure the future functioning of the system, for example, the illegal surveillance of political protesters by the Army and FBI, war crimes, and the assassination of foreign leaders. On the other hand, the crimes committed by the class that does not own the means of production are either accommodations or resistances to the conditions produced by capitalist production (Quinney 1977, p. 53). The protests against the Vietnam war, for example, were an attempt to participate in the political decision making process. That process was closed to the public, and in order to participate in the political process it was necessary to break or circumvent the existing legal codes.

Crimes committed by government and capitalistic agents are qualitatively different from crimes committed by the people. Government and corporate crimes against people are viewed as offenses to maintain the social and economic order, and crimes committed by the people against the government are perceived as offenses to change the existing structural relations of power.

Following our basic structural assumptions that political crime stems from differential economic power and flaws in the state of advanced capitalism, we designate both offenses committed by government agents and by capitalist agents against the people as political crimes. Because we are dealing with organizational crime, it is necessary to designate criminal patterns engaged in by government organizations and their agents, by corporate organizations and their agents, and by a combination of government and corporate organizations and their agents. Organizational criminal patterns against the government, whether they be in violation of conventional criminal laws (for example, assault, robbery, or theft), or in violation of laws applied as legalistic substitutes (such as loitering or parading without a permit), are considered to be political crimes should they be engaged in for political reasons. We define political crime as follows:

First, political crime includes organizational acts committed by government or capitalist agents that are defined as criminal by sectors of the population, whether or not they are illegal as defined by the government. Herbert Marcuse has summarized the issues in his *Essay on Liberation*. He asserts that the continued functioning of a capitalist society is a sufficient justification for its legality (1969, p. 67). "Functioning" is defined rather negatively as the absence of civil war, massive disorder, or economic collapse. Otherwise, considerable travesties are allowed, such as military dictatorships, plutocracies, and governments ruled by gangs and rackets. Genocide, war crimes, and other crimes against humanity are not considered criminal should they not interfere with functioning of the society. There is no enforceable law that could deprive a constitutional government of its legitimacy and legality.

Thus political crime by the government may be placed into the following categories: (1) Actions by government or capitalist agents that are not illegal in the government's criminal code but are illegal in the criminal code of a foreign government (for example, Lockheed's bribery in order to secure foreign contracts); (2) Actions by government or capitalist agents that violate international law (for example, CIA intervention in the sovereign affairs of a foreign nation); (3) Government or capitalist agents' actions that are deliberately designed to evade the enforcement of existing rules or statutes (such as the failure of regulatory agencies to regulate big business); (4) Government or capitalist agents' actions that are socially injurious but are beyond recognition by the people, either because of secrecy (in the case of violations of the law by the CIA and FBI), or because such acts are not yet definable in the criminal codes (such as certain injuries to the environment); (5) Acts committed by government or capitalist agents that clearly violate established local, state, or federal legal statutes (for example, assault and murder by local police, state troopers, or National Guardsmen) or federal regulatory agency and commission regulations and rules. In all of these cases, the state usually escapes criminal sanctions because it is supported and protected by the capitalist class.

Secondly, political crime includes organizational acts by the people against the government that are defined as criminal for reasons that the actors define as political. Marcuse observes that ". . . there is no (enforceable) law other than that which serves the status quo, and that those who refuse such service are *io ipso* outside the realm of law even before they come into actual conflict with the law" (1969, p. 67). Political crimes against the government consist of the following categories: (1) Symbolic acts in violation of established local, state, or federal legal codes that are committed for political reasons (for example, a bank robbery committed as a symbolic gesture to "liberate" the people from the dominance of capitalism); (2) The very existence of anticapitalist organizations such as the Socialist Workers party and the Weather Underground, which are not in and of themselves illegal but, as defined by the state, pose a threat to the existing political and economic system. Such organizations and their members are targets of political policing and are subject to legal processing in criminal courts.

A TYPOLOGY OF AMERICAN POLITICAL CRIME

Introduction

Renata Adler (1977) has suggested that the failure to understand political scandals (in our terminology—political crimes) in the United States results from the employment of two conflicting methodologies: the empirical, and the ideological. The first is that of the investigative journalist or television reporter who seeks out the "facts" at hand. This approach involves the intensive interviewing of everyone remotely connected with the scandal in an effort to gather corroborative evidence. A case is built on the reconstruction of individual personal accounts, and the "facts" supposedly speak for themselves. The second is that of the ideologue who begins his investigations with the assumption that the American system of government is corrupt. The evidence gathered on any particular case is then organized in a fashion to prove the "obvious," that the system is corrupt. Adler contends that neither approach is adequate, and suggests that researchers carefully study the mass of government documents that are available to most anyone close to a library. She claims that official documents provide greater insight into political corruption than do the revelations of an investigative reporter whose findings are consumed daily and forgotten quickly. Without a theoretical framework, empirical findings cannot provide a conceptualization of political crime.

Government documents may empirically refute the postulates of the ideologue who explains everything on the basis of an assumption that the system is inherently corrupt. According to Adler, for example, government documents suggest that the Watergate scandal did not result exclusively from internal corruption, but in part was provoked by illegal interventions in the American scene by foreign countries. She reports that Nixon was paid large sums by the South Vietnamese government to retain U.S. troops in South Vietnam, and that he purportedly resigned in order to keep this from becoming public knowledge.

The Typological Method

A type is an abstract category consisting of characteristics that have empirical referents; its basic focus is the empirical universe. A typology groups a number of types that are distinguishable from one another in at least one characteristic, though sufficiently similar to form a "set." Scholars in the physical and social sciences have always utilized typologies to order observed phenomena for analytical and comparative purposes. The social sciences employ a plethora of derived types, such as personality, family, community, social class, occupational, and deviant types (Clinard and Quinney 1973, p. 14). A typology is basically a collection of types that catalogues the various ways a given complex of characteristics are empirically connected, and it may be useful in an attempt to explain the behavior of acting units or individuals (Ferdinand 1966, pp. 28-38).

Typologies are distinguishable from classifications. A classification is a set of characteristics (or variables) that can be linked to form a number of logically possible categories. Classifications are more arbitrary and less discriminating than typologies, because all cases within a class are assumed to share equally the attributes of that class. In contrast, a type is a sensitizing construct—a point of reference from which to determine the degree to which any single empirical case approximates the abstract type.

Theories are concerned with the logical relationships that exist between analytic concepts. Typologies are not theories, but they are based on preconceived theoretical frames of reference, or ways of looking at the empirical world. Thus theories and typologies interact. The construction of typologies may lead to new theoretical constructs and systems (Hempel 1952, p. 84). Certainly, typology building is often the first step in theory building.

Typological Techniques

Typologists may reduce the complexity of the empirical world in two directly opposite ways: by reducing the number of types, so that many cases may be placed in one or a few types; or by reducing the heterogeneity of each type. The goal of typology construction, then, is to construct a minimum number of types, each of which displays maximum homogeneity. Kenneth D. Bailey (1973, pp. 291-92) describes two sociological examples of typology construction: empirical or extracted types; and heuristic types, which are based on theoretical constructs that are designed to be conceptually pure. The first approach utilizes quantitative computerized methods, such as cluster analysis or Q-factor analysis, which supposedly contrive types directly from the data without prior conceptualization. In our opinion, these are spurious. How does one type without some *a priori* considerations?

The second approach involves the use of theoretical constructs that are designed to be conceptually pure—for example, Weber's "ideal type." Although exacting empirical examples of the ideal type may not be found, it can be used as a criterion by which empirical cases may be compared. Another example of the heuristic type is the constructed type, which involves the purposive selection and abstraction of a set of criteria with empirical referents that then serves as a basis for the comparison of empirical cases (McKinney 1966, p. 25). The typologist is more likely to find examples of the constructed type than of the ideal type, because the former has conceptualized empirical referents.

The Typology

Our typology inheres in the basic assumptions clarified on pages 6-17, and it presents a constructed schema. Our concern was to construct types that have referents in the empirical world. These referents are, in fact, the dimensions of the typology. They are "first order constructs," that is, constructions of reality that have meaning to social actors in the real world. The types themselves are second-order constructs, or "typifications of typifications." Types are the constructions of social scientists; they are derived for the purpose of conceptualiation—to bring order to the multiplex phenomena in specific research settings (in this case, political crime). They might also serve as a basis for a general theory of political crime.

Our typology utilizes four dimensions: action patterns, the goal of the offender, the legal status of the offense, and the nature of the offense. Included in the four dimensions are the diverse phenomena associated with political crime: the systematic patterns of illegal political behavior, the intentions of the actors, the legal status of the offense, and the nature of the acts, along with the interactional setting in which the political crime occurs. The dimensions are described as follows:

Action Patterns. The political crimes under study occur as behavior patterns within formal organizations. Offenders are members of groups or organizations that are constantly attempting to improve or to maintain their relative positions with regard to other groups or organizations. Therefore, political crimes are a natural part of an on-going social process (Vold 1958, pp. 203–19). Action patterns are here confined to illegal actions to maintain and enhance the existing economic and political power structure, and illegal actions undertaken in an attempt to change the structure of political and economic power. We deem action patterns the most essential part of the typology, and therefore we devote more attention and space to this dimension than to the other dimensions.

Goal of the Offender. One critical feature of political crime is the political and economic character of the lawbreaker's objectives. The political offender is "convictional" (Schafer 1974, pp. 145–54). For reasons that are not entirely personal, he seeks a social order different from that currently existing. Those in power may also be "convictional" offenders in that they desire to maintain the particular social order of which they are a part. The political offender is therefore interested in maintaining or changing a set of structural conditions. We examine the organizational objectives (the "in-order-to" aims) of individuals or groups who commit crimes in the normal course of their work or activities as employees or members of organizations.

Legal Status of the Offense. Political offenses, as we operationally define them, fall into three categories: illegal offenses, surrogate-illegal offenses, and para-legal offenses. Political offenses are illegal when the actors violate established legal codes. Offenses are surrogate-illegal when selected legal codes are applied solely for purposes of punishment or social control for political reasons. There may be nothing inherently criminal in an act; but the actor is criminalized when persons in power attach the illegal label to his behavior. For example, this occurs when political dissenters are arrested for petty crimes such as criminal trespass and parading without a permit, or for more serious crimes such as treason, sabotage, or espionage. Because the "real" crime, which is political action, cannot be punished (the U.S. legal system does not officially recognize political crime), the actor is instead punished for legalistic substitutes.

Para-legal offenses comprise socially injurious interpretations of legality. For example, an executive committee or special agency appointed by the president may be beyond congressional control. Its authority may appear to have a legal base (it is derived from the executive branch of government), but it may not in fact have any legislative determination or definition (Borrosage 1975, p. 73).* Para-legal actions may also be undertaken by corporate agents who engage in collusive and evasive endeavors, among themselves or with agents of government, that are beyond congressional and regulatory agency control.

Nature of the Offense. It is assumed that the political offender's action patterns are rationally planned and are unrelated to abnormal psychological motivation. Action patterns may be violent or non-violent, secret or unconcealed (Minor 1975, pp. 385, 389). They may mesh with the existing political and economic system or they may not. We are also concerned with the extent of group support for these action patterns, and finally with the societal reaction to them.

Our typology delineates seven specific types of political crime: domestic intervention by government, foreign intervention by government, intervention against government, domestic surveillance, domestic confrontation, evasion and collusion by government, and evasion and collusion against government. The form of presentation is as follows. First, the major type is discussed in a general introduction. Then each type is examined along the four dimensions of study: action patterns (which are documented); the goal of the offender; the legal status of the offense; and the nature of the offense.

---

*The foreign activities of the CIA provide the best examples of para-legal actions; see Chapter 3 for documentation.

2

DOMESTIC INTERVENTION
BY GOVERNMENT

Intervention designates illegal attempts to change or control specific economic and political events, structures, or processes in a sovereign state in order to produce advantageous results for the changer. The changers may be agents of the government, capitalist agents, or a combination. Regardless of who the changers are, they systematically manipulate events, structures, or processes in order to promote the political or economic purposes of their formal organizations in the course of their everyday work activities. Manipulation can take the form of penetration or infiltration of agents, which could also be considered as actions preparatory to planned manipulation. The line between the two is difficult to establish. Manipulation includes direct actions such as war-making, paramilitary operations, militant lobbying, influence-peddling, and the hard-sale of arms. Penetration, on the other hand, refers to such acts as financial support and technical assistance to political parties or private organizations (including labor unions and businesses) and covert propaganda.*

ACTION PATTERNS

Within the United States, several government agencies and corporate groups have been involved in crimes (as defined in this work) against the American people. The following organizations were focused on for illustrative purposes: the White House, the Central Intelligence Agency (CIA), the Federal Bureau of Investigation (FBI), the United States Army, the Internal Revenue Service (IRS), and a variety of large multinational corporations based in the

---

*The concepts "manipulation" and "penetration" were gleaned from a study of CIA covert operations. For a brief overview see Marchetti and Marks (1974, pp. 63–73).

United States, such as Gulf, Exxon, and International Telephone and Telegraph (ITT). Interventions by these organizations designate the manipulation and penetration of the domestic scene. This chapter is concerned with transgressions designed to maintain the structure of wealth and political power in the United States.

The White House

The most noted domestic manipulations of the recent past were perpetrated by a White House cabal of government agents during the Nixon administration. The White House at this time represented the reactionary, politicized action arm of the corporate structure. In 1970, the Nixon administration brought dissenters to trial (such as the Gainesville 8 and New York 21), precipitating some negative reactions among members of the judiciary. Judges complained that indictments were loosely drawn, evidence was tainted, and defendants' rights were violated. Even so, this harassment of the left was successful because it burdened the dissenters with tasks such as soliciting funds from supporters, hiring lawyers, writing letters to the press, and drafting appeals. Consequently, they had little time to prepare for mass demonstrations and public protests. Despite some success at neutralizing the left, the administration was not completely satisfied. Furthermore, it was frustrated by a number of envisioned setbacks, including the failure to place a strict constructionist majority on the Supreme Court, the failure of J. Edgar Hoover to approve the Huston Plan, and John Mitchell's rejection of an outline for Watergate-like dirty tricks. The old semilegal approach to handling dissent was not working; the Plumbers were to serve as a solution of last resort (McCarthy 1974, p. 15).

The Plumbers

The Plumbers, the nation's first secret police force, were an investigation team organized under the aegis of the president and his staff. This group was planned shortly after publication of the Pentagon Papers by the New York *Times* in July 1971, which disclosed that the United States had provoked the Tonkin Gulf incident in 1964 in order to justify U.S. involvement in the Vietnam war. Moreover, the papers revealed that decision makers had disregarded evidence that the North Vietnamese could not be beaten in a guerrilla war. The president considered such leaks of highly classified information to be breaches in national security that imperiled the delicat Vietnam peace negotiations and impaired relations with the Soviet Union and Communist China (Reichley 1973).

The Plumbers' first task was to coordinate the congressional investigations into the leaking of the Pentagon Papers (U.S. Senate 1974a, p. 64). The administration hoped to secure prosecution of the individual who released the papers on grounds of espionage. When Daniel Ellsberg admitted leaking the secret report to the press, the Plumbers were assigned to find or fabricate derogatory information about his personal character and integrity—an assignment which led to some illegal liaisons with the CIA. One Plumber asked CIA director Richard Helms to provide the White House with a psychological profile of Ellsberg. Two inconclusive profiles were presented, but no derogatory information was ascertained. Consequently, G. Gordon Liddy and E. Howard Hunt sent a team to break into the office of Dr. Lewis Fielding, Ellsberg's psychiatrist, with the hope of obtaining discrediting information. Again, no dirt was found (U.S. Senate 1974a, pp. 65-71).

During this time, the White House staff gave the Plumbers another, similar assignment. In July 1971, a reporter learned, and leaked to the New York *Times*, the U.S. negotiating position formulated at the Strategic Arms Limitation Talks. This secret position was considered to be extremely sensitive, and its exposure alarmed the White House. Soon thereafter, the executive aide in charge of the Plumbers contacted the CIA and illegally obtained the personnel and equipment to conduct polygraph tests on State and Defense Department employees suspected of leaking the information to the press (U.S. House 1975, p. 241).

The Plumbers were also given individual assignments. E. Howard Hunt, a supervisor of the Plumbers' break-in teams, served on a number of such jobs. In July 1971, the Deputy Director of the CIA furnished Hunt with false identification, a wig, and a voice alterer. Hunt made use of these materials during the break-in of Daniel Ellsberg's psychiatrist's office in September 1971, and while seeking out damaging and derogatory information about Senator Edward Kennedy, interviewing ITT lobbyist Dita Beard (about a $400,000 campaign contribution that allegedly cleared ITT of antitrust charges), and supervising the break-in at the Democratic National Committee Headquarters on June 17, 1972 (U.S. House 1975, pp. 235-36). The Plumbers began as a specialized White House investigation unit, but ultimately handled such tasks as forging diplomatic cables and hiring thugs to disrupt peace rallies.

The Huston Plan

The Plumbers were by no means an aberration in the Nixon administration. From the beginning, the administration expressed the fear that a younger generation bent upon destroying the social order could disrupt the system and cause radical changes in society. One of the administration's reactions to the political protests of the late 1960s was the Huston Plan, created by Tom Huston, a young superpatriotic White House aide. Huston's plan called for illegal wiretappings, break-ins, and mail covers for domestic intelligence purposes. The scheme involved pooling the intelligence resources of four agencies (the FBI, the CIA, the National Security Agency, and the Defense Intelligence Agency), and was approved by the president and by the heads of three of the four cooperating agencies. Only FBI director Hoover objected, and his opposition blocked the plan's formal implementation (U.S. Senate 1974a, pp. 58-8). Nonetheless, evidence brought to light in late 1974 by Seymour Hersh of the New York *Times* showed that the U.S. intelligence agencies covertly engaged in many of the activities formulated in the Huston Plan (Hersh 1974). Huston admitted to a 1975 congressional committee that the plan was informally implemented (*Commercial Appeal* 1975a). The FBI, meanwhile, developed COINTELPRO, its own program of bugs, wiretaps, and break-ins.

President Nixon solidly supported the Huston Plan, and shared the belief of many of his aides that the social disorders of the late 1960s and the early 1970s could rip American society apart. The president's counsel, John Dean, supported the project because of his conviction that there was a domestic security crisis of critical proportions. Among the evidence he cited in support of this view was "a wave of bombings and explosions, rioting and violence, demonstrations, arson, gun battles and other disruptive activities across the country—on college campuses primarily—but also in other areas" (U.S. Senate 1974a, p. 58). Huston himself believed political dissidents to be "a major threat to internal security" (U.S. Senate 1974a, p. 58). The administration was obviously interested in thwarting any radical changes in American society and was willing to break the law in order to preserve the capitalistic economic system.

Nixon was fully advised of the illegalities involved in the intelligence gathering techniques in the Huston Plan. Huston's warning to the president was blunt: "Use of this technique is clearly illegal. It amounts to burglary. It is also highly risky and could result in great embarrassment if exposed" (U.S. Senate 1974a, p. 54). Huston justified this strategy by saying that ". . . it is also the most fruitful tool and can produce the type of intelligence which cannot be obtained in any other fashion" (U.S. Senate 1974a, p. 54). Nixon obviously felt that he, as a president, was above the law and could commit crimes with impunity in the name of national security.

Dirty Tricks

The radicals tabbed by the Nixon administration as intervention targets were not the only Americans who opposed the Vietnam war and other official policies. By the end of Nixon's first term, a majority of Americans questioned the continued presence of U.S. military forces in Vietnam. The White House responded with manipulative techniques designed to create the impression that the administration's war policies were widely supported. To achieve this objective, an elaborate public relations program was established by the White House staff, the Committee to Re-elect the President (CRP), and the Republican National Committee (RNC). For instance, within a few days following the president's announcement of renewed bombing in North Vietnam and Haiphong Harbor, the public relations staff of the Committee to Re-elect the President composed and mailed to the White House 1,200 phony letters conveying "public support" for the president's decision. Similar letters were sent to members of the Senate, and seventy letters were sent to the New York *Times* to counter a May 10, 1972 editorial criticizing the bombing decision. Additionally, a full page advertisement supporting the president and his position on Vietnam was planted in the *Times* by CRP members—paid for with $4,400 from the CRP campaign fund (U.S. Senate 1974a, pp. 238–39).

Political mail was sent by the Republican National Committee in 1972 to newspaper editors, television and radio stations, governors, congressmen, and other individuals or institutions capable of shaping or influencing public opinion. The mailing lists were prepared, duplicated, and distributed by the RNC. The CRP staff reproduced private letters and sent them by direct mail to persons whose names appeared on the RNC political mailing list. No acknowledgement was made that any of the RNC or CRP letters were mailed from the Republican National Committee headquarters. Persons receiving the letters thus received the impression that they were mailed by the person or company whose name appeared upon the letterhead. For example, a letter from Senator George Smathers supporting President Nixon for re-election was sent by direct mail to thousands of individuals. A reprint of a newspaper article indicating that Representative Pete McCloskey would consider backing a third-party candidate was mailed to thousands of people in plain number 10 envelopes with commemorative or unusual stamps to disguise the true mailing source (U.S. Senate 1974a, pp. 240–41).

Another strategy was the disruption of the campaigns of political opponents. The Committee to Re-elect the President hired Donald Segretti to formulate and distribute false and misleading literature about the Democratic contenders. Segretti was most successful in his work during the 1972 Florida primary, where he devised and distributed 300 posters that read: "Help Muskie in Bussing (sic) More Children Now" (U.S. Senate 1974a, p. 261). The posters were signed by the "Mothers Backing Muskie Committee," a fictitious organization (U.S. Senate 1974a, p. 261). The intention was to associate Senator Edmund Muskie with a strong pro-busing position, a position highly unpopular in Florida at the time. Additionally, Segretti and his associates printed and distributed 1,000 four-by-six inch cards that read: "If You Liked Hitler, You'll Just Love Wallace" (U.S. Senate 1974a, p. 261). The other side of the cards bore the inscription: "A Vote for Wallace is a Wasted Vote. On March 14, Cast Your Vote for Senator Muskie" (U.S. Senate 1974a, p. 261). The intent was to drive a wedge between the Muskie and George Wallace campaigns. Finally, the Segretti team composed a counterfeit letter on Muskie's stationery that alleged sexual improprieties by Democratic candidates Henry Jackson and Hubert Humphrey. Similar tactics by Segretti and his men were perpetrated in Wisconsin, Illinois, the District of Columbia, and California (U.S. Senate 1974a, pp. 261-62, 264-67).

The Incumbency Responsiveness Program

This program was devised to politicize the executive branch. On August 16, 1971 John Dean wrote to presidential advisors H.R. Haldeman and John Ehrlichman about how the administration could use its incumbency to deal with opponents by using federal bureaucracies to "screw" the White House's enemies (U.S. Senate 1974a, p. 59). Dean and his associates developed a plan in which diverse types of executive functions were adapted to the administration's goal of self-preservation. Key members of the president's staff were asked to suggest the names of persons who should be given a "hard time" politically. The project coordinator was then supposed to determine what kinds of dealings these individuals had with the federal government and how they could best be "screwed" (for example, through grant availability, federal contracts, litigation, and prosecution). Finally, the project coordinator was to enlist the full support of bureaucratic officials who were necessary to the neutralization of Nixon's enemies (U.S. Senate 1974a, p. 59). The "enemies list" scheme was another part of the Incumbency Responsiveness Program. Nixon's enemies (identified by his inner staff) were subjected to wiretapping, IRS audits, and physical surveillance. Other illegal political tactics utilized to insure Nixon's reelection involved personnel decisions (Nixon supporters got key jobs). Ethnic and regional groupings considered crucial to an electoral majority were targeted for special consideration in dealing with the government. Grants, contracts and loans were disproportionately awarded to these target groups (U.S. Senate 1974a, pp. 329–408).

The most direct criminal activity occurred in the administration's tamperings with the regulatory agencies created by Congress to curb the growth of corporate power and to protect citizens from being abused by employers and other large interests. In the Nixon administration's program, favorable but illegal decisions were granted to interest groups that supported (or could support) the administration, but whose activities might have been subject to criminal penalties. For example, the Equal Employment Opportunity Commission closed an investigation into discriminatory hiring practices by the University of Texas in 1972. By granting this favor to the university, the Nixon administration hoped to curry favor with influential Texans. Because of its large bloc of electoral votes, Texas was important to Nixon's reelection chances. Unions are another key source of support and funds for political candidates. In the early 1970s, when the leader of a Philadelphia dock and wharf builder's union was being investigated by the Department of Labor, administration officials intervened and persuaded the department to give the union a "clean bill of health" (U.S. Senate 1974a, pp. 382–84).

The Incumbency Responsiveness Program also engendered a number of strategies to centralize governmental power in the executive branch of government. Arthur Vidich (1977) maintained that there were five above-ground interventions by the Nixon White House to centralize government power in the executive branch:

First, the White House dominated foreign affairs by secret diplomacy, and the agencies normally involved in the formulation of foreign policy were left uninformed. Nixon and Kissinger ignored the established protocols of decision making and pursued their own seemingly contradictory policies, such as detente with the Soviet Union and China, and the secret bombings of Laos and Cambodia. Second, the Office of Management and Budget (OMB) was set up within the executive branch as a watchdog agency designed to monitor government operations in all spheres. Administratively, the OMB stood between the president and the executive departments. The cabinet's power was undermined by giving representatives of the OMB policy-making discretion over each government department. This served to formalize the Nixon inner circle's organizational control over all branches of government, and rendered impotent the more traditional sources of authority and policy. Third, the president impounded congressionally-approved expenditures, thus depriving congressmen of one of their main sources of rewards to their constituents. Impoundment also weakened the bargaining position of congressmen with lobbyists, who had already paid for their share of the blocked funds. Congressmen therefore became more dependent on the president for campaign funds and other patronage. Fourth, revenue-sharing, or direct grants to state and local governments, again deprived congressmen of credit for federal expenditures in their voting districts. This placed a hardship on urban liberal congressmen who had become accustomed to taking credit from blacks and other minority groups for delivering the federal dollar in the form of welfare, educational, urban renewal, housing, and other funds. Fifth, the traditional campaign apparatus of the Republican party was circumvented by the creation of the Committee to Re-elect the President, which solicited and controlled campaign contributions.

These five frontstage strategies suggest that the backstage tamperings by the White House were not aberrations but rather extreme portions of the president's general program of intervention into the domestic life and institutions of the United States. Both backstage and frontstage manipulations were motivated by fear. The public disclosures of these interventions resulted in the gradual withdrawal of public support for the president. The last group to withdraw support was the business class, which had benefited in many ways during the Nixon administrations. Nixon's 1972 campaign had attracted contributions from the major corporations because of favorable regulatory actions (or promises of such favorable treatment). The re-election committee, however, deemed these contributions insufficient and demanded that large corporations contribute additional, specified amounts of money. Many corporate officials felt this amounted to extortion, but they reluctantly contributed large amounts in fear of administration reprisal (Von Hoffman 1976, p. 6; Cockburn 1974, p. 8).

The CIA

The Central Intelligence Agency is barred from taking on clandestine functions within the United States, but this agency has engaged in many illegal domestic interventions beyond its involvement in Watergate. For example, the CIA illegally trained several local police departments in the arts of intelligence and provocation. Over 50 police officers from about a dozen American cities were trained by the CIA in the use of explosives, wiretapping, and intelligence management in the early 1970s (Burnham 1972). Victor Marchetti and John Marks claim that the agency's training of American police began in 1967, when

Chicago police were trained in intelligence tactics at the CIA's headquarters in Langley, Virginia, and at the special CIA training institution at Camp Peary, Virginia (Marchetti and Marks 1974, pp. 216-18).

In addition to establishing relationships with a variety of law enforcement organizations, the CIA worked surreptitiously through other institutions. The agency, for example, funneled $3 million to the National Student Association, the nation's largest student group. In return for this subsidy of 80 percent of its expenses, NSA, with chapters on 300 campuses, supplied the CIA with dossiers on foreign students, which were then sifted for evidence of tie-ins between leftist student leaders and foreign governments (Ross 1975). Phillip Agee provides a long list of public and private organizations, both domestic and foreign, that were controlled, supported, or used by the CIA for two decades (1975, pp. 600-21).

In the 1960s, the CIA owned several commercial airways in the United States, including Air America, Civil Air Transport, Intermountain Aviation, and Southern Air Transport. These airlines, dubbed "proprietary" organizations by the agency, reportedly served as "fronts" for intelligence activities. It is not known exactly what functions these airlines served, but the fact that they were owned by the CIA constitutes illegal intervention into private domestic affairs, that is, secret ownership of private corporations by a government agency (Marchetti and Marks 1974, p. 149).

The FBI

The FBI, like the White House and the CIA, went to extremes in order to protect the nation from what it claimed to be serious internal threats to national security, such as terrorism, violence, civil disorders, communism, subversion, and hostile foreign intelligence activity. Actually, FBI targets included law-abiding citizens and domestic groups defined as national security risks. This agency's misuse of power by political policing is illustrated in the following cases.

The Campaign Against Dr. Martin Luther King

FBI director Hoover feared that Dr. Martin Luther King would become a messiah for black people in the United States. The idea that King would eventually embrace the revolutionary tactics of the Black Panthers or Black Muslims alarmed the bureau. One month before Dr. King's assassination, a memo from FBI headquarters stated that one of the goals of the bureau's counter-intelligence program (COINTELPRO) was to prevent the rise of a black leader who could unify and electrify the black nationalist movement. As early as 1963, the bureau had labeled King the most dangerous and effective black leader in the country (Wise 1977). A longstanding concern of the FBI was the extent of communist influence among Dr. King's advisors—a concern that prompted the FBI to keep King's entourage under surveillance as early as the late 1950s (Wise 1976, p. 38).

The Kennedy administration was pressured by Hoover to wiretap Dr. King in order to substantiate the director's suspicion of communist influence in the civil rights movement. A tap on King's home phone in Atlanta remained in place for eighteen months, well beyond the one-month limit established by law. The FBI also wiretapped the Southern Christian Leadership Conference (SCLC) headquarters in Atlanta and New York. The longest FBI wiretap was in the Atlanta SCLC office and lasted from November 1963 to June 1966 (Wise 1976, p. 39).

The FBI supplemented these taps with electronic bugs in King's hotel rooms in Washington D.C. and six states. In tapes from the hotel room buggings, the FBI allegedly overheard Dr. King engaging in a series of extramarital affairs, and used this information to discredit him (Wise 1976, p. 40). Hoover aide Cartha DeLoach attempted to peddle the tape transcripts from the illegal bugs to journalists Jay Iselin and Benjamin Bradlee, but both refused to write stories based upon the transcripts (Wise 1976, p. 40). This effort having failed, the FBI on November 21, 1964, mailed an anonymous letter and a tape of the King hotel room bugs to King and his wife Coretta, advising King to commit suicide by the time he was to receive the Nobel prize in Oslo on December 10, 1964 (Wise 1976, pp. 40–41).

The vicious campaign against Dr. King included several other actions. In 1964, the FBI attempted to discourage Marquette University from awarding him an honorary degree, and approached Cardinal Spellman in an effort to dissuade the Pope from speaking with King. In 1968, the FBI covertly played a role in King's decision to stay at the Lorraine Hotel in Memphis, where he was assassinated. In March of that year, Dr. King went to Memphis to participate in a garbage workers' strike. On March 28, the FBI drafted a blind memo (bearing no FBI markings), intended for release to the news media, which criticized Dr. King for lodging at the Holiday Inn during his stay in Memphis. The Holiday Inn, according to the memo, was owned, operated and patronized by whites. The Hotel Lorraine, on the other hand, was owned by blacks and catered to a black clientele. No one is certain whether the memo was distributed to the press, but Dr. King did finally decide to change hotels. On April 4 King was assassinated at the Lorraine (Wise 1976, p. 42).

This campaign against King was characteristic of covert manipulations by the FBI, designed to disrupt and suppress individual freedom and the viability of legitimate social movements. The bureau often carried out these covert actions without notifying the attorney general or other executive branch officials, including the president. Such action suggests that the FBI was not what its name implies, but rather a politicized action agency that would go to any length to disrupt and destroy politically "subversive" activities. The FBI's definition of subversion has been a broad one, including the acts, ideologies, and goals of dissidents (New Left members, race leaders, radical student leaders, Puerto Rican Independence Movement members, members of the Socialist Workers party and of the Communist party, antiwar demonstators, civil rights movement members,

Black Nationalist movement members, Ku Klux Klan members, and members of any group that criticized property relations or free enterprise). All of these were perceived as members of a disloyal opposition and became targets of attack by the FBI (Chomsky 1975, pp. 9–38).

COINTELPRO

Aside from King, other individuals and groups have been illegally discredited by the FBI. During the mid 1960s and the early 1970s, draft counselors were deliberately and falsely accused of being FBI informants; contributions to black organizations were blocked; antiwar movements were falsely tied in with radical and communist ideologies; New Left members were intimidated by frequent and intense FBI interviews; pressures were placed upon university administrators to fire activist professors; and the bureau interfered with the free exchange of ideas among speakers, teachers, and writers (U.S. Senate 1976).

The FBI centralized its antisubversive campaigns into a single counterintelligence operation called COINTELPRO, which lasted from the late 1960s through the early 1970s. The purpose of this program was to expose, disrupt, and neutralize the memberships and the activities of various New Left organizations and radical groups (Viorst 1976, p. 21). COINTELPRO had four tactics: planting fictitious stories in the newspapers and other media; creating internal discord in "subvervise" movements; around-the-clock surveillance and intelligence gathering to implicate New Left leaders in actions they did not plan or organize; and direct disruptions of people and groups, either through burglaries, theft, use of informants, or agents provocateurs (Wall 1972).

The FBI attempted covertly to influence public opinion about certain persons and organizations by funneling derogatory information to the press anonymously or through friendly news contacts. For instance, the bureau planted a series of derogatory articles about Martin Luther King and the Poor People's Campaign through "cooperative news media sources." The same sources reported favorable images of the FBI and prevented critical articles about the bureau from being published (U.S. Senate 1976). According to former FBI agent James Wall, the FBI frequently leaked false stories to the press and television stations prior to mass rallies and demonstrations planned by New Left organizations. These stories characteristically predicted that the demonstrations would be large and violent. Leaders of the movement were erroneously linked with the North Vietnamese government. This served to evoke fear from the public and to discourage nonviolent members of the protesting organizations from participating (Wall 1972, p. 14).

Dissension among New Left groups was created by equally deceptive tactics. For example, a fictitious letter was the source of considerable confusion prior to a 1969 demonstration in Washington, D.C. that was planned by the National Mobilization Committee, a coalition of New Left organizations. The FBI sent a letter to the committee, stating that the blacks of Washington would not support the demonstration unless a $20,000 security bond was paid to a black organization in Washington. The letter was signed with the forged signature of a major black leader. At the same time, FBI informants planted in the black organizations in Washington suggested the idea of the security bond to black leaders. These actions produced misunderstandings within the National Mobilization Committee that had a significant effect upon the planning for the march (Wall 1972, pp. 14–15).

A 24-hour surveillance was utilized when it became necessary to implicate someone in a conspiracy. This was not difficult to do, because most any meeting between friends, colleagues, or family could be used to show a conspiracy. The conspiracy law created under the 1968 Omnibus Act did not require that any conspiracy plan be documented. All one had to do was prove that three or more persons established contact with one another to incite a riot or civil disturbance; and with a person under 24-hour surveillance, such "evidence" is easy to fabricate. Stokely Carmichael was a victim of such surveillance. When he moved to Washington, D.C. in December of 1967, he was followed constantly by agents on foot, in cars, and in lookouts (usually houses and apartment buildings). In the wake of the rioting in Washington following the assassination of Martin Luther King, 50 agents were assigned to follow him. These agents submitted voluminous reports to J. Edgar Hoover documenting Carmichael's minute-by-minute activities. The reports were heavily slanted to suggest that Carmichael plotted, planned, and directed the pillage that occurred in Washington, because the agents were assigned in the first place to prove Carmichael's role in a conspiracy. Participants and bystanders at the riot scene stated that Carmichael attempted to discourage the rioting (Wall 1972, p. 18).

Large numbers of warrantless break-ins have been conducted by intelligence agencies since World War II. In the 1960s alone, the FBI and the CIA conducted hundreds of break-ins, many against U.S. citizens and domestic organizations, and for such purposes as the installation of microphones and the theft of membership lists from organizations defined as subversive by the bureau (U.S. Senate 1976). An FBI memo obtained by the Senate Intelligence Committee in 1976 showed that the bureau had conducted 238 illegal burglaries or "black bag jobs" between 1942 and 1968 for "national security" reasons, and that numerous entries had been made against unnamed subversive targets. The targets of these illegal tactics have frequently not been threats to national security or persons intent on the criminal subversion of democratic society (Sykes 1978, p. 226; *Commercial Appeal* 1975b). Some writers have estimated the real number of black bag jobs to be as high as 1,000 (Ladner 1976). Ninety-two break-ins occurred at offices of the Socialist Workers party during the 1950s and 1960s and were specifically approved by the Washington FBI headquarters (*Commercial Appeal* 1976c, 1976d). Former FBI director Clarence Kelley claimed that all FBI burglaries ceased in 1968, but it is known that some break-ins occurred as recently as 1976 (Crewdson 1976).

Violent tactics were used to intimidate the more radical and quasi-underground organizations. Between 1971 and 1976, the FBI assaulted radicals, and burned or disassembled their cars (rendering them immobile for surveillance purposes). The car burnings were done with Molotov cocktails so that they would appear to be the work of other radicals (Horrock 1976). The extent of the FBI vendetta against the radicals is indicated by the 233 COINTELPRO actions taken against the Black Panthers from 1969 to 1971. In a crucial instance, the FBI supplied the Illinois state attorney's office with data on weapons in the Panther headquarters in Chicago and the layout of the apartment of Illinois Panther leader Fred Hampton (including the location of his bed and the fact that he slept there every night). Hampton was shot to death by Chicago police on December 4, 1969 (*Clarion-Ledger* 1976d).

The FBI also successfully fomented and incited violence between groups on the radical left. In San Diego, Los Angeles, San Francisco, and Chicago, the Bureau stirred up violence between the Black Panthers and other radical groups, such as the U.S. Organization and the Blackstone Rangers. Spencer Davis, a spokesman for the Senate Intelligence Committee, disclosed that in Los Angeles the FBI had used threatening telephone calls, firebombings, beatings, and shootings in order to prevent radical groups from working with one another. In San Diego, the tensions developed from FBI harrassment led to the killing of four radicals by opposing radical organizations (St. Louis *Post-Dispatch* 1976). In several instances the FBI falsely and anonymously labeled as government informants members of groups known to be violent, thereby exposing them to expulsion or physical attack. Additionally, the bureau anonymously attacked the political beliefs of targets in order to induce their employers to fire them, and mailed anonymous letters to the spouses of intelligence targets for the purpose of destroying their marriages. Misinformation was utilized to disrupt demonstrations through the broadcast of fake orders and instructions to demonstrators, false completion of forms for demonstrators, and anonymous letters to leaders of street gangs (U.S. Senate 1976).

In late 1977, further information came to light about the FBI's COINTELPRO program. A new series of documents released by the bureau showed that it sent anonymous letters to members of the Communist party (CPUSA), encouraging its informants to stir up dissension in the party ranks. For instance, an effort was made to persuade the Socialists Workers party to siphon off members from the rival CPUSA. Bureau agents subscribed to *The Militant*, a publication of the Socialist Workers Party, in the name of Communist party leaders. In a January 24, 1957 memo, FBI Director Hoover stated that the bureau "encourages increased participation by . . . informants in controversial discussions" designed to cause disunity at the Communist party's national convention in New York in February of that year (*Clarion-Ledger* 1977l). The FBI files also contain an October 1956 letter from Hoover to the Internal Revenue Service listing the names of 336 Communist party leaders who had gone underground, and requesting the IRS to investigate these persons for possible income tax violations. Hoover also asked this agency to provide him with any information concerning the employment or residences of persons on this list (*Clarion-Ledger* 1977l).

Documents published in 1977 showed that the bureau made concerted efforts to disrupt the Poor People's March on Washington, organized by Martin Luther King and the Southern Christian Leadership Conference in April 1968. When FBI agents in Pennsylvania learned that a steel company official had made a donation for the march, they attempted to dissuade him from lending further support to it. The FBI also edited, published, and distributed a student newspaper in Washington, D.C., discrediting antiwar movement leaders (*Clarion-Ledger* 1977m).

In order to maintain their credentials in violence-prone groups, FBI informants (in the pay of the bureau) have themselves engaged in violent activity. An FBI informant in the Ku Klux Klan who was present at the murder of a civil rights worker in Mississippi in 1964 later helped to solve the crime. While performing duties for the FBI, he had beaten people up, kicked people on buses, and beaten blacks in restaurants. The FBI requires agents to instruct informants that they may not engage in violence (U.S. Senate 1976).

The FBI infiltrators in the Ku Klux Klan publicly exposed Klan members and harassed them in a number of ways. FBI agents sent anonymous letters to Klan members threatening to expose their sex and drinking habits, or simply letting them know that someone knew of their secret membership in the organization. FBI agents cultivated friendly relationships with North Carolina journalists who printed unfavorable articles about the Klan in some of the state's newspapers (*Clarion-Ledger* 1977m; 1977n).

Court records in 1977 revealed that the FBI paid $2.5 million in Chicago to recruit an army of more than 5,000 spies who informed on Chicago-area residents and organizations between 1966 and 1976. During the same period, the FBI opened files on about 27,900 individuals and organizations in Chicago who were regarded as possible security risks or extremists. The same court records document an FBI break-in of the offices of the Chicago Committee to Defend the Bill of Rights, formed during the McCarthy era to oppose government repression. A list of financial contributors was taken and dossiers were subsequently developed on 46 persons whose names appeared on the list. These actions, were made public when Judge Alfred Kirkland of the U.S. District Court, ordered the FBI to answer written questions in a suit brought by the American Civil Liberties Union that alleged government spying (Tybor 1978a).

Of the $2.5 million paid to the Chicago informants by the FBI between 1966 and 1976, about $2.1 million went to persons who provided information about possible security risks, that is, about individuals and groups who were defined by the FBI as not necessarily violent but as espousing controversial or unpopular ideas such as opposition to the Vietnam war. A spokesman for the American Civil Liberties Union declared that most of the spying in Chicago was political spying, and that the massiveness of this illegal political policing signified that the FBI considered itself above the law (Tybor 1978a).

The IRS

The FBI and CIA have often cooperated with other agencies in domestic counterintelligence operations, especially with the IRS. The IRS abused its investigative powers in the 1960s and 1970s by granting the CIA and FBI illegal access to taxpayer returns. The IRS buckled under pressures applied by the intelligence community to take action against certain taxpayers for reasons having no bearing upon compliance with the tax laws. The FBI made 200 requests for tax returns as part of the COINTELPRO program. Over half of these returns belonged to members of New Left and Black Nationalist movements. A report of the Senate Intelligence Committee cited the case of a university professor in the midwest whose tax returns were audited by the IRS in order to distract him from engaging in a series of planning sessions for demonstrations at the 1968 Democratic Convention in Chicago. In another program apparently unrelated to the FBI's COINTELPRO operation, a special IRS unit conducted tax investigations between 1969 and 1973 on 11,000 politically active individuals as well as on some politically militant organizations (such as *Ramparts* magazine and the Southern Christian Leadership Conference). In this program, the IRS gave the FBI lists of persons and organizations who contributed financially to the SCLC. All of these tax investigations were initiated on the basis of political rather than tax criteria (New York *Times* 1976a; U.S. Senate 1976). Likewise, many persons, including George Wallace, were investigated by the IRS at the behest of the Nixon administration. In 1973, a Florida IRS agent utilized surveillance and break-in tactics to gather information on the sex lives and drinking habits of thirty political figures, including federal judges in Miami, Florida (New York *Times* 1975b; Horrock 1975).

Agents Provocateurs

Government agencies have suppressed political enemies through the use of "agents provocateurs" who infiltrated radical groups by posing as members and then encouraged the membership to commit crimes. Such entrapment is itself a crime. Agents provoked violent crimes by organized political groups in a number of cities in the late 1960s and early 1970s. In Chicago, government agents provoked violence between demonstrators and police at the 1968 Democratic National Convention and the killing of two members of the Black Panther party in 1969. In Los Angeles, the confrontation between the police and the Black Panthers and the raid upon the Black Muslim temple were also encouraged by the work of agents. Provocateurs engaged in violent incidents at the University of Alabama, Ohio State University, and other campuses during the late 1960s and early 1970s (Quinney 1975, p. 151).

The provocateurs were sponsored and paid by local, state, and federal law enforcement organizations who cooperated with one another from time to time in the disruption of dissident organizations. Sometimes the agents worked only for a single agency responsible for a limited jurisdiction, such as a local police force, county sheriff, or state bureau of investigation. Regardless of the type of arrangement the agents worked under, they were successful in disrupting the programs of radical groups. Often the provocateurs gained the respect and trust of the radicals to the point where they achieved leadership positions, a perfect cover. Provocateurs then initiated violent acts and later, after their true identities were made public, served as key prosecution witnesses (Karmen 1974). FBI agent Gerald Kirk, for instance, posed as an activist of the Students for a Democratic Society at the University of Chicago, and served as the secretary, treasurer, and chairman of the Communist party's regional student organization. Shortly before his graduation, at a student sit-in, he was exposed as an FBI agent. He later testified before the Senate about his role in organizing student activities on the Chicago campus (Karmen 1974, p. 212). In another case, William Frappoly, who worked as an agent of the Chicago Police Intelligence Division, joined the chapter of the Students for a Democratic Society at Northeast Illinois State College. He was expelled from that school for his involvement with a small group of militant students who threw the university's president off a stage. Using his college background as a stepping stone, he later became active in the protests at the 1968 Democratic Convention in Chicago. As a key witness for the prosecution during the Chicago Eight Conspiracy Trial, Frappoly admitted that during the convention he had attempted to persuade radicals to sabotage public facilities and military vehicles (Karmen 1974, p. 212).

At Kent State University in Ohio, an agent of the FBI and the campus police, Terrance Norman, was believed to have precipitated the volley of shots by the Ohio National Guard which killed four Kent State students. Norman posed as a photographer but was wearing a gas mask and brandished a pistol. He reportedly shot the pistol four times and may have shot a demonstrator. The National Guard volleys followed shortly thereafter (Karmen 1974, pp. 212-13). Two years after the Kent State shootings, a Kent State student named Reinhold Mohn began to visit the local chapter of the Vietnam Veterans Against the War, an organization of former soldiers dedicated to ending the war in Vietnam. He suggested that the organization adopt violent tactics as a means of ending the war. A few months later the local Kent police arrested Mohr for carrying a Chinese AK-47 machine gun, whereupon he confessed to being an undercover agent in the employ of the Kent State University security department (Karmen 1974; Powers 1972).

The vice squad of the Tuscaloosa, Alabama city police and the FBI jointly hired Charles Grimm in 1970 to serve as an undercover agent at the University of Alabama campus. Grimm eventually emerged as the fiery leader of the Student-Faculty Coalition. In his work as a student radical, Grimm openly urged violence, encouraged the setting of four fires on campus, solicited dynamite from other students, and made Molotov cocktails (Karmen 1974, p. 213). One noted undercover agent, M.L. Singkata Thomas Tonyai, alias "Tommy the Traveller," visited several campuses in order to instigate student violence.

"Tommy" frequented several upstate New York campuses during a two-year period and encouraged violence by offering students bombs, guns, and lessons in guerilla warfare techniques. He also allegedly made bombs, test-fired M-1 rifles, and experimented with dynamite detonations. He worked for the Ontario (N.Y.) County Sheriff, who admitted that Tommy's violent behavior was a front for his work as an undercover narcotics agent (Karmen 1974, p. 213). In another unusual case, Sheriff's Deputy Kevin Caffery posed as a campus radical at the State University of New York at Buffalo. Caffery made gasoline bombs and claymore mines during his short career as a student activist at the Buffalo campus (Karmen 1974, p. 213).

From an analysis of several case histories of agents provocateurs such as those given above, Karmen (1974) delineated seven steps in the provocation process. First, a group, territory, or situation is chosen for infiltration. Second, the agent selects a cover identity that fits his background, personality, inclination, skills, and required role. Third, in order to develop credibility (and to avoid suspicion) the agent builds his images and begins to fulfill his role requirements. This usually means doing party work and chores, picketing, demonstrating, or street fighting. Fourth, the agent begins to search out action-prone individuals or cliques within the target group. Fifth, once the agent's contact with militant members of the target group is established, he begins to direct the militant faction toward violent tactics. The agent purchases the needed materials for violence, and he may participate in the illegal acts of violence that he provokes. Sixth, police close in at the most compromising moment, and the agent's active phase terminates. Finally, at the trial, in carefully rehearsed testimony, the agent denies any acts of entrapment, but admits complicity with the criminal events.

Within the anti-establishment movements of the 1960s and 1970s, provocateurs were extremely destructive because they fomented an atmosphere of fear, distrust, and animosity in the targeted groups. They widened a gulf between groups espousing legal reformation and groups advocating underground activity. They obstructed the growth of the antiwar movement by endangering all participants, and destroyed the movement's development by interfering directly or indirectly in policy making. Provocations decimated the movement's leadership, destroyed close relationships between leaders and followers, and forced the movement to adopt a defensive posture in the face of costly court cases and unfavorable publicity (Karmen 1974, p. 224).

In the final analysis, the exploits of the agents provocateurs were successful, as evidenced by the fact that most radical groups after 1970 either folded or split into factions. Some factions advocated violent means of revolution, whereas others advocated non-violent means of revolution. In cases where the provocateurs were exposed, the members of the group felt that they could no longer trust any present or future members. The provocateurs had frequently been group leaders, so it was evident that most anyone with cunning and skill could infiltrate a target group and eventually turn state's evidence against it. In cases where the government agents were not exposed, the violence they perpetrated tended to alienate the majority of the student activists who did not advocate violent tactics. The subsequent bickering among leaders and followers led to the decline of many movement groups. The pro-violence factions tended to go underground and engage in terrorist bombings and guerrilla warfare (Karmen 1974).

Drug, Behavioral, and Bacterial Experiments

One of the more frightening ways in which some agencies of the government planned to deal with dissenters was by the manipulation of behavior with mind-altering drugs, aversive therapy, and "behavior modification" techniques. Some of these programs were originally justified on the basis that foreign enemies of the United States were already using them (New York *Times* 1977b).

CIA

The CIA's program of mind-control experimentation, MK ULTRA/ DELTA. operated for about 25 years (estimated 1950–75) at a cost of $25 million. The purpose of the project was to find the most efficient means of controlling human behavior through such means as hypnosis, drugs, and brainwashing. The idea for the program germinated during the 1949 treason trial of Hungarian dissident Joseph Cardinal Mindszenty, whose vacant expression and robot-like behavior on the witness stand convinced CIA officials that the communists had discovered a way to control people's behavior. The CIA decided to emulate these techniques with full knowledge of their illegality (New York *Times* 1977b).

MK ULTRA/DELTA encompassed several secretly-funded research projects involving drugs (LSD, alcohol, and tranquilizers), undetermined substances, and sensory deprivation. Experiments were conducted at several respected institutions, including 44 colleges and universities, and several hospitals, prisons, and pharmaceutical companies. Many prominent professors and medical doctors supervised this CIA-funded project wherein research subjects were often unknowingly and unwillingly fed a variety of substances (New York *Times* 1977a). In some cases the subjects willingly took part in the experiments, but neither the subjects nor the researchers were aware that the research was funded by the CIA. Such a case occurred at the Boston Psychiatric Hospital in the 1950s, where 200 people volunteered to take LSD in a controlled experiment (New York *Times* 1977a).

A highly disturbing aspect of this CIA program was the quality of the individuals and institutions who participated in carrying out the experiments. Twenty-six universities have admitted receiving money and carrying out research of this kind for the CIA, including Columbia, Cornell, George Washington, Harvard, Illinois, Indiana, Maryland, McGill, Minnesota, Ohio State, Oklahoma, Pennsylvania, Pennsylvania State, Princeton, Rutgers, Texas, and Texas Christian

(Thomas 1977). The contributions of these universities to MK ULTRA/DELTA lent the program a legitimacy that was unwarranted given the brazen illegalities of the research

A New York *Times* reporter's inquiries in 1977 found that CIA campus research varied from innocuous sociological surveys to tests aimed at finding better ways to administer drugs to unsuspecting subjects. At many universities only the professor supervising the research knew its real sponsor and purpose. Research funds were often disbursed by independent research organizations who told only the professor that the research funds were actually financed by the CIA. For instance, sociological, cultural, and anthropological studies were financed through the Society for the Investigation of Human Ecology, based at Cornell University. Biomedical and medical research was often financed through the Geschickter Fund for Medical Research of Georgetown University (Thomas 1977). Unfortunately, a number of factors have made it impossible to pinpoint the professors involved and how much university administrators knew about the covert funding arrangements. The passage of time, in some cases 20 years, has made it difficult to reconstruct the important events in any detail. Moreover, the CIA's secrecy during the projects and the incomplete nature of the records provided by this agency have made it difficult to document completely these questionable and in some cases illegal projects (Thomas 1977).

The CIA's secrecy regarding MK ULTRA/DELTA was reprehensible because the effects of the experiments on unwitting subjects were negative or even fatal. Frank Olson, an Army biochemist who was given LSD in 1953 as part of the ULTRA program, jumped to his death from a New York City hotel window while under the influence of the drug. The CIA kept Olson's intake of LSD from his family until 1975, when the whole case was published in the press (Horrock 1977). Some of the experiments were not only illegal but absurd. One of the CIA's most bizarre experiments with mind control and behavioral modification was a project called "Operation Midnight Climax." A CIA employee hired prostitutes to covertly slip their customers an exotic chemical or biological agent while operatives watched the proceedings through a two-way mirror (*Clarion-Ledger* 1977f).

The full extent of MK ULTRA/DELTA and the use made of its research findings may never be known because of the CIA's veil of secrecy; internal CIA accounting procedures were waived in these cases. One physician who conducted research in the program reported that drugs were tested for their suitability in interrogation and "knockout" operations, that is, their capacity to disable a human target temporarily (Horrock 1977). Given the tensions and fears during the Cold War years, it is likely that such drugs were used against American dissidents. A plan presented by G. Gordon Liddy to the Committee to Re-elect the President in 1972 called for a security force at the 1972 Republican National Convention that would inject radical protesters with "knockout" drugs. The protesters could then be transported to Mexico and detained until after the convention. Jack Anderson, a long-time critic of the Nixon administration, found in

1977 that Liddy had collaborated with a CIA doctor in a plan to drug him. The drug was to be slipped to Anderson in order to make him appear drowsy during a public appearance, thus discrediting him as a source of information (Anderson 1977).

Prisons

In several prison programs throughout the country, dangerous drugs, hypnosis, electroconvulsive shocks, brainwashing, psychosurgery, and sensory deprivation have been added to a group of therapies prison officials call "behavior modification." U.S. Bureau of Prisons institutions as well as a number of state correctional facilities have sponsored these so-called treatment programs. Some correctional facilities, faced with failure at rehabilitation, have been willing to resort to most anything to prevent recidivism. Researchers in these facilities speak in terms of behavioral engineering, the science of building and eliminating behaviors to suit the researcher's fancy. Inmates have been subjected to dangerous "treatment" programs that in reality exist for punishment and experimental and behavioral control purposes. Electric shock, as well as Anectine (which paralyzes muscles without dampening consciousness or the ability to feel pain), Librium, Thorazine, Ampomorphine, Prolixin, and Asklepienion, all dangersous drugs with negative side effects, have been combined in "treatment" with severe sensory deprivation, hypnosis, and a rigid manipulation of reward and punishment to gain almost complete control over an inmate's behavior. These various treatment programs frequently have been operated to segregate and sedate troublemakers and black militants, punish recalcitrants, and undermine some inmates' personality structures. As a result, many inmates have suffered physical disabilities and confusional states of mind (Sage 1974).

Some court systems, the federal judicial system, and the American Civil Liberties Union are beginning to realize that many of these treatment schemes do not constitute therapy but punishment of a cruel and unusual kind. Some prison administrations, fearing court action and public criticism associated with these illegal programs, have made euphemistic changes in the nomenclature of their treatment schedules (Sage 1974).

The Army

The army has also conducted studies similar to the CIA's covert drug projects. Drugs have been administered to unwitting subjects in unprofessional, unethical and illegal scenarios. At the U.S. Army installation at Edgewood, Maryland, 19 different hallucinatory and delirium-producing drugs were tried on 300 to 400 unwitting volunteers annually for an undisclosed period prior to 1963. Congressional investigators believe the programs began around 1953. During this time, an additional 585 enlisted men and officers were unknowingly given LSD for experimental purposes. Overall, servicemen at 900 army bases were given LSD in drug experiments; approximately 30 servicemen per month were tested between 1953 and 1975. LSD in these experiments was given surreptitiously in drinks. Further, 100 to 200 prisoners at Philadelphia's Holmesberg State Prison received drugs in army drug programs between 1967 and 1973 (Richards 1975).

The CIA and army tests documented above were limited to a specific number of subjects. Other tests utilizing bacteria exposed millions of U.S. citizens to illness, infectious diseases, and death between 1950 and 1966. The army tested the spread of the bacterium *serratia mercenscens* in eight U.S. cities and military bases. The tests were designed to chart the spread of bacteria so that defense analysts could assess America's readiness to combat a foreign enemy's biological warfare attacks. What the army program really amounted to, however, was a biological war against millions of unwilling Americans. Hundreds of citizens became ill, and a few died because of the army program (Cummings and Fetherston 1976). These tests were conducted in Key West and Panama City, Florida; San Francisco, California; New York City; Point Mugu and Port Hueneme (Los Angeles); Fort McClellan (Anniston, Alabama), and a naval facility in Mechanicsburg, Pennsylvania. The *serratia* bacteria were released in all of these sites. In the Mechanicsburg test, the army used an additional fungus that is known to be fatal when administered to humans (Cummings and Fetherston 1976).

The spread of illnesses in the wake of these bacteria projects has been documented. For instance, during 1952, when the army conducted the bacterium test at Fort McClellan, the number of pneumonia cases more than doubled in the surrounding county. This area in Alabama, though it comprised less than 3 percent of that state's total population, accounted for more than 12 percent of the reported cases of pneumonia. There was also a tenfold increase in pneumonia cases in the Key West area in the year after the army's test in that city, and a sevenfold increase in pneumonia deaths. According to the medical literature, the serratia bacterium is identified as a rare cause of pneumonia (Cummings and Fetherston 1976).

In the 1950 army test in San Francisco the germs spread to Stanford University Hospital, where one man died from *serratia* infection; but despite this knowledge, the army continued using the bacteria. The most vicious bacteria test was conducted in New York City, where a light bulb containing *serratia* was dropped from a moving subway train, and the spread of the bacteria through the subway tunnels was monitored (Cummings and Fetherston 1976).

The foregoing drug, behavioral, and bacterial experiments killed people and violated the Food and Drug Administration's regulations requiring that any person involved in medical or drug research be given: (1) A full explanation of the nature, expected duration, and purpose of the study; (2) A full and fair explanation of the procedures to be followed, including an identification of those that are experimental; (3) A disclosure of appropriate alternative procedures that would be advantageous to the subject; (4) A description of discomforts and risks; (5) A description of expected benefits; (6) An instruction that the subject is free to decline participation or terminate participation at any time without prejudice; (7) An offer to answer any questions (Winfrey 1978).

Destruction of the Environment

We discuss under this topic the destruction of the physical environment by corporations and by the government itself. Unfortunately neither of these formal organizations has recognized or heeded the findings of the Club of Rome, which clearly tie the environmental problem to an increase in population and industrial growth. This failure in itself is socially injurious. The Club of Rome, with the aid of large foundation grants, commissioned a detailed study of the likely effects of sustained growth patterns. The study was conducted by a Massachusetts Institute of Technology research team that used complex computer models to generate projections extending well into the twenty-first century. The report of this team, entitled *The Limits to Growth*, was published in 1972. The researchers concluded that mankind probably faces an uncontrollable and disastrous collapse of society and the economy within a hundred years unless we quickly establish a global equilibrium whereby population growth and industrial output remain constant. Should the human population continue to multiply, industrialize, consume resources, and pollute at its present rate, the planet's environmental system will be devastated beyond the point of sustaining industrial civilization or large numbers of people (Meadows et al. 1972). In great part, the following illustrations of corporate and government destruction of the environment inhere in the commitment to the capitalist ideology of the maximization of profits and growth.

Occupational Killers

The powdery pesticide Kepone has spectacularly brought the issue of occupational chemical pollution to the public eye. In 1974 and 1975, employees of the Life Sciences Product Company, Inc. of Hopewell, Virginia (now closed) were exposed to this substance. Many of these 149 workers suffered various nerve disorders as a result of their contact with Kepone, and several became permanently disabled. Many will probably contract cancer in the future from this exposure (*Clarion-Ledger* 1978e).

Approximately 100,000 U.S. citizens die annually from occupationally-related diseases, and many others suffer from a variety of pathological conditions caused by their work-site condition (lung ailments, liver ailments, black lung diseases, cancer, and heart trouble, among others). These ailments result from a few years to a life-time exposure to some of the thousands of industraial chemicals, radiation, excessive noise, and stressful work situations (U.S. Department of Labor 1972). We are primarily concerned at this point with occupational exposure to toxic chemicals and hazardous substances which could be reduced to safe levels or eliminated. The technology is available to accomplish this aim, federal regulatory agencies exist to oversee toxicity (the National Institute for Occupational Health and Safety, a part of the Department of Health, Education, and Welfare, and the Occupational Safety and Health Administration [OSHA], a part of the Labor Department), and the corporations have the money to pay for the job. The task is not accomplished because the political and economic system in the United States is structured and operated to maximize corporate profits at the expense of industrial workers. Corporations, with the compliance of weak regulatory agencies, avoid cleaning up unhealthy operations that result in disease and death (Swartz 1975).

Even when regulatory agencies take a stand against industry, industry fights back. As a case in point, the Occupational Safety and Health Administration in 1978 proposed a crash program to identify and control carcinogens, or cancer-causing agents in occupational work sites. In response, 40 companies, many of which are in the chemical industry, put up $1 million dollars to establish the American Industrial Health Council, a corporate council specially chartered to challenge the OSHA proposal. In 1978, the American Industrial Health Council filed an 85-page brief recommending that a select panel of scientists, rather than the government, should decide what substances cause cancer. It also recommended a narrower definition of carcinogens than that proposed by OSHA (Burnham 1978). OSHA claims that more than 1,000 Americans die every day of cancer, that from 60 to 90 percent of these cancers are caused by substances in the environment, and that millions of workers are exposed to an increasing number of known or suspected carcinogens. Industry, through its American Industrial Health Council, argues against this claim and denies that the increased use of industrial chemicals is causing an increase in cancer in the United States (Burnham 1978).

An often repeated scenario (historically documented) follows. Workers are exposed to toxic substances such as asbestos, vinyl chloride, beryllium, coal tar distillation products, arsenic, and cutting oils for many years without receiving any information about their dangers. First, a few articles pro and con about these substances appear in the scientific literature. Then in-house scientists, on the basis of rigged research projects, sanitize them. When it becomes public knowledge that these chemicals are related to disease and death among industrial workers, corporations mount a last ditch stand. They hire researchers to disprove the truth, have company doctors minimize the relationship between the workers' illnesses and the prevailing toxicity and thus minimize workers' compensation claims, threaten to close down shop operations should employees continue to complain about safety measures, and persuade regulatory agencies (whose enforcement procedures are already inadequate) to permit them a gradual reduction in toxicity safety levels for the substances under consideration. In regard to the latter strategy, it is obvious that a standard approaching zero is necessary to protect workers against some substances. Corporate agents postpone the elimination of work-site toxicity because the cost of the engineering improvements necessary to eliminate these hazards would greatly reduce corporate profits (Swartz 1975).

The case of asbestos exemplifies the process. The public is now aware that occupational exposure to asbestos has resulted in a large number of lung diseases, including cancer. Ironically, the link between asbestos and asbestiosis has been known about since 1900. From 1935 to 1965, reports in the medical literature indicated that asbestos was a probable cause of lung cancer, but the government bureaucracy and the medical community ignored this knowledge. Company doctors at the Johns-Manville plant in Manville, New Jersey diagnosed many lung diseases in the early 1970s among asbestos workers, but failed to inform them that their lung diseases were associated with asbestos. Following a study by the Statistical Research Unit of the British Medical Council, which concluded that lung cancer was related to the industrial hazards of certain asbestos workers, the asbestos industry funded a spurious study undertaken by the Industrial Hygiene Foundation (a front supported by industry). This study concluded that it was safe for employees to work with asbestos (Swartz 1975). Initially, under the Walsh-Healy Act, the government set a maximum asbestos exposure level at 12 fibres per cubic meter. In the early 1970s, inspections of an asbestos plant in Tyler, Texas disclosed that 117 of 138 samples in the plant exceeded the minimum standard, and that asbestos concentrations were ten times the allowable limit in parts of the plant. Yet, these violations were listed as "non-serious" by U.S. Government inspectors. Eventually, Pittsburgh-Corning, the owner of the plant, was fined a mere $210. By the time this plant closed in 1972, approximately half of the long-term workers had already developed asbestos disease symptoms (Brodeur 1974, p. 75). Of the 875 workers employed at closing time, 260 were expected to develop cancer within a period of 20 to 30 years. Ninety employees had already died of cancer, and several others were expected to be severely incapacitated by asbestiosis (Tieded 1978). Once asbestos fibers are ingested, they remain in the body.

Moreover, it is known that even secondary contact with asbestos can be crippling or fatal. Relatives of asbestos workers have become diseased (and died) because of exposure to asbestos dust brought home by the workers on their clothes. Although the asbestos plant in Tyler was dismantled in 1972, other workers in the industrial park where the plant was located were also exposed to asbestos. Waste material from the plant containing asbestos had been transported in trucks to huge open dumps. A half-million burlap bags impregnated with asbestos were sold to a nursery, which used the bags for packaging plants. In a similar case in the Pennsylvania town of Ambler, a corporation dumped asbestos wastes over a ten-block area in the heart of the town in 1974. Youngsters used the dump as a playground (Conot 1974, p. 5).

Chemical Pollution: Land and Water

Pesticides, products of corporate enterprise, are currently destroying the environment and endangering the health and safety of millions of Americans.

More than 300,000 chemicals are produced by chemical companies each year, and many of these are inadequately tested for their environmental and social safety. Birds, vegetation, fish, insects, and other wildlife have been known to die from chemicals sprayed along roadsides or in fields of crops. The vegetables sprayed with pesticides also carry residues, and thereby millions of Americans have become contaminated (Brody 1977; Hill 1977; Stevens 1977a). For example, the chemical DDT was widely applied on vegetable and crop-growing lands prior to its banishment in 1972. The contaminated crops were eaten by farm animals and eventually consumed by the public in the form of roast beef and steaks. In 1970, the average American carried pesticide residues in the amount of 12 parts per million in his fatty tissues. DDT levels in milk were .15 and .25 parts per million. American babies have consumed four times the maximum daily intake of DDT recommended by the United Nations and five times the amount of DDT that is usually allowed in interstate shipments of cow's milk.

A stark example of the ravages of water pollution is provided by the Great Lakes. In the late 1960s it was discovered that Cleveland, Detroit, Buffalo, and other cities were pouring untreated sewage and phosphorus into Lake Erie. At this time, Monsanto's Trenton, Michigan plant was dumping 5,000 pounds of phosphate wastes per day into the Detroit River. Approximately 3,800 metric tons of this compound, which is found in most brands of laundry detergent, were deposited into Lake Erie from Michigan washing machines during the late 1960s. This contamination nourished algae in the lake which killed the fish. Phosphates generally accelerate the natural aging of lakes, a process called eutrophication. A eutropic lake is one where algae and larger plants are increasingly taking over the water. The middle stages of eutrophication may actually enrich a lake's environment, but in the latter stages (as was the case in Lake Erie) this process depletes oxygen, chokes lakes with green plants, and kills off animal life. The phosphorus in the Great Lakes, together with mercury pesticides and PCBs from industrial wastes, are known to have killed fish in the Lakes in the 1960s. An additional hazard was presented by the Reserve Mining Company of Silver Bay, Minnesota, which discharged 67,000 tons of tacarite tailings (a refuse of steel production) daily into Lake Superior for 21 years (from the mid 1950s to the mid 1970s). This action contaminated the drinking water of Duluth, Minnesota with asbestos fibers (*Clarion-Ledger* 1976g; Stevens 1977b).

Occasionally, the damages of pollution are registered instantly. More than 50 persons along the Ohio River in the Louisville, Kentucky area became ill in March 1977 due to chemical fumes. Twenty-five employees of a sewage treatment plant required treatment after inhaling gases from a chemical called *hexachlora cyclopentadiene*, which was used in the production of pesticides. Twenty-seven employees of the U.S. Census Bureau in Clarkesville, Indiana, across the river from Louisville, also became ill from inhaling similar gases. All of these illnesses probably resulted from the 100 million gallons of raw sewage dumped into the Ohio River every day during this time (*Clarion-Ledger* 1977d).

Each year, half a million tons of crude oil are leaked or dumped into the oceans. Tons of phosphates in the form of agricultural fertilizers are carried by rivers to the sea. Lead, DDT, pesticides, and other poisons eventually wind up in the ocean. Consequently, fish and marine life die and the ocean declines as a source of food (McKee and Robertson 1975, p. 86).

Oil Spills

Oil spills resulting from off-shore drilling by big oil companies have contributed to the pollution of the oceans. Large spillings have had a destructive effect upon the ocean flora and fauna. The most publicized case occurred at Santa Barbara, California, in 1969, where a spill of 18,500 barrels of oil contaminated the beaches, killed birds, interfered with marine life, and disturbed the ecology of the ocean. Drilling continued despite a loud public outcry and numerous city, county, state, and individual lawsuits brought against the oil companies (Molotch 1973). The companies in this case paid small fines for heavy damage. Similar spills occurred three times off the Gulf Coast between 1967 and 1970, but received much less publicity (Crider 1975). The right of corporations to spill oil continues unabated. In late 1976, a series of spills off the Atlantic coast were reminiscent of those in the 1960s. The Department of the Interior sold off-shore leases along this same Atlantic coastline to oil companies in early 1977, prompting a wave of court fights to stop them.

The government itself sometimes blatantly engages in direct pollution of the environment. These instances rarely come to the attention of the public, because the government is perceived by many to be totally legitimate and immune from culpability regardless of what it does. For example, the Mayport, Florida Naval Station dumped 637,000 gallons of waste oil off the Florida coast into the oceans in 1972. The Defense Department failed to investigate the case. Such dumping violated the National Environmental Policy Act of 1969 (Lieberman 1972, p. 196).

Air Pollution

Air pollution is another threat to public safety that is a direct consequence of industrial activity. A citizen on the streets of New York inhales into his lungs the equivalent in toxic materials of 38 cigarettes a day, and atmospheric pollution cuts down on the amount of sunlight reaching this city by up to 25 percent. Other cities are worse off: pollution cuts out up to 40 percent of Chicago's sunlight. And cities are not the only areas affected by air pollution. Smog generated in urban and industrial areas has been sighted over the oceans and even over the North Pole. At present, the United States dumps more than 200 million tons of per person (Rienow and Rienow 1969, p. 141; Ehrlich and Ehrlich 1972, p. 146; Auchincloss 1970).

Air pollution comes from four main sources: transportation, power generation, industry, and waste incineration. It has been known for a long time that the most serious contributor to air pollution is the private automobile. Annually, U.S. cars release into the air some 66 million tons of carbon monoxide, one million tons of particulate matters, and a number of other noxious substances. Pollution control measures are directed at only a few of the gases and particles released through auto exhausts, and auto pollution is increasing. Power generation and industry produce in enormous quantities a large number of pollutants including sulphur oxide, carbon monoxide, nitrogen oxides and particulate matter. Waste incineration produces millions of tons of particulates and nitrogen oxides (McKee and Robertson 1975, pp. 83–84).

Air pollution on such a large scale poses a grave threat to public health. Deaths resulting from lung cancer and bronchitis are doubling every ten years, and emphysema, a lung disease, is the fastest growing cause of death in the United States. Air pollution has been directly implicated in these trends. The director of the National Institution of Environmental Health Services estimates that a tenth of the nation's annual bill for health services goes to treating illnesses resulting from atmospheric pollution (New York *Times* 1970).

Radioactive Wastes

Radioactive wastes generated by nuclear power plants pose another environmental problem. These wastes emit radiation which causes cancer or birth deformities in small doses and death in large doses. Low-level radiation has caused workers at the government's nuclear facilities in Hanford, Washington to die at a rate 5 percent greater than the general U.S. population (*Clarion-Ledger* 1978c). Shipyard employees who worked on the nation's first nuclear submarines at Portsmouth Navy Yard following World War II have died from cancer at a rate more than double the national average, with deaths from leukemia occurring at a rate 450 times higher than average (*Clarion-Ledger* 1978d).

One prototype nuclear power breeder reactor built outside Detroit in 1966 was closed down in 1975 after a "near miss" accident that violated the Atomic Energy Commission's safety specifications. Such a highly dangerous and experimental plant should never have been built so close to a densely populated industrial area. After the near accident, the Atomic Energy Commission (AEC) refused to file an official statement on the environmental impact of the breeder reactor program. Subsequently, private conservationist groups took the AEC before a federal court which declared that the "program presents unique and unprecedented environmental hazards to human health for hundreds of years" (McKee and Robertson 1975, p. 91).

Potential radioactive wastes are also carried by the 1,000 American and Soviet satellites which have been orbited in the past two decades. Many of these have carried uranium power packs involving tons of uranium in total. When such vehicles self-destruct on reentry into the atmosphere (as a Russian satellite did over Canada in 1978), a severe danger is posed to the ecosystem in the form of dispersed radioactive dust. Though the vehicles themselves self-destruct, the uranium dust remains and eventually enbeds into sea, soil, or living organisms. The dust forms a highly mobile radioactive dust cloud which follows worldwide weather tracks, poisons the air we beathe, and contaminates the rain, the soil, and the food we eat (Stevens 1978).

Food

After World War II, the food industry—dominated by a few large corporations—began to manipulate the public away from staples and toward synthetic foods. Due to the production and clever advertising of junk foods, U.S. citizens now consume between 21 and 25 percent fewer vegetables, dairy products, and fruits than 20 years ago, and 75 to 80 percent more snacks and soft drinks. Additionally, manufacturers have substituted artificial elements into many foods. Bread is made to appear as if it is made with butter and eggs, whereas in reality the elements that give the "buttery" essence are artificial coloring and flavoring. Pizza is made to look like the "real thing" with artificial tomato sauce. This adulteration and substitution is profitable to the food industry but unhealthy to consumers. Artificial bread, pizza, and other foods are cheaper to produce than products made with eggs, butter, tomatoes, and so on. The artificial products are chemically treated so that they may remain on the distributor's shelves for months. This suits both manufacturers, who can hold back food reserves in order to manipulate prices upward, and the chemical companies, whose business in food preservatives increases. There is now evidence that artificial foods are a major threat to public health. In testimony before the U.S. Senate in 1973, it was divulged that the artificial colorings and flavorings extant in 95 percent of all processed foods cause hyperactivity in children. A distinguished physician in a controlled experiment claimed that 15 of 25 research subjects (all children) were cured of hyperactivity simply by abstaining from processed foods (U.S. Senate 1973a).

In the quest to market flour quickly and profitably, baking corporations bypass the time-consuming processes necessary to the production of a nutritious brand of flour. The outer layer of the wheat berry is very nutritious, but the large food corporations do not take the time to use these layers. Without the layers, 14 key nutrients are left out and replaced by synthetic substitutes. In the language of the baking corporations, this is "enriched" flour. One of the key nutrients which "enriched" flour lacks is magnesium, and magnesium deficiencies have been linked to heart disease in humans (Jacobsen 1974, p. 47). The bleaching and refining of wheat products, including flour, also eliminates fiber or roughage from the diet, and fiber-poor diets are related to cancer of the intestine and rectum (Jacobsen 1974, p. 22). Evidence indicates that the American diet of these diseases and deficiencies are in part a consequence of the deliberate manipulation of the public by the food industry. Political reactions to this manipulation· have been weak because substitutions and adulterations by the food industry have been kept secret in the past. For instance, a study commissioned by the Nixon administration found that the American public was either malnourished or prone to develop nutritional problems. The study reported only preliminary results because once the embarrassing statistics began to surface the administration cancelled the project (Jacobson 1974, p. 1).

Corporate Resistance

The destruction of the environment and harm done to public health caused by corporate pollution were eventually challenged in the early 1970s by consumer advocates and environmentalists. Activists and a concerned public became aware of the fact that pollution directly violates the public's economic, political, and human interests. As a result of this awareness and subsequent public pressure, some laws have been passed prohibiting certain kinds of pollution. Corporate polluters have fought (and still fight) against the movement to clean up the environment and insure the production of nutritious foods. Pollution control interferes with corporate rights to increase production and profits—even at the expense of public health and safety.

The Reserve Mining Company of Duluth dumped thousands of tons of asbestos wastes into Lake Superior and stalled the public's efforts to place pollution control devices in its plants. While the case was held up in court litigations during the early 1970s, the company continued to dump its carcinogens into the lake, daily polluting the drinking water. The company manipulated its way through the litigations and fought stubbornly to resist pollution controls. Similarly, in 1977 the Detrtoit auto makers were still holding out on pollution controls that would render automobiles pollution-free. While new autos are now 95 percent free of pollutants, the companies are deliberately stalling the implementation of devices that would be 100 percent effective. The corporations claim that the cost of implementing the final 5 percent of the pollution controls would be roughly equivalent to that of the first 95 percent—a cost they fought bitterly (*Clarion-Ledger* 1976g; Hill 1977).

In yet another case, Michigan manufacturers of soaps and detergents strongly opposed a 1977 state law prohibiting phosphate waste discharges. The position of the soap industry was that sewage treatment plants should be improved so that they would screen out phosphorous wastes. The industry did not want to spend the money necessary to create new phosphorous-free products, but instead wanted to pass on their problems to sewage treatment plants. The soap industry challenged the new anti-phosphate legislation right up to the moment when it became law. In late September 1977 (the law went into effect on October 1, 1977), the industry proposed an injunction that would have prevented the phosphate ban from taking effect. The injunction was refused by a circuit court judge in Detroit (Stevens 1977b).

As a last resort, some corporations have chosen to export their pollution to other countries. For instance, after the Consumer Product Safety Commission banned the sale of cancer-causing Tris-treated children's sleepwear in 1977, some corporations sold this item in Argentina, Brazil, Peru, and in African nations where the product could be legally marketed. This callous disregard of the health and safety of children in foreign nations illustrates perfectly the corporate commitment to profit rather than to human life (Anderson 1978a). In April 1978, within hours after HEW secretary Joseph A. Califano, Jr. announced support of a bill that would require pharmaceutical companies to disclose test data on the safety and effectiveness of newly manufactured drugs, the president of the Pharmaceutical Manufacturers Association (PMA) denounced it. He warned that if this bill passed, with its new requirement for disclosure of test data on drug safety and effectiveness, many drug houses would test and introduce their drugs in countries where testing regulations are less strict. According to the president of the PMA, the new bill would worsen "drug lag," thus withholding needed new medicines from U.S. consumers because of outdated safety and efficacy requirements. He failed to mention the significant import of his threat to release large quantities of untested drugs on foreign populations (Wehr 1978).

Militant Lobbying by Corporations

The close relationship between government agencies and large corporations is manifest on Capitol Hill, where corporations often lobby successfully for self-serving benefits to the detriment of the consuming public. The following cases illustrate this lobbying process.

The ITT-Hartford case

The International Telephone and Telegraph conglomerate (ITT) decided in the 1970s to acquire more companies in order to sustain an adequate cash flow. ITT's sagging subsidiaries in France and Spain required an economic boost, and acquisition of the Hartford Life Insurance Company appeared to be the most lucrative option available for this purpose. ITT had to receive special treatment from several government bodies and agencies, including the Justice Department, the IRS, a Senate subcommittee, and the Connecticut Insurance Commission, in order to acquire Hartford. To this end, ITT intervened in the affairs of these departments and agencies with a militant lobbying program.

The first task in 1969 was to clear the merger with William Cotter, the Connecticut Commissioner of Insurance. In December 1969 Cotter ruled against the ITT-Hartford merger because the people in Connecticut and local insurance company executives opposed it. Harold Geneen, ITT's board chairman and chief lobbyist, led a team into Hartford, the state capital, to pressure Cotter and his staff into reversing the decision. Geneen also enlisted the lobbying skills of a local attorney who pressured Cotter's office in ITT's behalf. ITT agreed to build a new civic center and a new Sheraton hotel in the city of Hartford, thus aiding a civic improvement program favored by local politicians (Sampson 1973, pp. 152-256). The merger was cleared at the local level in 1970.

At this time, federal antitrust officials appeared to oppose the concept of corporate mergers in general, and were apparently specifically opposed to the ITT-Hartford merger. In order to surmount this obstacle, Geneen exerted pressure on as many federal departments as he could possibly reach. He personally pressed ITT's case to many influential government officials, including Secretary of Commerce Maurice Stans, Secretary of the Treasury David Kennedy, and his successor, John Connally, Federal Reserve Board chairman Arthur Burns, Nixon advisors Charles Colson, John Ehrlichman, Pete Peterson, and Peter Flanigan, Paul McCracken, chairman of the Council of Economic Advisors, and congressmen and senators such as Phillip Hart, Vance Hartke, Emmanuel Celler, and Bob Wilson (Sampson 1973, p. 244). Geneen met with Attorney General John Mitchell on August 4, 1970, while the ITT-Hartford case was under review by the Justice Department, and tried to persuade him that ITT's economic interests were synonymous with the national interest in a healthy economy (Sampson 1973, p. 245).

ITT public relations director Ned Gerrity visited the Justice Department's antitrust chief, John McLaren, to explain the "merits" of ITT's case, and to argue that ITT should not be harassed by antitrust suits such as the one threatened by the Justice Department. Gerrity dispatched a number of his own underlings and hirelings all over the United States to push ITT's case. Special foci were Washington and New York, where congressmen, journalists, and editors were pursued by the lobbyists. The general idea of the lobbying blitz, as Gerrity explained to a senator, was "to tell anyone who would listen that we thought the antitrust policy being pushed by the administration was not in the national interest . . ." (Sampson 1973, p. 246). Gerrity further explained that ITT picked out the leading cities in the United States and sent lobbyists to call on business editors, editorial writers, and radio and television stations. They were sent out "with the gospel" and "tried to acquaint everyone as widely as possible" with the ITT position on the merger with Hartford (Sampson 1973, p. 246).

This campaign was especially successful in Washington. Attorney General Richard Kleindienst (who succeeded Mitchell) was confronted at a social gathering in suburban Washington and pressured by one of Gerrity's men. ITT also cultivated Jack Gleason, a special contact on the White House staff, who enlisted the services of a staff aide in the Justice Department on ITT's behalf. When Gleason resigned from the White House staff in 1969, he went to work for ITT as a lobbyist (Sampson 1973, p. 253). In the meantime, Geneen had been busy pressuring two more key contacts. One, Judge Lawrence Walsh of New York, eventually intervened with Kleindienst, McLaren, and Solicitor General Erwin Griswold. He argued that failure to approve the ITT-Hartford merger would have a devastating effect upon ITT and the nation's economy as well. The other contact, an influential New York stockbroker named Felix Rohatyn, visited Kleindienst and his antitrust staff and pushed ITT's lobbying position on the merger.

Rohatyn followed up his lobbying with three subsequent visits to Kleindienst's office (Sampson 1973, pp. 248–51).

The lobbying of Geneen, Gerrity and the others peaked in July 1971, when the Justice Department was close to deciding the fate of the ITT-Hartford merger. At about this same time, the ITT-Sheraton hotel in San Diego contributed $400,000 to the Committee to Re-elect the President. This contribution supposedly was an attempt by ITT-Sheraton to secure San Diego as the convention site for the 1972 Republican National Convention. Suspicions arose immediately that the $400,000 pledge was really made in order to "fix" the final outcome of the anti-trust settlement. A highly incriminating internal ITT memo, published by columnist Jack Anderson in February 1972, appeared to confirm these suspicions. The memo suggested that the $400,000 commitment was in fact a bribe to buy a favorable ruling at the Justice Department. Whether or not the payment was a "quid pro quo" arrangement between ITT and the Justice Department is still debatable. However, Attorney General Kleindienst was subsequently convicted of perjury (in Judge Sirica's court) for failing to accurately relate how much he knew about the payment to a Senate subcommittee investigating the ITT scandal (Time 1975).

Lobbying by Defense Contractors

A more subtle brand of lobbying than that of ITT has been the lobbying of government procurement officers by defense contractors. These contractors have attempted to win their way on Capital Hill by wining, dining, and entertaining key Defense Department procurement officers. Of 41 leading defense contractor firms investigated in 1977 by a congressional committee, 30 admitted giving Defense Department procurement officials tickets to sports and cultural events and then furnishing "hospitality suites." At least 16 of these corporations actually sponsored sporting events to which the government officials were invited, ranging from golf matches to hunting trips. Some firms paid for a wide range of expenses incidental to these events, such as transportation, hunting licenses, ammunition, meals, lodging, hunting, and guide fees (Anderson and Witten 1977c). In return for this largesse, it is likely that contractors obtained advance information on government requirements and specifications, pricing policies, and bidding procedures, thereby gaining an unfair advantage over competitors. In any event, government procurement officers accepted gifts and favors from firms conducting business with the government, thus violating a 1965 executive order prohibiting this conduct (Anderson and Whitten 1977b).

Lobbying by the Ad Hoc Consumer Issues Group

Jack Anderson and Les Whitten reported in 1977 that several large corporations secretly banded together in that year to defeat the proposed bill to create a Consumer Protection Agency. This new lobby, called the Ad Hoc Consumer Issues Group (a euphemistic twist if there ever was one), includes such companies as Armour, Armstrong Cork, Bethlehem Steel, Exxon, Firestone, Georgia Pacific, Maytag, Shell, Sun Oil, and United Airlines. The Ad Hoc Consumer Issues Group holds that a consumer protection agency would harass business. As a spokesman for the Ad Hoc Group commented, "The better the (Consumer Protection Agency) bill, the worse it is for us" (Anderson and Whitten 1977d). The journalists alleged that this lobbying group has pressured congressmen and provided them with anti-consumer speeches (Anderson and Whitten 1977c).

Lobbying by the Business Roundtable

Another group of corporate officials, the Business Roundtable, has engaged in low-key, covert, behind-the-scenes lobbying in Congress. This secret organization was formed in 1974, but was not publicly acknowledged until late 1975, when Jack Anderson and a New York *Times* reporter documented its lobbying efforts on specific pieces of legislation. Journalists did not have concrete evidence to write a feature article on this organization until late September 1977, by which time the lobby's success on Capitol Hill was patently evident.

The Business Roundtable, a mouthpiece and action arm of the corporate structure, consists of top officers of 180 of the nation's largest corporations, including General Motors, Dupont, IBM, and Coca Cola. The organization helped defeat a common situs picketing bill in 1976 that construction unions wanted badly, and lobbied hard (though unsuccessfully) against a hike in the minimum wage in 1977. In other efforts, the Roundtable sought a major revision of labor-management laws in favor of corporate management, and pressed for tax law changes to encourage more investment in U.S. businesses. This lobby opposes the proposed consumer protection agency and bills providing for mass antitrust action on behalf of consumers. The Roundtable entered the battle over the Carter energy bill. It has lobbied for fewer environmental controls (it claims they slow the development of new energy sources), and a decrease in business taxes in order to provide energy companies with money to develop new energy sources (Hager 1977). These two objectives are detrimental to the consuming public and the U.S. Treasury, but very helpful to corporate profits.

The success of the Business Roundtable lies in personal contacts with legislators. Roundtable lobbyists are corporate heads, and congressmen and senators stand in awe of these important personages who take the time to visit them personally. The lobby's access to members of Congress is unquestioned. As a House of Representatives staff aide put it, "You can be sure that there would be very few members of Congress who would not meet with the president of a Business Roundtable corporation, even if there was no district connection" (Hager 1977). Mark Green, a longtime Ralph Nader assistant, has reported that the Roundtable is the most effective invisible lobby on Capitol Hill. "They are the quintessential big business lobby, because of the way they can push a button and get scores of Fortune 500 chief executive officers to descend on impressionable legislators" (Hager 1977).

Lobbying by the Tobacco Institute

Industries that produce a single product frequently form lobbies to protect their interests. The companies that produce cigarettes, cigars, pipe tobacco, and other tobacco products have joined forces in the Tobacco Institute, with head-quarters in Washington, D.C., and a staff of forty persons. It represents big tobacco companies such as R.J. Reynolds, Phillip Morris, Brown and Williamson, American Brands, Lorillard, and Liggett. Faced with new anti-smoking initiatives by the government and by such health organizations as the American Cancer Society, the Tobacco Institute has stepped up its lobbying and public relations activities. Its lobbyists have worked to promote the tobacco industry's point of view at the White House, in the Congress, in city halls and court rooms, at television and radio stations, and with newspaper and magazine publishers. Its representatives, the finest and most persuasive lawyers, public relations men, and lobbyists that money can buy, include former senators, congressmen, and friends of presidents. The tobacco companies' point of view is that smoking is not harmful to health. The increase in cancer, according to them, has nothing to do with smoking, but is related to an increase in the average length of life. According to health officials, someone in the United States dies every minute and a half as a result of smoking, but the Tabacco Institute and tobacco company officials deny that this health issue is conclusive. They spend considerable time and money attempting to discredit the antismoking forces by challenging their research, motives, accuracy, and objectivity. Moreover, they pump their own dollars into research, a good deal of it aimed at finding other causes of cancer (Jensen 1978).

Because much of the lobbying battle is being fought in Washington, the tobacco industry persistently tries to win the loyalty and votes of influential officials and congressmen, and it appears to be successful in this goal. For example, Frank Saunders, Phillip Morris's director of public relations, was the only big business representative on President Carter's election campaign in 1976. It was probably no coincidence that the White House medical advisor in January 1978 issued a pro-tobacco industry statement on the very same day that HEW Secretary Califano called for a $6 million program to encourage Americans to quit smoking. This advisor declared that the government should not make outcasts of smokers, a view that took some of the sting out of Califano's drive (Jensen 1978).

The Tobacco Institute's use of former congressmen also helps its political clout. The Institute is headed by Horace Kornegay, who served as a U.S. Representative from North Carolina from 1955 through 1960. As an influential member of the House Interstate and Foreign Commerce Committee, he argued forcefully and effectively for the tobacco industry. Like Mr. Kornegay, many of the tobacco industry's most powerful figures come from the tobacco-producing states. Mr. Kornegay's predecessor as head of the institute was Earle C. Clements, a widely acquainted former Democratic senator from Kentucky and a friend of Lyndon Johnson. Mr. Clements still consults with his tobacco colleagues and serves as chairman of the steering committee of the institute's political fund. He lobbied vigorously in 1974 for the appointment of Senator Wendell Ford to the Senate Commerce Committee, where the tobacco industry lacked a strong advocate. Within two years, Mr. Ford had been named chairman of the Commerce Committee's consumer subcommittee, which has oversight jurisdiction over the Federal Trade Commission (Jensen 1978).

Securities and Exchange Commission investigative reports have disclosed a pattern of illegal behavior engaged in by big tobacco companies in their efforts to pressure politicians. The R.J. Reynolds Company, for example, used $190,000 in company funds between 1968 and 1973 for illegal domestic political contributions. Reynolds diverted some money from a foreign licensee and also employed dummy invoices to build up its political fund, which was then used for congressional and presidential campaign contributions. Some tobacco companies gave government officials cigarettes and rides on corporate planes and employed other questionable practices to curry favor. Two Georgia congressmen, for example, were reported to have accepted $900 each from Brown and Williamson for touring this company's plant in Macon, Georgia, and meeting its executives (Jensen 1978).

Corporate Campaign Contributions

Several corporations solicited favors from the Nixon administration through direct monetary campaign contributions. These companies did not lobby or wait to be lured by the promise of favorable government action, but attempted to buy favors outright. Hughes Tool Company, ITT, and Charles "Bebe" Rebozo received favorable treatment from the IRS and the antitrust division of the Justice Department in this way (U.S. Senate 1974a, pp. 206-09, 539-56; Anderson and Clifford 1974, pp. 65-71; U.S. House 1975, pp. 253-57). Such favorable treatment motivated Gulf Oil to undertake an elaborate political campaign contribution program geared toward presidential and congressional candidates.

In 1977, Gulf was fined $229,000 for secretly bringing money across U.S. borders for illegal contributions to the political campaigns of Richard Nixon and members of the Congress. This action violated the Bank Secrecy Act, which stipulates that a report be filed with the Customs Bureau on all cash in excess of $5,000 that is carried into or out of the country. A Gulf official had brought $470,000 into the United States on nineteen trips. This was part of a "laundering" operation, whereby monies were cashed in at foreign banks and then brought back to the United States as new funds in order to concel the fact that the cash had originated with Gulf Oil. Contributions by a corporation to a political campaign are illegal (*Commercial Appeal* 1977), but Gulf was not the only corporation to contribute to political campaigns. The Committee to Re-elect the President in 1972 received at least $5 million from oil sources, including illegal cash contributions of $100,000 each from Phillips and Ashland Oil (Engler 1977, p. 62).

Gulf has intervened with government officials to win favorable treatment at other times. It was fined $36,000 in November 1977, after pleading guilty to giving illegal trips to an Internal Revenue Service auditor in charge of a Gulf Oil tax account. The plea marked one of the first times a major U.S. company acknowledged that gifts to public officials were illegal, even when such favors were asked for or expected by these officials. The auditor, Cyril J. Niederhoffer, supervised the IRS agents who audited Gulf's 1959–1964 tax returns. The audit team concluded in 1974 that Gulf was not liable to pay taxes on its Bahamas-based political fund. The government charged that Niederhoffer received a trip to Pebble Beach, California on the day the favorable audit was filed. Nieder-hoffer also made trips to country clubs in Florida, New Jersey, and Las Vegas (New York *Times* 1977c). In a similar case in 1963-64, the Colonial Pipeline Company, owned by major oil companies and operated by a veteran oil execu-tive from their ranks, paid $110,000 in cash through the Bechtel Corporation to New Jersey municipal officials. Sought and received were rights-of-way and building permits for storage tanks, without the public hearing required by law, so that Colonial could complete a $400 million pipeline (Engler 1977, p. 65).

The Arms Race: Domestic Considerations

The Military-Industrial Complex

We deal here with conventional arms, that is with small arms pistols, machine guns, tanks, cannons, airplanes, and helicopters, and exclude nuclear arms. Arms production policies of the United States interfere with the welfare of the domestic economy and contribute to the military-industrial complex, the interlocking network of politicians, Pentagon officials, military chiefs, and corporate executives who supply military hardware to the Department of Defense and to foreign nations. Prior to World War II, the United States had no armaments industry. The arms business since that time has become institu-tionalized because corporations have increasingly depended upon arms sales as a source of profit, and because workers in the arms industry have increasingly looked to arms production as a source of livelihood. Politicians at all levels have supported this institutionalization and the arms race by giving in to military and corporate armsmakers and to civilian pressures for jobs (McKee and Robertson 1975, p. 229).

The economy is so geared to military production that it would be severely dislocated if weapons manufactures were significantly reduced. When Lockheed found itself on the brink of bankruptcy in 1971, the federal government came to its aid with a loan of $250 million—a remarkable step in a society priding itself on a free enterprise system in which government does not aid or interfere with the free operation of the marketplace. Secretary of the Treasury John Connally said that the loan was made to protect the 31,000 workers who would have lost their jobs had Lockheed gone bankrupt (Fitzgerald 1973, p. 18).

Evidence of the military-industrial complex at work was available in 1960, when the Pentagon awarded contracts worth a billion dollars or more to four defense companies: Lockheed, Boeing, North American, and General Dynamics. All of these corporations maintained a patronage relationship with the Pentagon for the next decade; they were dependent upon the Pentagon for their economic survival. Each of the companies brought political pressures to bear on Washington through their influence with senators and congressmen. The Pentagon awarded defense contracts on the basis of a balance between the demands of the armed services and the aerospace companies. The Defense Department's goal was to keep the aerospace plants open and the politicians contented. When one project came to an end, or when a company was in serious financial difficulty, a new contract would be awarded in keeping with the "follow on" or "bail out" imperative. Meanwhile, the aerospace companies posed as the guardians of the nation's defense, the keystone of prosperity, and the guarantor of jobs (Sampson 1977, pp. 101–02).

The F-111 Case

One of the most widely criticized defense contracts was that granted to General Dynamics to build the F-111, an all purpose supersonic fighter-bomber. The contract appears to have been awarded to the wrong company for economic and political reasons. Cost overruns during production reach high levels and the finished product fell far short of design specifications (Fitzgerald 1973). When the Pentagon originally decided to develop the F-111 in the early 1960s, Boeing and General Dynamics submitted contract bids. A panel of military experts recommended that the contract be awarded to Boeing on the basis of facilities for development and realistic costing, but the contract was awarded to General Dynamics. Frank Pace, a former secretary of the navy, was president of General Dynamics at this time. Contract decisions appear to have been based on the fact that General Dynamics had lost $400 million in the preceding years and needed a large defense contract to survive. Secretary of the Navy Fred Korth, previously president of a Texas bank that had loaned money to General Dynamics, strongly recommended that the contract go to that corporation (Fitzgerald 1973).

The original price of the F-111 was $2.4 million each, and the Pentagon initially ordered 1,700 planes. The first planes produced did not meet basic design specification and, more importantly, had a high crash rate. The first contingent sent to Vietnam either crashed or were shot down so readily that they were all grounded within a few weeks. Foreign governments also cancelled orders for the F-111, costing the United States hundreds of millions of dollars in anticipated export earnings. Furthermore, the cost of the planes had increased to $8 million each by the end of the 1960s. At this point the Pentagon cancelled the original contract and paid General Dynamics compensation in the amount of

$215.5 million. In 1975, General Dynamics was producing a modified version of the F-111 at a price of $13 million each, and the Pentagon was buying them (McKee and Robertson 1975, p. 234).

Critics of the F-111 have claimed· that its production exemplifies the diminishing relationship between military procurement and genuine defense considerations. They assert that procurement of the F-111 was determined by military-bureaucratic and industrial considerations, and that the prime reasons for building the planes were to save the largest company in the military industrial complex from collapse and to appease Pentagon chiefs who would not concede that the F-111 was an inferior airplane. Billions of dollars that could have been used to eliminate poverty were squandered as "welfare" payments to the Pentagon brass (Stone 1969, p. 6).

The F-111 has also been criticized in Congress on the grounds that it was obsolete before it was built and never needed in the first place. Disenchanted former employees have held that the Pentagon's massive support of losing or incompetent corporations undermines the free enterprise system. One such employee, Ernest Fitzgerald, has maintained that the principal threat to American capitalism is the government's support of inefficient and incompetent corporations such as General Dynamics. He holds that an open economic system cannot function with a wasteful and arbitrary military-industrial complex. He argues further that the national administrations always support the demands of the large corporations belonging to the military-industrial complex, with the result that "the Pentagon and its supporting cast of contractors unite to pick the public pocket" (Fitzgerald 1973, p. 18). In fact, the relationship between the Pentagon and the leading corporate suppliers of military equipment is hardly distinguishable from the relationship between government and industry under socialism, except that in the case of the United States the corporations make great profits.

Arms Sales and the Domestic Economy

In the 1970s, arms sales became increasingly important to the viability of the domestic economy. Politicians and civil servants view arms exports as a necessary component of the whole national balance sheet, like any other trade figure (Sampson 1977, p. 118). The Treasury desires to earn foreign currency, the separate states want to maintain employment, and the armed forces wish to reduce costs by increasing production. The United States has entered into co-production agreements with European nations in order to meet these goals; arms are made in Europe under the license of European nations. Under this arrangement, the European countries benefit from the employment of nationals in defense jobs and also gain new technologies in the weapons field as co-partners of the U.S. government and U.S. corporations. American arms companies (private corporations) make high profits under this licensing partnership, and the Treasury spends less on foreign aid (Sampson 1977, p. 115).

The export of armaments is currently an "essential" U.S. industry. According to a recent Department of Labor report, military sales have become a major source of employment for Americans since 1973. In June 1975, each $1 billion of arms sold abroad required the employment of about 52,000 U.S. workers, or about one-sixth of all defense jobs in the aircraft industry (U.S. Department of Labor 1975, pp. 25, 28). In this same year, 7 percent of all U.S. aeronautical engineers were working on military sales (U.S. Department of Labor 1975, p. 33). In 1977, the U.S. Treasury counted 29 states where a 40 percent reduction in new arms orders would cause the loss of two or more jobs out of every thousand (U.S. Department of State 1977). Furthermore, in 1977 the United States was expected to deliver $6.8 million in military goods and services to foreign buyers. This meant that in 1977, some 350,000 people were working either directly or indirectly to deliver military sales (U.S. Department of Labor 1975, pp. 20, 25, 28).

In 1978, the arms industry is likely to increase the numbers of jobs it requires to over 430,000. This will mark a great increase since 1973, when 100,000 U.S. workers were so employed. Such industrial growth is unparalleled in the civilian economy. Military exports already require the services of more people than are at work in eleven states. The United States, in October 1977, had a stock of unfilled military sales orders worth $32.8 billion, and this backlog will not be cleared until 1983 (U.S. Department of Labor 1975). As the scope of the military export economy grows, economic pressures will make it increasingly difficult to reduce the volume of arms sold by American corporations (Rothschild 1977a).

The foregoing suggests that the permanent arms industry yields profit for large corporations and forces workers to depend upon that industry for employment. Politicians encourage this state of affairs in order to please both the corporations and the people who depend upon the arms industry for jobs. We must eventually restrict arms productions for the benefit of the domestic economy, and in order to do this the link between military production, domestic prosperity, and political influence must be broken (Rothschild 1977a).

The Carter administration appeared to be making strides in this direction in 1977 when the president decided to cancel production of the B-1 bomber, the most expensive aircraft project in U.S. history. In the wake of the president's cancellation, however, arms makers began scrambling for a share of the $25 billion that they believed would be available for other projects over the next five years. Unfortunately, this suggests that Carter's decision will not produce a de-escalation of the arms race. Based on administration budget forecasts for fiscal 1979, some analysts see a 1 percent annual growth rate ahead, in contrast to a 3 to 4 percent growth in recent years. It is likely that the arms race will continue to grow, but at a lesser rate than in the past. The B-1 cancellation means that billions of dollars will be channeled into other projects. How many billion, and where they are spent, will be the subject of intensive lobbying by the three military services and their corporate allies in the future (Lindsay 1977).

Cancellation of the B-1 project has already resulted in a competitive scramble at the Pentagon. The army is trying to get some of the money originally intended for the bomber to purchase more helicopters and to contract for an expensive Chrysler-built tank. The navy wants more ships, submarines, and anti-submarine warfare equipment. The air force is trying to divert some of the B-1 money to an F-111 conversion bomber project, to be contracted by General Electric. The latter project is backed by some very influential patrons, including the Texas congressional delegation, long supporters of the General Dynamics Corporation, and the Massachusetts congressional delegation, which desires work for the General Electric plant in Massachusetts hurt by the B-1 cancellation. The arms companies are also lobbying for some of the anticipated displaced billions. The Grumman Aerospace Corporation, a major subcontractor jolted by the B-1 decision, is trying to persuade the air force to buy large fleets of its F-14 fighter. Lockheed wants to divert some of the B-1 money into its C-141 and C-5A transports. Finally, General Dynamics and Boeing will be competing for cruise missile funds to compensate for the loss on the B-1 project (Lindsay 1977).

Manipulating the Rate of Employment

Another way the corporations and the government have intervened in the economic and political process is by manipulating the rate of employment. This is less direct or open than pollution and some other interventions, but it is just as costly. Unemployment can destroy the personal life of an individual. Though the social costs of unemployment can never be pinned down precisely, the Joint Economic Committee of Congress has attempted to measure the effects of unemployment as precisely as possible. Figures and calculations released by this committee in October 1976 indicate that a substantial number of deaths, suicides, and murders between 1970 and 1975 were related to a dramatic rise in the unemployment rate. The unemployment rate rose 1.4 percent in 1970, a rise that was correlated with 26,000 stress-related deaths (stroke, kidney and heart ailments), 1,500 suicides and 1,700 homicides. The committee attempted to control for other variables that may have accounted for these deaths, such as race, age, sex, and medical history. However, deaths were only positively correlated with the rise in the unemployment rate. No direct cause-effect relationship between unemployment and the rate of voluntary or stress deaths was claimed, but the evidence suggests that unemployment does have serious, negative human consequences (Hicks 1976).

The committee estimated the financial cost of these unemployment-related ills to be $21 billion. This figure covers lost income, mortality, and institutionalization. In terms of the human costs, the following estimates were given: The effects of unemployment accounted for 5.7 percent of all suicides; 4.7 percent of mental hospital admissions; 5.6 percent of state prison admissions; 8 percent of homicides; 2.7 percent of deaths from cirrhosis of the liver; and 2.7

percent of cardiovascular and renal diseases. If the number of illnesses due to unemployment could be documented (due to lack of proper nutrition or health care, for example), it is likely that the scope of unemployment's harmful social effects would be magnified (Hicks 1976)

How can unemployment and its negative consequences be constructed as intervention? The answer is that the rate of unemployment is often manipulated by corporations and government. Industry blames employee layoffs on oversupplies, underdemands, or employee demands (especially the latter). Regardless of where the blame is placed, unemployment tends to decrease the militance of workers and condition employees to accept the status quo. Unemployment may thus be profitable to the corporation, and corporations may actually encourage it. Persons without work are (as corporations see it) the victims of their own tamperings with the free enterprise system. Corporations oppose federal legislation that creates jobs, because such legislation depletes the available corporate pool of workers and diminishes corporate control over workers. Further, the government itself may cause unemployment by its monetary policies. Decisions to increase or decrease the money supply are important. Restricting credit to businesses (except the large ones) may encourage firms to lay off workers, while at the same time enhancing the "financial health" of the nation (Gordon 1975). The only group whose "financial health" improves, however, is the corporate group.

GOAL OF THE OFFENDER

The primary, underlying goal of government and corporate intervention at home has been the maintenance of the current distribution of wealth, property, and political power. This goal is clearly discernible in some intervention action patterns, but in others it is subtle, indirect, clandestine, or ambiguous. Frequently the primary goal is subsumed under secondary goals, because purported goals of the social actors engaged in intervention tactics sometimes mesh with real goals. In other cases, purported goals camouflage hidden agendas, represent propaganda ploys, or provide umbrellas for the legitimation of naked power.

The Nixon administration's interventions were perpetrated in the name of defense, national security, and the maintenance of a strong executive branch of government. The real aims centered on two ends: to keep, entrench, and expand the powers of Richard Nixon and his colleagues (all true agents of the capitalist class), and to enhance and strengthen executive control over the other branches of government and the people of the United States. The Plumbers acted to discredit the administration's enemies, and to discover and thwart the leakage to the media of classified and secret government data. The planners and implementers of the Huston Plan wished to stop and neutralize antiwar dissidents and protesters. Dirty tricks were performed to discredit and malign Nixon's political opponents. Nixon's Incumbency Responsiveness Program was organized by his staff to gain control over the federal bureaucracy by stocking it with pro-Nixon bureaucrats.

The CIA's purported primary intention was to maintain national security. Secondary goals subsumed under this shibboleth encompassed the prevention of civil disorders by dissidents and the discovery of tie-ins between foreign communists and domestic movement leaders. Though the ideal domestic goal of the CIA might have been national security, ensured by counter-intelligence, it was also concerned with mundane ends, such as control over some domestic organizations and the suppression of the right of dissident groups to express their views and ideologies publicly. The FBI claimed that its domestic intelligence intervention program was necessary to combat terrorism, civil disorders, subversion, and hostile foreign intelligence activity (U.S. Senate 1976). Its real aim was to discredit the ideas and plans advocated by socialist, radical, and dissident groups and individuals, and to neutralize the actions of those who proclaimed legal dissenting political views (U.S. Senate 1976). The common goal of the CIA and FBI was political policing.

Illegal intervention actions by the IRS were ostensibly performed to investigate delinquent federal income taxpayers. The real purpose was to derogate and harass people on Nixon's enemies list. *Agents provocateurs* reputedly acted to control "subversive" domestic groups. The real objective here was to harass, punish, and disrupt "subversive" groups' members, to incite subversives to violence against one another, and to subject subversives to court action and incarceration. Drug, behavioral, and bacterial experiments were allegedly conducted to gain knowledge about techniques that foreign nations might use against the United States. Prison experiments were conducted under the rubric of rehabilitation. CIA and army drug tests and prison experiments were actually employed to discover new ways of controlling and sometimes punishing political dissidents, subversives, and prisoners.

In the case of the destruction of the environment, corporations claimed that a limited amount of pollution is the price that we all must pay for the operation and growth of business enterprises. Industrial growth, in short, is necessary in order to preserve U.S. citizens' high standard of living and the capitalistic system that supports and makes possible our political and economic democracy. On the contrary, the corporate structure's chief interest in the present levels of pollution and its proliferation is clearly increasing profits at the expense of the environment and the health of the citizenry. The economic goal underlying pollution has been and is irrational because the capitalists poison themselves at the same time that they poison others. Even slave owners throughout history have been concerned, if only for economic reasons, with the health of their slaves.

Corporate interests claimed they lobbied (as did other interest groups) to promote healthy business enterprises necessary to the U.S. economy, and to prevent excessive governmental regulatory controls (controls defined as socialistic measures not needed in a free capitalistic society). The real intention was to maintain and increase profit margins by: promoting the passage of bills favorable to big business but unfavorable to consumers; circumventing laws, rules, and procedures that inhere in the government's business regulatory process; and soliciting the favors of government agents responsible for the disbursement of government contracts. Corporate campaign contributions were supported by big business in the guise of the rights and privileges of all interest groups in a democracy to financially assist their favorite candidates. The pragmatic objective of corporate campaign contributions was to buy the candidate's good will and future services.

Government and corporate proponents of arms sales supported the military-industrial complex on the basis of several professed ends: to protect the United States against the militant incursions of communist or socialist aggressors; to offset the unfavorable balance of payments resulting from essential U.S. military deployment abroad and importation of crude petroleum; and to sustain the multitude of employees engaged directly or indirectly in the production and distribution of arms and arms technology in the United States. All of these objectives were spurious in terms of future economic and political considerations and in terms of the destruction and loss of human life incurred in arms production and sales. The actual ends pursued by government and corporate agents in the arms race encompassed these major aims: the support of the military-industrial complex in the United States; the protection and enhancement of the military and political position of the United States in relation to the communist bloc nations; and the provision of employment for an army of workers engaged in the manufacture of arms for domestic and foreign deployment. Finally, corporate and government agents (corporate directors and the chairman of the Federal Reserve Board), in manipulating the rate of employment, claimed that their actions were essential to the maintenance of a healthy economy. The real purpose behind the manipulation of the employment rate was to condition the working class to periodic unemployment, and to provide the corporations with a large pool of docile workers.

LEGAL STATUS OF THE OFFENSE

The vast majority of interventions discussed in this chapter were illegal, and in violation of established criminal statutes. Some were para-legal violations. The Plumbers and implementers of the Huston Plan were guilty of breaking and entering and theft. Dirty tricksters violated federal political campaign laws and criminal libel laws. Members of the Incumbency Responsiveness Program violated the Hatch Act, which prevents federal employees from engaging in partisan political activity.

The CIA and the FBI domestic action patterns exceeded the restraints on the exercise of governmental power imposed by the Constitution, laws, and traditions of the United States. They violated the civil rights and rights to privacy of U.S. citizens. Many of these activities were carried out covertly, without the authority of a statute or executive order. Criminal law procedures regarding the collection and use of evidence were often ignored, but the targets of domestic surveillance had little opportunity to discover and challenge the legality of such practices.

Legitimate tasks, such as preventing criminal violence and identifying foreign spies, were frequently expanded to include gathering information about the lawful acts and political beliefs of U.S. citizens, even when these incorporated no threats of violence or illegal acts on behalf of foreign nations. Groups and individuals were harassed because of their political views and life styles. These agencies often committed excesses in response to pressures from high officials in the executive and legislative branches. They also resorted to illegal practices which they then concealed from superiors. Both agencies appealed to a higher moral order that existed above the law and interpreted this moral order as they saw fit, defending their moral right and exclusive duty to break the law in the cause of national security. Richard Helms, then CIA director, in an address to the National Press Club in Washington, D.C., justified the CIA's secret operations, saying, "You've just got to trust us. We are honorable men" (Agee 1975, p. 8).

Official guidelines and regulations imposed on these two intelligence agencies have been limited and vague. Executive officials, including presidents and senior executive officials, appear to have abdicated their constitutional responsibility to oversee and set standards for intelligence activity. Therefore, these two agencies have assumed broad mandates without the strict interpretation of law. Congress has also failed to exercise meaningful oversight. Most domestic intelligence issues have never reached the courts, and in cases where they have the judiciary has been reluctant to deal with them. There has been a sustained failure by those responsible for controlling the intelligence community to control it and to insure its legal accountability (U.S. Senate 1976). Agents of the FBI and CIA found guilty of illegal interventions might claim immunity against criminal prosecution on the grounds that their illegal acts were ordered by higher authority. For instance, the United States Court of Appeals for the District of Columbia overturned the convictions of Bernard Barker and Eugenio Martinez for the burglary of Dr. Fielding's office (Dr. Fielding was Daniel Ellsberg's psychiatrist). The court argued that the lower court was in error in not permitting the defendants to show that they had acted in good faith on a command from legitimate authority (Marro 1976).

The IRS violated tax and civil rights laws by investigating a select group of U.S. taxpayers. *Agents provocateurs* violated entrapment laws, civil rights laws, and criminal laws (in inciting targets to violate the law and resort to violence). Those engaging in drug, behavioral, and bacterial experiments violated regulatory agency regulations (Food and Drug Administration regulations governing medical research), the right to privacy laws, and proscriptions against murder. The action patterns resulting in the destruction of the environment by government and corporations were widespread, variegated, and diffuse. These transgressions sometimes violated statute law (oil spills off the coast of Florida in 1972 violated the Environmental Protection and Quality Act; some air pollutants violated the National Air Quality Standards Act of 1970; and asbestos concentrations in several factories violated the Occupational Safety and Health Act). Others violated regulatory agency and commission rules and guidelines (air pollution in Pittsburgh violated the Environmental Protection Agency's rules). Still others were beyond specific statutory, regulatory agency, or commission control because current rules and laws did not cover them. We consider the latter to represent para-legal violations.

Many regulatory agencies and commissions vested with the authority to monitor, challenge, and regulate practices desctuctive to the environment have not had the staff or resources to carry out their duties. Frequently these regulatory agencies have relied upon the cooperation of the private corporations that they are supposed to monitor and sanction for pollution practices. Corporate clients expect bargaining procedures instead of strict enforcement, loose controls, and weak penalties. We single out the legal aspects of corporate occupational health violations as an illustrative case. The Occupational Safety and Health Administration (OSHA), under the Labor Department, has responsibility for setting and enforcing the federal regulations pertaining to occupational health, in compliance with the Occupational Safety and Health Act. This agency's sources and staff are inadequate to the tasks placed upon them (Swartz 1975). Few work-site inspections have been made, the average fine in 1972 for work-place violations was $22.60, and $$99.00 was the average total per work-place. Such fines present no clean-up incentives for giant companies like General Motors or Standard Oil. In reality, the most profitable method for a corporate employer is to violate the law with the hope that no inspection will take place. Should an inspection occur and indicate a violation, the corporation cleans up a little and pays only a small fine. In the case of the Pittsburgh-Corning plant in Tyler, Texas, asbestos concentrations were ten times above permissible levels in some parts of the plant. The company was fined only $210.

Corporations systematically break laws set up to protect the health of workers. The regulatory apparatus (an accessory to crime) permits this to happen because it is a captive of big business and because its enforcement procedures and legal sanctions are weak. Scientists and doctors in the pay of industry have wittingly distorted the facts and claimed that known toxic substances were not dangerous, thereby becoming offenders themselves. Industry "safety" programs (such as the National Safety Council, a corporation-founded institution) have erroneously placed the blame for occupational disease and mishaps on the shoulders of "careless and lazy workers" (Swartz 1975). Others have argued that corporations whose violations of occupational safety and health standards result in serious health impairments and death should be prosecuted for murder and manslaughter (Swartz 1975).

With regard to corporate militant lobbying, some intervention patterns clearly violated statute law. Antitrust laws were not invoked in the ITT-Hartford merger case; lobbying by defense contractors violated a 1965 executive order prohibiting federal employees from receiving favors from persons with whom they were conducting government business; and corporate tobacco lobbyists broke federal election campaign contribution laws. Other lobbying groups, such as the Business Roundtable and the Ad Hoc Consumer Issues Group, committed para-legal offenses (socially injurious offenses perpetrated in secrecy). Corporate campaign contributions (by Hughes Tool Company, ITT, Gulf, and Colonial Pipeline) were clearly illegal because they broke the 1972 Federal Election Campaign Act, the Bank Secrecy Act, and the 1965 executive order prohibiting federal employees from receiving favors.

Government and corporate agents acted together in para-legal violations involved in the domestic arms race. These patterns were socially injurious because they supported the military-industrial complex and rendered the domestic economy artificially dependent upon the production of arms, thus weakening the economy in the long run. Many of these violations were conducted in secrecy and in defiance of regulatory controls. Corporate and government manipulations of the employment rate comprise socially injurious para-legal offenses.

NATURE OF THE OFFENSE

The White House

The White House interventions constituted covert, non-violent offenses. The social actors consisted of the president, his inner-circle staff, and his staff's paid thugs—all employees of the U.S. government who engineered a conspiracy to neutralize those citizens deemed subversive and to aggrandize power in the executive branch. The criminal acts of this cabal were committed by various individuals during the course of their everyday work activities as employees of a formal organization and in the interests of that organization. The interventions to neutralize subversives were supported by corporate and government agents as well as by the general public. The White House interventions negated the divisions of power existing among the various branches of government. Neither the legislative branch nor the judiciary was pleased with Nixon's power plans, but big business supported Nixon until he was flagrantly exposed as a "persona non grata" to the government as well as to the people. At this point he had neither the time nor the power to help the capitalist class. The Nixon cabal, once exposed, was supported only by members of its peer group and a few loyal Republican congressmen. Public support slipped away when the Watergate tapes were released to the media. In the final analysis, government, corporate, and public reaction to these interventions was negative; however, legal sanctions for the guilty social actors were minimal. Nixon is still at large. Leon Jaworski failed to prosecute several individuals and groups known to have committed crimes in the Watergate scandal. Several of Nixon's henchmen, after serving brief prison sentences in medium security institutions, were released and subsequently made fortunes out of the mess they created through books, magazine stories, and media appearances.

Domestic Intelligence

Domestic intelligence interventions by the CIA, the FBI, the IRS, and *agent provocateurs* were covert, and in most cases non-violent, though the FBI and provocateurs encouraged violence among some of their targets. Government agents, including those in the legislative, judicial, and executive branches, went along with and frequently lent support to illegal domestic intelligence operations. The corporate structure favored these tactics which appeared to protect, maintain, and sustain the capitalist class against its enemies. The public, with the exception of a few liberals, radicals, and intellectuals, acquiesced.

There is a certain amount of tension between order and liberty in any society, and intelligence activities conducted within the confines of the law and government control are probably necessary to a society's viability. On the other hand, intelligence activity in the United States in the past two decades has been in many cases patently unlawful and counterproductive to a democratic society. Despite this fact, such activity has been interwoven throughout the U.S. political and economic system. Peer groups that engaged in domestic intelligence interventions gave little thought to the legality of their actions and were only interested in pragmatic results. Peer group members worked for formal organizations (government organizations), and their offenses were committed in the normal course of their work as employees of these organizations and directed toward organizational goals. Employee aims and the aims of the organization were synonymous—national security. For the most part, their actions were supported by peer groups and by most sectors of the general public. Societal reaction to misconduct in the domestic intelligence field was passive. Legal sanctions were weak: former CIA director Richard Helms was permitted to plea bargain and pay a very small fine.

Former FBI director L. Patrick Gray and two other former key FBI officials were indicted in April 1978 in connection with bureau wiretappings and break-ins. Attorney General Griffin Bell stated that the charges developed from FBI activities earlier in the decade, when the agency was pursuing radical fugitives. The federal grand jury in Washington indicted Gray, former associate director W. Mark Felt, and former assistant director Edward S. Miller on a single charge of conspiring to violate the rights of citizens. This charge carries a maximum penalty of 10 years in prison and a fine of $10,000. Bell also said that the Justice Department had dropped its prosecution of John J. Kearney, a former FBI supervisor in New York, indicted in 1977 in connection with the same activities. He announced that 70 other FBI agents would receive disciplinary actions ranging from censure to dismissal. Most of these agents were members of the New York unit that conducted anti-radical activities under Kearney's supervision (*Clarion-Ledger* 1978h).

Drug, Behavioral, and Bacterial Experiments, and Destruction of the Environment

Drug, behavioral, and bacterial experiments, and incursions into the environment, with the exception of air pollution, were covert and violently destructive both to the health of individuals and to the environment. Social actors committed these crimes during the normal course of their work as employees of organizations and at the behest of these formal organizations. Such actors worked for corporations and for government bureaucracies. In most cases, corporate agents and government agents, though working for separate bureaucracies, formed collusive teams in the commission of these transgressions. Such teams, marked by strong peer group support, were contrived by the capitalist class and functioned in its interests. The drug, behavior, and bacterial experiments were conducted exclusively by governmental agents. Most sectors of the population appear to be indifferent to these violations, and the regulatory agencies that are supposed to have jurisdiction over them are ineffective.

Militant Lobbying

Militant lobbying and corporate campaign contributions constituted covert and non-violent offenses committed by teams of corporate and government agents on the behalf of corporate and government bureaucracies. These acts were perpetrated by organizational employees during the normal course of everyday work assignments. Social actors experienced strong peer group support, government support, corporate support, and public support for their crimes. Militant lobbyists received no legal sanctions and most corporate campaign contributors escaped penal sanction. A few of the latter were fined under the 1972 Federal Election Campaign Act.

The Domestic Arms Race

Corporate and government teams comprising the military-industrial complex engineered the domestic arms race. The individuals and groups engaged in these interventions were employees of formal organizations working for either government or corporate interests. These overt, non-violent actions received strong support from peer groups, the government, the corporate structure, and the general public. The public viewed employees of the arms industry as respectable citizens occupied in projects necessary to the health of the U.S. economy and national defense. Societal reaction to the domestic arms race has been positive.

Manipulating the Employment Rate

Corporate and government agents working as members of organizational teams manipulated the employment rate by covert and nonviolent means and methods. A team of corporate executives, officials of the Federal Reserve Board, and members of the Business Council (a corporate policy-planning organization) cooperated in this action. Support from the peer group, the government, and the corporate structure was strong. The general public, in a state of ignorance, acquiesced. The societal reaction, therefore, has been indifference.

3

FOREIGN INTERVENTION
BY GOVERNMENT

Most of the manipulative or penetrative strategies (interventions) employed by the U.S. government and corporations at home have also been used abroad. Infiltration, coercion, influence-buying, bribery, destruction of the environment, intelligence—all of these have been performed abroad by government and corporate agents in the interests of U.S. government influence and power and corporate profits. These interventions are frequently made in the name of national security and the survival of the capitalistic system.

ACTION PATTERNS

We discuss five joint foreign interventions by agents of the U.S. government and U.S. corporations: the Vietnam war, the foreign arms race, government intervention in foreign countries on behalf of the oil industry, CIA foreign intervention, and the foreign corporate bribery scandals of 1945-1976.

The Vietnam War

The Vietnam war lacked a "front" (Quinney 1975, p. 155). Guerilla warfare in this conflict varied greatly from conventional fighting in that opponents rarely confronted each other directly in a battle front. The National Liberation Front was hidden from view virtually everywhere in the Vietnamese countryside (in both South and North Vietnam) and thus the entire geographical area of Vietnam was the enemy. In order to "save" Vietnam from communism it was therefore necessary to destroy the entire country. In South Vietnam, rural villages were often bombed, a practice not usually taken against an ally in conventional warfare. In North Vietnam, efforts were made to destroy all institutions of organized human life, including schools, railroads, harbors, factories, churches, hospitals, private homes, dikes, and dams (Gerassi 1968). These vicious attacks, both in South and North Vietnam, helped to explain the excessive loss of life during this conflict.

During the course of the war the United States committed a variety of criminal offenses, and some scholars have argued that the war itself was illegal because formal hostilities were never declared. Other writers have pointed out instances of American conduct during this conflict that violated international law. A few of these follow. The massacre of 500 South Vietnamese civilians at My Lai is the most commonly acknowledged example. The Senate Subcommittee on Refugees estimated that in the years from 1965 to 1969 over a million refugees were killed and 2 million were wounded by the U.S. armed services. A CIA-funded counterinsurgency program was designed to eliminate Viet Cong infiltrators from U.S. and South Vietnamese police, military, and intelligence units (Quinney 1975, pp. 153-54; Marchetti and Marks 1974, pp. 236-37).

There have also been numerous reports of murder and ill-treatment of Viet Cong prisoners of war by the U.S. and South Vietnamese military. A member of the American Special Forces (Green Berets) testified before the Bertrand Russell International War Crimes Tribunal that he had been instructed in torture tactics and was ordered to kill four Viet Cong prisoners. Others testified before the tribunal that torture and execution were in fact carried out. Testimony revealed beheadings, murder by expulsion from airborne helicopters, and intensive torture followed by execution. These cruel and illegal methods were characterized in testimony as "expected combat behavior" and "standard operating procedures" (D'Amato et al 1969, pp. 1075-81).

Finally, the use of certain gases and sprays by American forces violated the 1925 Geneva Protocol. Approximately 14 million pounds of CS gas, which incapacitates both combatants and civilians, was dispersed during the war. American and South Vietnamese troops sprayed over 100 million pounds of herbicidal chemicals over 5 million acres, about half the arable land in South Vietnam. The purpose here was to defoliate trees serving as cover for the enemy, and to kill rice and other plants harvested by enemy forces (D'Amato et al 1969, pp. 1091-93).

The Arms Race: Foreign Considerations

General Background. Another form of intervention into the affairs of foreign nations has been arms peddling by the U.S. government and American arms manufacturers. The economic benefits of arms sales were noted during the 1960s by George Thayer (1969, p. 220), who reported that these sales were made to offset the unfavorable balance of payments resulting from essential U.S. military deployments abroad. Thayer documented the economic considerations that played a larger role in U.S. arms sales than the usual justifications proffered by corporations, for example, that arms promote the defensive strength of our allies and promote the concept of cooperative logistics with friendly nations. Since the 1970s, the United States and the chief Western European arms exporters (France, Britain, and West Germany) have justified arms sales as an important instrument of foreign policy, and as a means of easing the unfavorable balance of payments in an era of costly oil imports (Kandell 1978). The spiral of arms sales by the United States following the end of the Cold War and the Vietnam conflict displayed the continued importance of arms sales as a significant part of the economy. Several scholars in the early 1970s (including Barnet and Muller 1974) began documenting the fact that U.S. arms corporations had become American-based multinationals owing allegiance only to profits and growth. Sampson's (1977) historical study on arms has shown how corporate and government profit maximization has been the primary goal of arms sales since the late 1800s, and how this goal has contributed to a dangerous proliferation of arms and armed conflicts.

Thayer explained how the sales of arms by the U.S. government had set ally against ally and neutral against neutral, polarized the world into many armed camps, and heightened world tensions. Further, he pointed out that these sales led to an increase in anti-Americanism, a dissipation of U.S. influence, and a world-wide glut of arms. He also demonstrated that arms sales have led to the bankruptcy of nations, the downfall of friendly governments, a collapse in the mechanisms of arms control, and war (Thayer 1969, p. 378). In fact, in the 24 years between 1945 and 1969, there were 55 wars fueled by the arms race (Thayer 1969, p. 1). Thayer thought it ironic that the United States, the world's most vocal proponent of disarmament, was also the world's largest seller of arms; U.S. arms sales doubled the total of all free world suppliers combined in 1965. The relative importance of the other major Western arms suppliers at that time was that of a "corner shop to a supermarket" (Thayer 1969, p. 258). The United States has remained by far the greatest arms seller in the world, with arms accounting for close to half the value of all exports in 1978. In the fiscal year ending October 1, 1977, U.S. foreign sales totalled $11.3 billion dollars and, according to Defense Department estimates, arms sales would rise to $13.2 billion in fiscal year 1978, despite Mr. Carter's arms cutback propaganda. On the other hand, according to the best estimates available, the Soviet Union sold $4 billion in armaments to foreign countries in 1977 (Kandell 1978).

The U.S. government became actively involved in propping up the arms sales of multinational corporations following World War II. The government reasoned that it was in its interest to give away surplus military equipment to allies so that they could maintain a credible military posture against communism. In the mid-1950s, the U.S. government's Military Aid Program began to buy from the three services (army, navy, air force) brand new equipment to be given away to its allies. This program gave the U.S. military services an additional source of funds without having to ask Congress for more. In other words, the Defense Department, the administrator of the military aid program, bought from its own army, navy, and air force war surplus arms that were then given free to foreign countries. Thus, the three services possessed a lucrative means of clearing inventories and acquiring large sums of money to buy new equipment outside the purview of direct congressional control. The emphasis shifted from "give away" to sale under Robert S. McNamara, secretary of defense in 1961 (Hovey 1966).

The International Logistics Negotiations Section of the International Security Affairs Division of the Defense Department (ILN) became the government's official arms sales office in 1961. Henry Kuss, Jr. and a staff of 42 people ran this office, which specialized in arranging U.S. arms sales to various parts of the world. The staff was divided into four teams. The "Red" team, for instance, was responsible for sales to Canada, the Far East, Scandinavia, France, and the North Atlantic Treaty Organization (NATO) forces. Overall, Kuss's salesmen were responsible for $2 billion in sales per year between 1962 and 1969 (Thayer 1969, pp. 185-86). The Department of Defense which housed the ILN was the most influential American agency in determining sales of arms to foreign governments. Mr. Kuss testified at hearings of a subcommittee of the Senate Foreign Relations Committee in 1967 that it was his responsibility to sell arms, and that he determined a country's capacity to purchase arms without endangering its economy (U.S. Senate 1967, p. 17). Domestic considerations were also important in arms sales. One of the ILN objectives was to offset the unfavorable balance of payments. This office lent an aura of legitimacy to the policy of selling arms strictly for monetary reasons (Thayer 1969, pp. 251-54).

Additional insights into the government's promotion of arms sales came from General Robert J. Wood, a former director of the Military Aid Program. He explained to a House Appropriations Committee in 1964 that foreign officers were trained in the United States in a manner that would induce them to purchase American arms at a later date. "We have a program to train certain countries in some of our equipment in the expectation that they will buy it. This is really sales promotion" (McCarthy 1967, p. 83). Wood cited the Paris Air Show, the largest and most prestigious arms market in the world, as a target of the Defense Department's sales promotion effort. The department spent more than $750,000 in promoting U.S. arms at the 1967 show which lasted ten days (New York *Times* 1968). Private U.S. firms as a group spent $2.25 million to sell their wares at this show (Thayer 1969, p. 175).

Since 1974, the director of the Defense Security Assistance Agency (DSAA) has been the controller of arms sales in the Defense Department. About 95 percent of U.S. arms deals are negotiated by the Pentagon staff through DSAA in behalf of the arms companies. These deals are finalized in government-to-government negotiations known as "foreign military sales" (Sampson 1977, pp. 288-90). Though arms sales are coordinated through this new agency, an accurate assessment of the total arms sales by U.S. companies is impossible because corporations scatter arms production among various subsidiaries, and arms sales profits are not properly itemized in corporations' annual financial reports. This camouflage of financial reporting is hard to understand, because the U.S. government has been the largest arms purchaser and should have required corporations with whom it was doing business to keep accurate and decipherable financial reports (Thayer 1969, pp. 295–319).

CIA Cases. The sale of arms to foreign countries has often led to international altercations. Between 1949 and 1961, the CIA actively supplied arms to a group of Chinese Nationalists in Burma. When Chiang Kai-shek fled to Formosa in 1949, many who wished to accompany him were not able to do so. Some 12,000 nationalist troops fled across the Yunnan border and set up camp in the lush, poppy-growing area of northern Burma. Occasionally they conducted hit-and-run raids into China, but soon they settled down and became rich by growing opium. Nevertheless, the CIA saw these troops as Mao's enemies and continued to supply them with money and arms. Many supplies were air-dropped by a CIA-backed company called Air America, a firm that later supplemented the U.S. military effort in Vietnam (Thayer 1969, p. 158).

In the early 1950s, the CIA secretly supplied arms to Chinese Nationalist guerrillas who conducted hit-and-run raids from Quemoy and Matsu onto the mainland. In another case, operating under a dummy company called Western Enterprise, a purported trading firm, the CIA ran gun agents to China between 1951 and 1954. Again in 1958, the CIA smuggled arms to the anti-Sukarno rebels in Indonesia. B-11s were ferried in and out of a rebel air-strip in North Celebia from Clark Field, a U.S. Air Force base near Manila (Tully 1962, pp. 32, 196–99, 201–02; Wise and Ross 1964, pp. 106–09, 129–46).

The equipment supplied by the CIA for the 1961 Bay of Pigs invasion of Cuba was American in origin. Much of the small arms ammunition was manufactured in U.S. government arsenals, given fake head stamp designations, and packed in unmarked boxes. Some of the heavier ordnance appears to have been foreign-made, but was purchased from American sources. The military vehicles, B-26 bombers, JC-46 and C-55 transports, trucks, jeeps, and landing craft were surplus stock taken directly from the U.S. military inventory. Some of this equipment was smuggled to Retahuller and Puerto Barrios in Guatemala or to Nicaragua, and then to the Bay of Pigs with the invasion forces. Other equipment was taken directly to the beaches from the United States by U.S. Air Force planes, U.S. Navy ships, and CIA transportation agents (Wise and Ross 1964; Tully 1962; Blackstock 1964; Meyer and Szulc 1962).

Sales to Western Europe. The United States and its corporate allies have sold to a number of European countries, including Germany, Holland, Belgium, and Italy. One German case demonstrates this partnership. In March 1959, a contract was signed between Lockheed Aircraft Company and West Germany for 96 Lockheed Starfighters. Thus began what was later referred to as the "Starfighter Affair," which lasted for six years. Lockheed and U.S. government officials pressured the German government to buy a number of these planes, which proved to be dangerous, inadequate, and expensive. The representatives of Lockheed and the U.S. government, with their hard-sell tactics, did not promote the defensive strength of an ally in this case (New York *Times* 1966b). West German Chancellor Erhard in 1961 conducted talks with the U.S. deputy secretary of defense, during which he pointed out that Germany's military financial need could equal the foreign exchange costs of stationing U.S. troops on her soil. The West Germans agreed to purchase through the ILN office $1.3 million worth of U.S. military equipment (including Starfighters) over a two-year period. The agreement was later continued for two further two-year periods. Despite denials from Secretary McNamara that the U.S. was using West Germany as a dumping ground for U.S. arms, the United States was forcing Germany to purchase military weapons it did not need. By 1965, West Germany had such an oversupply of arms that it had to sell them to other nations. Consequently, Germany faced a prospective budget deficit for 1967 of $1 billion. The United States refused relief in this situation and the Erhard government fell, in large measure because of this force-feeding of arms (Thayer 1969, p. 223).

Sales to the East. The attempt by the United States to create a military balance in the Middle East prior to the 1967 War resulted in each side having missiles, offensive bombers, jet interceptors, and the most advanced conventional weaponry. Following U.S. encouragement, West Germany in 1960 agreed to supply Israel with $80 million worth of arms as a "moral debt." The U.S. desired to strengthen Israel without being blamed for it by the Arabs. The arms aid was given by Bonn under the guise of a strictly German-Israeli agreement. The American involvement in this transaction became known in 1965 when the United States reluctantly admitted that it had secretly agreed to the transfer of 200 U.S. tanks from Germany to Israel. Later the State Department admitted that it had supported the clandestime move (New York *Times* 1966a). From February 1965 to February 1966, the United States supplied arms directly to Israel, and at the same time supplied surplus tanks to Jordan. In May 1966, the United States sold Israel a number of tactical jet bombers and, in December 1966, shipped $7 million worth of arms to Jordan. All of this equipment was used six months later in the Seven-Day War. Patton tanks faced Patton tanks in this conflict (London *Times* 1966; New York *Times* 1966d).

Arms have been sold to Iran in exchange for oil, to redress the balance of payments, and to buy friendship in an oil state. The State Department has insisted that the arming of Iran was a very special case for security needs. Iran, however, has set a pace in armaments that her Arab neighbors have been determined to follow. For example, the Saudis have desired to keep up with Iranian arms, and by fiscal 1976 American arms sales to Saudi Arabia totaled $2.5 million (Sampson 1977, pp. 292, 311). Thus arms sales to one nation in a given region trigger compelling arms demands from other countries in that area. Arms companies have offered contradictory justifications for their huge sales to Iran and the Arab countries. The corporations claim that arms sales are essential to Western security, and that they are not dangerous because the purchasers cannot effectively deploy them. This claim is erroneous, because along with arms sales goes the sale of technology. The Saudi and Iranian arms purchases were followed by an auxiliary army of civilian technicians and engineers. The Vinnell Corporation of California, which was hired to train the Saudi National Guard, served in the manner of mercenaries. The biggest technical services supplier in Saudi Arabia has been the U.S. Army Corps of Engineers, whose contracts there approached $1 billion in 1976 (Sampson 1977, p. 311).

In the 1960s, the United States encouraged developing nations to buy arms by providing them with enabling financial aids. Arms were purchased by foreign governments through a financing procedure called the Military Assistance Credit Account, whereby Defense Department funds served as credit for arms sales. This procedure dates back to 1957, when under the Mutual Security Act $15 million was authorized to provide credit for arms sales. Credit was made available in the transition period between the giveaway arms programs (through "arms grants") and the arms payment programs. From yearly appropriations ranging from $21 to $23 million, the fund grew to approximately $383 million by 1967. Additional legislation in 1961 rendered the fund a "revolving account." Future repayments by borrowing countries were recontributed into the fund to finance more loans (Thayer 1969, p. 212). Another source of arms credit was the Export-Import Bank of Washington, D.C., which extended loans (through the ILN office) to underdeveloped countries considered poor credit risks. Thus the United States, through its liberal credit procedures, supplied arms to foreign nations who neither needed nor could afford them.

Fourteen underdeveloped countries in some of the most explosive areas in the world (names kept secret by the ILN office) were granted loans under these procedures. The developing countries paid out approximately $4 billion in foreign exchange for debt service in 1964, much of which had been incurred through large arms purchases (New York *Times* 1967). These loans have allowed the underdeveloped countries to prepare themselves for wars. In fact, 95 percent of all post-World War II conflicts have been fought in underdeveloped areas of the world with imported weapons. Restrictions on the resale and end-use of weapons by the producing and selling countries have proven ineffective, as have arms embargoes. This situation has led to armed conflicts among developing nations (Thayer 1969, p. 362).

In the India-Pakistan War of 1965, the Sherman tanks of the Indian Army battled the Patton tanks of the Pakistani Army. All of these tanks had been sold to the two countries with the understanding that they were to be used only defensively in the control of communist aggression. The amount of military equipment sold to Pakistan totaled more than $730 million. The United States and other nations had armed India to help the Indians protect themselves against border attacks by the Chinese. The United States, in other words, supplied arms to stop one war that were used in the initiation of another (Thayer 1969, pp. 202–33).

Sales to the Third World. The 1970s have seen an arms race among the countries of the Third World who can least afford it. Many of these nations are buying weapons instead of food and health and welfare services. The U.S. government and corporate agents have supplied weapons to these developing countries where, in many cases, repressive regimes reign and potential war zones exist (Kandell 1978). Military aid to Latin American countries following World War II has been ostensibly designed to contribute to the stability of Latin nations, to counter Western European arms sales, to coordinate hemispheric military efforts, and to augment U.S. influence over the training and supply of various military forces. This policy has rested on the assumption that Latin American countries have been threatened from within and without by communist aggressors. Critics of U.S. arms policy have shown, however, that U.S. arms have entrenched military dictators in power, stifled reform, and diverted money from badly needed economic and social programs into wasteful military ones (McArdle 1964; Lieuwen 1967, p. 208). This policy, in addition to promoting armaments to countries that do not need them, flatters their nationalistic ambitions.

The destination of U.S. arms has moved from developed countries to oil-exporting countries, and more recently to poor developing countries that do not export oil. From 1972 to 1976, orders for U.S. arms from developing nations without oil were up from $240 million to $2.3 billion (Sampson 1977, p. 316). According to Defense Department figures, the developing countries that do not export oil accounted for 24 percent of U.S. military orders in 1976, compared to 10 percent in 1975 and only 5 percent in 1974. Since the late 1960s, most arms exports have been sent as trade, not aid; companies and government arms salesmen now collaborate in selling for dollars. Most military sales are still arranged between governments. The Defense Department and the armed services promote these sales, and supervise the corporations as they produce arms for export. Thus the factory of a defense corporation, much like a General Motors plant producing parts for blue sedans and pink station wagons, might make parts for a Jordan "Main Battle Tank," a tank for the U.S. Army, an Israeli tank, or a tank for Saudi Arabia (Rothschild 1977a, p. 24).

A big boom in the arms business exploded in 1974 when foreign countries ordered $10.6 billion worth of U.S. military equipment. This compares with $3.3 billion in 1972 and less than $1 billion in 1970. Foreign military sales orders were worth more than $7 billion in 1976 (U.S. Department of Defense 1976). Deliveries of arms to foreign countries (actual exports) are also increasing as the backlog of orders is filled. Since 1975, the U.S. has actually made a profit on its worldwide military involvement. Twelve years after American combat troops arrived in Vietnam, the U.S. government received more money for its foreign military sales than it spent abroad on defense (Rothschild 1977a, p. 24). At the height of the Vietnam war, U.S. arms exports were worth $1 billion per year, compared to defense procurements of over $42 billion a year. Now, with U.S. companies no longer sending planes to forces in Vietnam, exports are worth some $4 billion a year in actual deliveries and twice that in orders, while procurement for national purposes is still $42 billion (Rothschild 1977a, p. 25). In 1976, all the increase in arms sales came from sales to developing countries (oil exporting countries excluded) such as Kenya, Ethiopia, and Zaire. In 1977, the Carter administration proposed to supply arms to such African states as Somalia, Chad, and Sudan (Rothschild 1977b, p. 10). Britain and France are competitors, but they each account for less than a fifth of the value of U.S. arms exports to developing countries (Stockholm International Peace Research Institute 1977, p. 309).

Current Policy. By 1975 even high U.S. government officials were conceding that arms were being sold for economic reasons. In a 1975 speech, Henry Kissinger spoke on the value of U.S. arms sales in terms of prosperity and justice. He explained that arms assistance programs provided needed jobs for workers, enabled us to maintain a more favorable balance of payments, and contributed to the strength of the defense industries and the armed forces (Kissinger 1975). Obviously, Kissinger spoke for the military-industrial complex, that is, for its profits. Given the economic pressures that encourage a spiral in arms sales, it is likely that little will be done to limit them.

Many senators and congressmen were skeptical of President Carter's 1977 plan to place a ceiling on arms sales to the Third World nations and to reduce arms exports during fiscal 1978. Some feared that under this proposal Israel would not be supplied with the level of arms that it had received in the past. Additionally, there was increasing pressure to sell new equipment to Iran, Israel, and Saudi Arabia. It was estimated that these nations desired $6 billion of arms above Carter's proposed ceiling level. The South Korean government also wanted to buy more arms in the wake of the withdrawal of U.S. troops from Korea (Burt 1978). Further pressure on the administration escalated when the Egyptians tied military aid to a settlement in the Middle East. In January 1978, President Anwar Sadat accused Israeli leaders of sabotaging the Arab-Israeli peace negotiations. In a speech before the Egyptian parliament, he claimed that Israeli intransigence resulted from U.S. arms sales to the Jewish state. Sadat requested that the United States sell Egypt the same kinds and quantities of weapons being sold to the Israelis, and promised that the arms would not be used against Israel, but rather to strengthen Egypt's defenses in Africa (Antar 1978). Carter's arms policy plan included a package sale of $4.8 billion of arms to Saudi Arabia, Egypt, and Israel. Saudi Arabia was to receive 60 F-15s; Egypt, 50 F-5 fighters; and Israel, 75 F-16s and 15 F-15s (Kaiser 1978; *Clarion-Ledger* 1978i).

President Carter announced in February 1978 a $6 billion lid on arms sales for fiscal 1978. The so-called ceiling actually disguised a sellout to economic and political pressures for greater arms sales. The lid applied only to nonallied nations and did not include some major purchasers of arms such as NATO member nations and Japan. The ceiling also permitted the continued sale of arms to Israel and the Arab nations, and veiled an overall increase in total arms to be sold. Adding to the $6 billion lid all sales under the Foreign Military Sales program (including such items as cranes, generators, compressors, commercial trucks, telephones, and ambulances), the total expenditure the United States can devote to arms production for sale during 1978 is $13.2 billion, contrasted with

$12.1 billion for 1977 (*Clarion-Ledger* 1978b). Carter's proclaimed arms limitation policy is sheer rhetoric.

In the light of U.S. arms sales, President Carter's criticisms of the Soviet Union for peddling arms in order to provoke warfare are absurd. In January 1978, Carter accused the Soviet Union of massive arms shipments to the horn of Africa (Gerstenzang 1978). He claimed that the United States has avoided shipping arms to Somalia and Ethiopia. While it is true that the USSR has been guilty of selling arms, their participation is miniscule in relation to sales by the United States.

Government Intervention on Behalf of the Oil Industry

The international oil companies, like the arms companies, have benefitted greatly from government intervention on their behalf. In fact, government agencies have probably done more for the international oil cartel than for any other corporate entity. Oil companies operating in foreign countries have enjoyed tax favors at home along with diplomatic assistance abroad, including the direct aid of the CIA, the U.S. Information Agency, the State Department, and other agencies. The State Department, for example, cleared the way for the oil cartel's foreign oil concessions and investments through a so-called oil "open door" policy. Whenever and wherever this "open door" policy was employed, in Iran, Kuwait, Saudi Arabia, Indonesia, Mexico, Peru, or Venezuela, the State Department intervened in support of the oil cartel when it had legal or financial difficulties with host countries. American support for oil companies' interventions abroad has extended into the highest reaches of the national security apparatus and protected the oil industry from antitrusters, revenue agents, and foreign and domestic enemies (Engler 1967, pp. 182–309). Oil interventions in Iran, Iraq, and in Latin America serve as illustrative cases in this type of political crime engaged in by government and corporate agents.

Iran. In 1951, when the Iranian government nationalized the properties of the Anglo-Iranian Oil Company (British Petroleum) without compensation, the U.S. State Department helped bring the Iranian Government to terms by persuading independent oil companies to abstain from seeking concessions there. In May 1951, the State Department issued a press release stating that U.S. oil companies, in face of the unilateral action against British Petroleum, would not be willing to undertake operations in that country (U.S. Senate 1975). The major oil companies (including those in the United States) also contributed to the submission of the Iranian government to the oil cartel. In 1951, the eight major international oil companies imposed an effective embargo on Iranian oil. Consequently, Iran's oil exports decreased from over $400 million dollars in 1950 to less than $2 million dollars in the two-year period from 1951 to 1953. The oil cartel compensated for its temporary loss in Iranian oil by increasing oil production elsewhere in the Middle East (Blair 1976, p. 78).

Unable to market its oil and starved for revenues, the Mossadeq government fell. The CIA helped to depose Mossadeq and restore the Shah to the throne (U.S. Senate 1975), and the Shah, a dictator, has cooperated with the oil cartel ever since. Subsequently, the U.S. State Department, the Iranian government, and nine international oil companies (Iricon, British Petroleum, Shell, Mobil, CFP—a French company, Exxon, Texaco, Gulf, and SoCal) negotiated an agreement in 1954 to bring Iranian oil production, transportation, refining, and marketing back into the control of the major oil companies. An oil production output formula was worked out to keep Iran's oil production equivalent to that in other Middle East countries (U.S. Senate 1974c). Iran's oil remains within the control systems of the international oil cartel though, along with other exporting nations, it has raised the price of crude oil sold to the major oil companies.

Iraq. In 1964, the Iraqi government established the Iraq National Oil Company under Public Law 80 to mine oil in areas confiscated from the Iraq Petroleum Company (IPC), owned by British Petroleum and a few other companies comprising an oil cartel. IPC had refused to develop Iraqi oil to its fullest extent in order that the oil cartel might maintain a balance of oil production throughout the Middle East. In 1972, Iraq nationalized all of IPC's holdings (Blair 1976, pp. 85-90).

When the newly formed Iraq National Oil Company (INOC) solicited foreign companies to develop oil concessions (excluding British Petroleum), the State Department interceded on the behalf of the international oil cartel. It warned independent companies to stay out of Iraq's underdeveloped fields. The State Department claimed that the entrance of independent oil companies on the scene would limit corporate negotiations over cancelled concessions, and that the intruders would risk legal actions by older interests. The State Department wished to keep Iraq National Oil Company's oil from flowing to consumer nations without the control of the oil cartel. In short, the U.S. State Department pressured American independent oil companies to stay out of Iraq pending a settlement between the Iraqi government and the IPC related to the confiscation and nationalization measures (Blair 1976, p. 86). The State Department also threatened American retaliation against foreign consumer countries who would permit their oil companies to enter the Iraqi oil fields (Engler 1977, p. 125).

The major concern of IPC throughout its difficulties with the Iraqi government was to hold Iraq's oil production down. This had to be done to offset the high growth rates of oil production in Libya and to sustain the growth rates in Iran and Saudi Arabia. The oil cartel, with the help of the U.S. State Department, tried to prevent Iraqi oil from flowing to consumer nations to avoid a "price-reducing surplus" (Blair 1976, pp. 83-85). To date the case of Iraq marks the singular success of an oil-producing nation over the international oil cartel.

Latin America. American foreign aid to some Latin American countries has been cut since 1960 because they have demanded that the control of oil production, marketing, refining, and transportation be returned to indigenous oil companies.

In 1964, the government of Peru attempted to expropriate the International Petroleum Company (owned by the international oil cartel), and as a result U.S. aid to this country was revoked. The State Department and the U.S. embassy in Peru identified with the International Petroleum Company (accepting its facts, figures, interpretations, and legal positions), and even allowed the company to negotiate U.S. foreign policy positions with the Peruvians (the most important being the oil position) in the early 1960s. The State Department made it clear to the Peruvian government in 1964 that unless it came to terms with the company, foreign aid would be cut off. Peru ignored the threat and U.S. aid was cut (Engler 1977, p. 106).

Latin Americans have often correctly perceived huge U.S. investments in their countries as a sign of economic imperialism. To counteract this image, the U.S. Information Agency helped the international oil firms in the early 1970s to improve their "public relations" in Latin America. In Ecuador, for example, the U.S. Information Agency prepared pamphlets for Texaco and Gulf to be distributed to the public (with no sponsor's credit indicated) that proclaimed the advantages of private development over the menace of public control and "communist solutions" (Engler 1977, p. 106). American taxpayers unwittingly financed this activity.

At least once, U.S. public relations schemes in the interests of international oil companies failed; Cuba is the case in point. In the late 1950s, a number of developments in Cuba caused consternation among officials of the U.S. government and large oil companies. When Castro came to power, Cuba expropriated the Shell, Esso, and Texaco refineries (that were built under favorable terms during the Batista regime), seized the records of oil exploration companies, increased the Cuban government's percentage of refinery ownership from 10 to 60 percent, and authorized service stations to sell brands other than those supplied to them by their oil company owners. Among other things, this created outlets for a nationalized Cuban refinery. Cuba, without water power, coal, or crude petroleum, had to rely upon imports. The U.S. State Department took the position that whoever supplied petroleum to Cuba controlled Cuba (U.S. Senate 1974c, p. 11). When the Cubans demanded that the major oil companies refine Russian oil (which the Cubans had obtained through barter) as a means of government payments to the refining companies, the companies objected. They feared the competition of Russian oil because it would interfere with their marketing of oil brought in to Cuba from Venezuela. Shell, Esso, and Texaco therefore refused to refine the oil on the spurious basis that low-quality Russian oil would seriously damage their refineries (Tanzer 1969, pp. 317–20). Secretary of the Treasury Robert Anderson, a Texas oil man, told the major oil companies in Cuba (Esso, Texaco, Shell) that their refusal to accede to the Cuban government's request would be in accord with the government's policy toward Cuba. He also advised the companies that a joint refusal on their part would not incur any penalties under American antitrust laws. Finally, he informed the companies that the Anglo-Dutch company that owned Shell would also refuse to refine Soviet oil. Shortly after this statement, the three oil companies separately informed the Cuban government that they would not refine Russian oil, giving the impression that each company's decision had been arrived at independently (Bonsal 1971, p. 149). In addition to this move the United States suspended Cuba's sugar quotas. These blows were made in the interests of big oil and to bring about Castro's downfall. Despite these actions, the Cuban government seized the three refineries, and Russian technicians supplanted Shell, Esso, and Texaco technicians in the nationalized oil refineries (Engler, 1977, pp. 106–08). Oil was processed as easily in red refineries as it had been in red, white, and blue refineries.

The CIA

Introduction. Evidence from Senate investigating committees and other sources indicates that the CIA has been involved in at least 900 foreign interventions during the past 20 years. CIA interventions have included the surreptitious manipulation of foreign governments, assassinations, an extensive program of domestic surveillance, and secret paramilitary operations responsible for the deaths of thousands of people. Concerning the last part of this process, the congressional committee investigating the CIA, at the request of the agency under investigation (the CIA), has not published casualty figures (*New York Times Magazine* 1976). The thin line between manipulation and penetration is evident in an examination of CIA interventions in the affairs of several nations. The first step in such CIA actions called for the penetration of key political institutions in the target nation. Political and economic conditions created by virtue of this penetration set the scene for manipulation, usually calculated to overthrow left-wing governments. The new government, usually right-wing in orientation, often neglected the human rights of its citizens. These new regimes, unlike the former leftist regimes, favored "free enterprise" capitalism and welcomed U.S. business expansion within their jurisdiction.

CIA interventions have also lined the pockets of oppressive ruling minorities in foreign nations. Phillip Agee, a former CIA agent in Latin America, has claimed that foreign ruling minorities are often responsible for great injustices and extreme poverty. These ruling elites enjoy a high standard of living at the expense of the dispossessed masses. Foreign aid and business investments disproportionately benefit the ruling elites, while the masses suffer from inadequate educational, health, and welfare facilities (Agee 1975, pp. 503–04). Agee contends that CIA interventions cannot be separated from these structural conditions. In Latin America the CIA has trained and supported police and military forces and intelligence agents, and provided economic aid for military and social programs. This aid does not help the majority of citizens, but rather enables the elites to stay in power and maintain their disproportionate share of wealth and income. CIA activities designed to penetrate, neutralize, or eliminate left-wing political parties and organizations also serve to strengthen the ruling minorities (1975, p. 504).

CIA intervention in Ecuador in the early 1960s served as the model for this agency's interventions in several nations during the 1960s and 1970s.* In Ecuador, CIA agents infiltrated into labor organizations, the press, and anti-communist political groups. CIA funds were dispensed to each of these entities, which combined forces to dispose of the left-wing Arosemena regime in 1963 (Morris 1975, p. 77). In the last 25 years, the CIA has been involved in plots to overthrow governments in Iran, the Sudan, Syria, Guatemala, Ecuador, Guyana, Zaire, and Ghana. In Indonesia in 1965, the CIA engineered a bloody coup that removed Sukarno from office and led to the slaughter of at least 500,000 people. In the Dominican Republic this agency arranged for the assassination of the dictator Rafael Trujillo, and later took part in the invasion that prevented Juan Bosch, the liberal ex-president, from returning to power. The CIA paid for and directed the invasion of Cuba that failed at the Bay of Pigs. According to Agee, it is difficult for most people to believe or comprehend that the CIA could be involved in all of these subversive activities all over the world (Agee 1975, pp. 8-9).

The Chile Case. The case of the CIA's and ITT's penetrations and manipulations in Chile serves as an excellent illustration of corporate and government interventions in a foreign country. For this reason we discuss it in some detail. Latin America had been a lucrative source of profit for ITT for 40 years prior to the CIA-ITT intercession in Chile. Beginning in the 1920s, ITT bought up or built telephone companies in Puerto Rico, Cuba, the Virgin Islands, Peru, Chile, and other Latin American countries. With the rise of nationalism, many of these countries resented having their telephone companies owned and operated by a U.S. company, and they threatened nationalizations. Cuba's ITT holdings were expropriated without compensation under Castro, whereas in Argentina, Brazil, and Peru, ITT telephone companies were expropriated with compensation. The general trend toward nationalism threatened ITT's telephone business in Latin America, and following the expropriation of the telephone business in Peru, ITT built a new Sheraton hotel in Lima. The change from telephones to hotels provided a new and safer source of investment. Expropriations in Latin America left ITT with only three telephone companies, which its officials were determined to keep, in Puerto Rico, the Virgin Islands, and Chile. The Chilean operation employed 6,000 workers and was worth $150 million. The apparent absence of revolutionary nationalist parties in Chile seemed to insure that ITT's telephone companies would not be expropriated. The 1966 election looked promising. The

---

*For example, the CIA funneled money to the Israeli government in 1957, the same year CIA money was sent initially to Jordan's King Hussein. Since 1957 CIA payments to Israel totaled $80 million, although it is not certain when the payments were curtailed. The Israelis at first used the cash to underwrite Israeli aid programs for Black African nations, and in return hoped to earn black political support in the United Nations (Anderson and Whitten 1977a).

moderate Christian Democrat Eduardo Frei, a reformist but not a radical, was not hostile to big business. ITT offered campaign funds for Frei to be channeled through the CIA. The CIA refused this indirect arrangement, and instead gave Frei $20 million in direct campaign contributions (U.S. taxpayers' money). In 1966, when the Chileans expanded their telephone system, ITT received the contract despite a Swedish company's lower bid (Sampson 1973, p. 263).

In the 1970 Chilean elections following Frei's term in office, ITT worked assiduously against the popular candidate Salvador Allende Gossens, a socialist. ITT, in consultation with the CIA, planned to offer campaign funds in the amount of $1 million to the conservative candidate Jorge Allesandri. ITT also suggested to the CIA additional plans for Allende's defeat: the bribing of Chilean legislators who would cast electoral votes, sponsoring advertisements in the conservative newspaper, *Mercurio*, placing propagandists on Chilean TV and radio, and publicizing *Mercurio*'s editorials throughout Latin America and Europe. The CIA rejected this plan in lieu of its own plan to block Allende's election. Banks were to be asked to delay credits, U.S. companies were to be persuaded not to invest any money in Chile and to stall shipping deliveries, savings banks and loan institutions were to be asked to close down, and technical economic assistance was to be withdrawn. To what degree ITT inaugurated this CIA plan is not known (other government agencies contributed to the plan). The CIA eventually withdrew its plans in face of solid support for Allende among the congressmen who were to cast the decisive votes. Allende was elected in October 1970 (Sampson 1973, pp. 259-81).

After Allende's victory, ITT lobbied State Department officials and senators in an attempt to toughen the U.S. position toward Chile. ITT's most specific goal was to prevent Allende from expropriating its companies in Chile without compensation. In 1971, when it appeared that its property would soon be expropriated, ITT implemented an aggressive plan of intervention with the aid of the U.S. government. A special White House task force put pressure on Chile by breaking off all loans and aid to Chile from the United States and from banks, fomenting discontent in the Chilean military establishment and labor unions, provoking labor strikes, disrupting Chile's diplomatic efforts, and subsidizing the right-wing newspaper *Mercurio*. ITT contributed $350,000 to the effort (*Commercial Appeal* 1978; Petras and Morley 1975; Sampson 1973, pp. 285-86; Agee 1975, p. 583). The CIA spent millions to destabilize the Allende government and set up the junta that followed (Agee 1975, p. 8). Allende was assassinated in September 1973 amidst right-wing violence and a military takeover.

Dramatic social, economic, and political changes followed the 1973 military coup in Chile. The ruling military regime discarded completely the Allende government's nationalist foreign policy, adopted a program of unconditional support for U.S. policies and business interests in Chile, and outlined a new development strategy designed to encourage foreign capital investment. The vast majority of foreign and domestic enterprises nationalized during the three years under Allende were returned to their original owners. The junta also agreed to compensate expropriated U.S. copper companies in Chile (Petras and Morley 1975, p. 140). The overthrow of the Allende regime resulted in denials of human rights to the Chilean people (Birns 1973).

Recent CIA Disclosures. In addition to the plot on Allende's life, the CIA is suspect in plots against two other foreign heads of state; concrete attempts were made against the lives of five other foreign leaders (Weisman 1975). Cuban leader Fidel Castro was the target of 24 separate assassination attempts by the CIA (Schorr 1977). The aftermath of CIA intervention into Ecuador, Chile, Zaire, Brazil, Somalia, Indonesia, Iran, and other nations has left a trail of poverty, social chaos, and political repression (New York *Times* 1976b; Baraheni 1976; Anderson 1976d). Nations subject to intervention have become more receptive to expanding foreign business operations. Roger Morris calculated that ITT, Dow Chemical, and other U.S. interests account for 60 percent of foreign investments in Ecuador as a result of CIA intervention (1975, p. 77). The oil cartel, including the Texaco-Gulf consortium, owns a large share of these investments (Agee 1975, pp. 586-89).

During the Ford Administration journalists learned that the CIA had penetrated the electoral politics of Angola, Italy, and Portugal in endeavors to neutralize socialist parties in those nations, and that King Hussein of Jordan had been paid by the CIA (from 1957 to 1977) to provide it with intelligence information about countries in the Middle East (Wicker 1977). Journalists also recorded a long-term effort by the CIA to shape foreign opinion in support of U.S. policy abroad by channeling information and misinformation through a network of 50 newspapers, news agencies, and other communications entities (most of them based overseas) that it has owned, subsidized, or heavily influenced over the years. Nearly a dozen prominent American publishing houses have printed at least 250 English-language books financed or produced by the CIA since the early 1950s (New York *Times* 1977). The CIA's specific efforts to mold foreign opinion have encompassed tampering with historical documents (as with the 1956 denunciation of Stalin by Nikita Khrushchev), embellishing and distorting accounts that were otherwise factual (such as the provision of detailed quotes from a Russian defector), and fabricating misinformation (as with a report that Chinese troops were being sent to aid Vietnamese Communists). The CIA's favorite medium for launching what it terms "black" or unattributed propaganda has always been the foreign-based media in which it has had a secret financial interest. Reporters and editors in these foreign media have been paid by the CIA, and at one time numbered as many as 800. Former CIA Director Colby, when asked in a 1977 interview whether the CIA ever told these agents what to write, replied "Oh sure, all the time" (New York *Times* 1977e).

Some claim that the disclosures of such illegal activities have had the effect of temporarily modifying CIA interventions. The alarm of Senate investigating committees and the general public have apparently attenuated CIA foreign interventions, at least for the moment. The Carter administration proclaims opposition to the more blatant past interventions, and the new CIA director has promised that the CIA will not meddle again in the domestic affairs of sovereign states. The opposition is probably more cosmetic than real. The corporate structure requires such an arm.

The Foreign Corporate Bribery Scandals of 1945–1976

The ITT-Chile case is significant because it illustrates the lengths to which a company will illegally go to make money. It also shows that government agencies have been involved in illegal corporate behavior abroad. Other examples follow in a discussion of the foreign corporate bribery scandals of 1945-1976.

Corrupt payoffs to foreign government officials by U.S. corporate officials in the years since World War II became a major scandal during the 1970s. Over 350 firms subject to the jurisdiction of the Securities and Exchange Commission (SEC) admitted to making payments in the amount of $750 million to foreign government officials for the purpose of influencing a favorable flow of business. These payments have included so-called facilitating payments and commissions as well as outright bribes (Hershey 1977; Proxmire 1978). Corporate bribery not only tarnishes the image of U.S. democracy abroad, especially among the developing nations, but it violates the legal codes in host countries. Bribery also destroys what little competition remains between American companies. For example, a company that develops a good product for sale at a fair price may find itself excluded from a market because its competition, which produces an inferior and higher-priced product, has rigged the market with a bribe. Investors in corporations (public companies) have a right to know about corporate management, corporate expenditures and cash flows, and corporate financial status. Many corporations have set up accounting systems to hide massive payments (bribes) to foreign officials, so the maintenance of these slush funds masks the true corporate financial condition. U.S. companies and their foreign subsidiaries do not maintain an accurate set of books and records that can be checked for bribery practices (Proxmire 1978). The SEC has sued two dozen corporations for failing to inform their stockholders of payoffs overseas, and for deducting bribes from tax payments as legitimate expenses. In one notable case, Lockheed stockholders were unaware that this company had funneled $25 million to foreign politicians in order to sell its planes (Hershey 1977).

Some corporations claim that bribery is necessary to economic survival, that without bribery international markets could not be expanded, and that without such expansion corporate enterprises would collapse. Bribes have permitted corporations to escape domestic taxes in host countries. Foreign bribes have been usually engineered by middlemen, thereby protecting the company offering the bribe and the government receiving the bribe. The middlemen, normally natives of the host countries, have often enjoyed close ties to high government officials. Serving as corporation agents in some cases, the middlemen would approach agents of their governments with the foreign corporate bribe offer. In other cases, officials of the target countries accepted kickbacks on a continuing basis. In both cases, U.S. government agencies have facilitated bribery. The Northrop Corporation, for example, hired Adnan Khashoggi in 1971, with the encouragement of the Defense Department, to negotiate an arms deal with Saudi Arabian government officials. Northrop, like many other firms in the arms industry, had turned to the Middle East as a source of profits following the Vietnam war. Khashoggi demanded and received from Northrop the sum of $450,000, which he passed on to two Saudi Air Force generals, who in turn closed the arms deal with the Saudi Arabian government. Khashoggi received his commission from his employer, Northrop (Gwirtzman 1975, p. 106). Since that time he has operated as a middleman-agent for several corporations and governments throughout the world. Khashoggi's immense wealth and sumptuous life style are typical of that found among many other arms agents, who in reality are long con men (sophisticated confidence men who earn large scores).

In the Northrop case it was obvious that this corporation did not need to place pressure upon the U.S. government in order to sell its planes to Saudi Arabia. The Pentagon, in fact, encouraged Northrop to seek out the Saudis as a new market. Government agents have helped other companies sell arms to foreign countries. For example, the Iranian government became disenchanted with middlemen in 1975 (fed up with the money they were making and the adverse publicity entailed), and adopted a new arms policy providing that U.S. firms selling arms to Iran could no longer deal through indigenous middlemen or agents. In the same year, a Lockheed regional manager joined with U.S. embassy officials in Iran and with officials of the Iranian government to work out a new policy that would allow Lockheed to operate in Iran and to conduct bribery as usual (Jones 1975).

The close cooperation between industry and government in the foreign arms corporate bribery scandals is not surprising when one considers the fact that agencies such as the CIA have often cooperated with corporations in facilitating bribes and payoffs in foreign countries. The aforementioned CIA and ITT political manipulations in Chile entailed payments to the Chilean labor unions, press, and military.

When agents left the employ of the CIA for jobs in industry, they often found their new duties similar to past tasks. When the American press uncovered the CIA's covert subsidization of the National Student Association in 1966, the agency decided it needed a deeper cover, and turned to the multinational corporations for this purpose. A special CIA office was created in Washington in 1967 to place former CIA agents in the overseas offices of American-based corporations. Some retired agents from the CIA who had formerly facilitated the bribery of foreign officials in an official capacity for the U.S. government commenced a new career, bribing the same foreign officials, as employees of private enterprise. For example, Kermit Roosevelt, Jr., became an "international consultant" to Northrop following his career in the CIA. In his new vocation, he used the same network of contacts he had utilized earlier as head of the CIA operations in the Middle East (Gwirtzman 1975, p. 104).

At times the government-industry linkage has constituted collusion. It is known, for example, that the CIA paid Ashland Oil $99,000 between 1969 and 1973 for an unspecified purpose. At the time, Ashland utilized a Saudi prince as a middleman in order to arrange a contract in Saudi Arabia. There is a suspicion (unconfirmed) that CIA agents helped Ashland in the Saudi Arabian influence-buying scheme, and that the $99,000 CIA payment to Ashland was made in order to reimburse CIA operatives who had posed as Ashland employees (Birmingham *News* 1975).

Oil Company Bribes. Gulf Oil was one of the largest offenders in the foreign bribery scandals. The SEC charged this company in 1977 with falsifying reports to conceal a $10 million fund for political payments made to foreign government officials between 1960 and 1974; the money was channeled through a Bahamas company. In a consent decree, Gulf agreed to refrain in the future from such violations (U.S. District Court 1975). A Gulf reform committee, established by this company in the wake of the SEC charges, determined that the total of Gulf's political contributions at home and abroad exceeded $12 million between 1960 and 1974. The same company committee described the Bahamas Company as a "vehicle for accumulating cash with which domestic political payments were made and for recording charges resulting from transfers of funds abroad for political purposes" (Securities and Exchange Commission 1975). Between 1970 and 1973, Mobil Oil contributed nearly $2 million to the Italian Social Democratic and Christian Democratic parties, concealing this information from its own stockholders and internal auditors. In 1975, Exxon admitted to the subcommittee on multinational corporations chaired by Senator Frank Church that it had given over $50 million to Italian politicians from 1963 to 1972, including at least $12 million to the Christian Democrats, $5 million to the Social Democrats, $1 million to the Socialists, and $86,000 to the Communists. Evidence suggested that the U.S. State Department, the CIA, and the American ambassador to Italy knew about these activities. Devices used to facilitate these payments included secret bank accounts, adjustments in bank interest rates, inflated prices, dummy invoices, and kickbacks—all to further the so-called democratic process. These practices also deprived the Italian government of tax revenues. Exxon officials referred to these false accounting procedures as errors in business judgement. Mobil supported its bribes to Italian political parties in the name of supporting the democratic process (Engler 1977, pp. 111-12). Exxon's contribution to the Communist party in Italy probably appears to be an anomaly to many, but the Communists do have some political power in Italy and Exxon knows that political power is economic power—in short that political power brings profits. And what else matters?

Arms Company Bribes. Lockheed, under investigation by the Church committee and the SEC in August 1975 (after first stubbornly denying any wrongdoing), admitted to the Church committee that it had spent at least $22 million between 1970 and 1975 on payments to officials and political organizations in foreign countries. The committee found that Lockheed had paid kickbacks and bribes in countries ranging from Indonesia and Iran to Saudi Arabia and the Philippines during this period (U.S. Senate 1975, Part 14). On the basis of information aired in testimony, the committee determined that Lockheed had paid Prince Bernhard of the Netherlands a sum of $1 million (through Swiss bank accounts) from October 1960 through 1962 for his service as an undercover arms agent. He was supposed to arrange sales of Lockheed planes to the Dutch government. During the 1960s, the Northrop Corporation had employed the Prince as an arms middleman in the Netherlands and Germany (U.S. Senate 1975, Part 12). The Prince was forced to resign following these revelations. The Church committee reported that three Italian ministers of defense and their political parties collected bribes from Lockheed in the amount of $2 million from 1970 to 1971. These defense ministers arranged a $60 million Hercules transport plane sale to the Italian government. Two Italian government ministers were indicted by the Italian parliament in 1977, and their indictment created a national political crisis (Sampson 1977, pp. 133-278).

The Church committee also found that Lockheed had paid $12 million to Japanese government officials for the Tristar plane deal in 1972 in which Japanese Premier Tanaka was involved. Tanaka had resigned after being charged with other shady financial dealings. Earlier, Japan had ordered 230 Starfighter airplanes from Lockheed, nearly all of which were produced under license by Mitsubsi in Japan. Lockheed was estimated to have paid $1.5 million in bribes to Japanese officials and $750,000 to a middleman-agent for this transaction. The details of these bribes were passed on to the CIA. In total, the Lockheed scandals had nearly toppled a monarchy (the Netherlands), influenced three elections (in Italy and Germany), and caused the arrest and trial of a former prime minister in Italy (Sampson 1977, pp. 227-81).

Lockheed and Northrop were not the only arms companies that paid bribes overseas in order to do business. SEC investigations published in 1976 disclosed that U.S. embassies overseas had given advice about bribes on a regular basis, and that the Defense Department had encouraged arms salesmen to utilize the customs of the host countries in sales work. The SEC found that one in ten of the 500 largest American corporations (including Boeing and McDonnell Douglas) had admitted questionable foreign payments in the amount of $100 million over a five-year period. Lockheed and Northrop had devised secret money channels for domestic and foreign bribery, and kept bank accounts in Switzerland, beyond the reach of any official inquiry (Sampson 1977, p. 286).

In order to reduce foreign corporate bribery, the House of Representatives proposed legislation in November 1977 making it a crime for an American corporation or its overseas subsidiaries to bribe foreign officials. The bill (net yet passed), which is similar to one passed by the Senate, sets a maximum $1 million penalty for a U.S. business caught violating the law, and authorizes a $100,000 fine and five-year jail sentences for company officials involved in a bribe (*Clarion-Ledger* 1977k). Such penalties, however, will not eliminate bribery. Though most corporations have denounced bribery many of them feel that this practice is necessary in obtaining business contracts abroad. Some corporations have set a maximum of $100 for "facilitating payments" which shall continue upon the approval of senior management (Hershey 1977). It is likely that many corporations will still manage to engage in bribery (business as usual) for the following reasons: the U.S. government allows corporations to accumulate large international slush funds; corporations maintain secret money channels and foreign bank accounts; multinational operations extend throughout the world and include divergent subsidiaries through which cash flows may be hidden; and corporate financial reports are vague and incomplete.

GOAL OF THE OFFENDER

The purported goal of the U.S. government and corporate agents in the Vietnam war was to protect an ally, South Vietnam, from communist aggression. The real political aim was to prevent the existence of a socialist state in Vietnam. The economic intention was to secure valuable raw materials in South Vietnam for corporate U.S. interests, and to maintain open trading avenues between U.S. corporations and Southeast Asian nations (Kolko 1969).

Government and corporate proponents of arms sales to foreign countries pursued several purported ends: to protect U.S. allies against the militant incursions of communist or socialist aggressors; to promote the defensive strength of one nation vis-à-vis another; and to offset the unfavorable balance of payments. The actual ends pursued by government and corporate agents in the foreign arms race encompassed three major aims: support of the military-industrial complex in the United States, protection and enhancement of the military and political position of U.S. allies with respect to the communist bloc nations, and promotion and dissemination of capitalist ideology throughout the world.

The publicized objectives of U.S. corporate and government agents' foreign interventions in behalf of the oil cartel were: to insure an adequate supply of crude petroleum for the United States and its allies, to keep viable the U.S. oil industry, a necessary part of our business economy whose interests were equated with national interests, to prevent the nationalization of oil by the oil producing countries, and to block the divestiture of oil at home. Specific rationales were often invoked by the social actors in the rhetorical language of national security, competition, freedom vs. socialism, expansion of foreign markets, corporate survival, employment maintenance, maintenance of a high standard of living for U.S. workers, and even "energy for a strong America" (Exxon's ludicrous T.V. advertising slogan). The actual goal of the oil cartel and the U.S. government agents who supported it was an ever-increasing corporate profit margin and the preservation of the vertical integration of oil, keeping mining operations, transport, refinery processes, pipelines, and the marketing of crude petroleum in the hands of the international oil monopoly.

The CIA's purported motivation for foreign interventions was to contain the spread of communism throughout the world. The CIA's functional goals were to overthrow left-wing regimes and to supplant them with right-wing regimes more amenable to U.S. political and economic control. CIA agents also acted to sustain and enhance the immediate corporate interests of big business abroad at a high cost to the ordinary American taxpayer. It is hard for some people to realize that the CIA has no money of its own other than what it gets from the taxpayer.

Corporate participants in the foreign corporate bribery scandals claimed that foreign bribes did not violate U.S. laws, were necessary to corporate survival, and were in keeping with normal business practices in foreign countries and thus could not be circumvented by U.S. corporations. The true purpose of these illegal briberies was the maximization of corporate profit in the host countries without consideration for national or international laws—in short, profits to the U.S. corporations at the expense of corporate shareholders, the U.S. Treasury, foreign taxpayers, and the tax assessments of competing U.S. corporations abroad.

LEGAL STATUS OF THE OFFENSE

The intervention in the Vietnam war by the U.S. government violated international law. Specific international, criminal, and war crimes violations were also committed by the U.S. military during this conflict, as in the My Lai incident. Government agents and corporate agents worked as partners in several world-wide para-legal violations tied in with the arms race. We list a few of these joint political violations: the United States has been the largest producer and seller of arms for export in the world since World War II; the United States has force-fed arms to foreign countries; the United States has encouraged Third World nations to buy arms they could not afford and did not need; the United States has sold arms to conflicting parties in several volatile areas throughout the world; and the CIA has supplied arms to right-wing revolutionaries in various parts of the world.

The oil industry's interventions into the economic and political affairs of oil producing countries, engineered by corporate and government agents, broke international laws and laws of the host countries. The CIA aided the rightist party that forcibly deposed Mossadeq from power in Iran in 1953. Such interventions enabled the oil cartel to violate U.S. antitrust statutes and to maintain and expand the vertical integration of oil. CIA interventions in Chile, Ecuador, Angola, Portugal, and several other foreign countries violated the United Nations charter, which prohibits one sovereign state from interfering with the political affairs of another.* In fact, some of these interventions involved criminal offenses

---

*See Falk (1975) for a discussion of CIA violations of international law.

such as assault and murder. The foreign corporate bribery scandals violated tax laws in other countries, as well as the Securities and Exchange Commission's rules safeguarding stockholders' rights to know about corporate management, cash flows, and financial status.

NATURE OF THE OFFENSE

Social actors engaged in the Vietnam war, the foreign arms race, oil interventions in foreign countries, CIA interventions, and the foreign corporate bribery scandals committed intervention offenses as members of work teams employed by corporate or government bureaucracies—in most cases tied together by the same collusive acts and aims. For example, corporate and government teams worked together abroad in the financial interest of the oil cartel, the arms industry (the military-industrial complex), and in the political and economic interests of the U.S. government and corporate structure. CIA and ITT teamwork in Chile is illustrative of the latter. Corporate and government agents' interventions in the foreign arms race and in the oil industry were overt, whereas foreign bribery interventions were covert and nonviolent. These interventions for the most part were non-violent, except in the cases of Iran, Cuba, Vietnam, and Chile. Strong peer group support, government support, corporate support, and public support existed for all these actions, with the exception of the Vietnam intervention in its latter stages. Only when it became clear that there was no chance for military success did massive public support for this engagement wither away. There appears to be a belated but weak reaction to the CIA interventions in Chile, as illustrated by the following cases.

In March 1978, the Justice Department charged two ITT executives with felonies in connection with their testimony about ITT's intervention in the 1970 Chilean election. Edward Gerrity, an ITT senior vice president, and Robert Berrellez, another ITT official, were charged with giving false testimony to the Senate Foreign Relations Committee's Subcommittee on Multinational Corporations and to the American Arbitration Association, both of which were probing ITT cooperation with the CIA to block Salvador Allende's election to the presidency of Chile.

Gerrity was charged with three counts of perjury, one count of obstructing governmental proceedings, one count of subornation of perjury, and one count of making a false statement in a government matter. The Justice Department charged that Gerrity gave false testimony about a $1 million fund raised to bar Allende's election. Gerrity had testified in 1973 that ITT, rather than covertly raising funds to interfere in the election, desired to engage in a U.S. government plan to improve relations with the anticipated Allende government. Gerrity was also charged with suborning Harold Hendrix, a former ITT Latin American public relations director, to give false information to the Senate subcommittee. Hendrix received a suspended one-month jail sentence and a $100 fine after pleading guilty to a charge of withholding information from Congress. He was also named as an unindicted co-conspirator in the charges against Berrellez, which included one count of conspiracy, three counts of perjury, one count of obstructing governmental proceedings, and one count of lying to official investigators in a governmental matter. Berrellez conspired with Hendrix and other persons to obstruct the Senate subcommittee's proceedings, to commit perjury, and to defraud the United States (Ostrow 1978). To say the least, sanctions are weak for known and convicted intervention offenders.

4

INTERVENTION
AGAINST GOVERNMENT

DOMESTIC INTERVENTION

A mélange of organized groups that emerged in the United States during the 1960s and 1970s have intervened against the establishment (the government and the corporate structure). Interventions were manifest in several forms of manipulation including assault and assassination, malicious bombing, trashing, intimidation, and thefts or "expropriations." Left-wing organizations (including the Students for a Democratic Society, Weather Underground, Black Liberation Army, People's Liberation Army, Puerto Rican Armed Forces of Liberation, Symbionese Liberation Army, and Black Panther party) had evolved from non-violent organized social movements of the 1960s such as the civil rights move-ment, the New Left movement, and the antiwar movement. Right-wing organi-zations (such as the John Birch Society, Minutemen, National Socialist White People's Party, and National Youth Alliance) evolved from groups of disen-chanted superpatriots, anti-liberals, and racists. The Ku Klux Klan, an older organization, was rejuvenated. Right-wing groups were hostile to the political system's membership but not to the social structure; they planned intervention against the government only if a communist takeover was imminent.

Both left-wing and right-wing organizations reflected an urgent sense of dissatisfaction with existing political and economic institutions, a dissatisfaction stemming from the frustration of attempting to effect social change through nonviolent means. Consequently some of these groups resorted to violence. The Weather Underground, in a May 1970 communiqué, stated that its members had felt frustration in trying to change the American political system in a peaceful fashion during the 1960s, and that revolutionary violence was the only remain-ing alternative (U.S. House 1974b, p. 217). Right-wing splinter groups such as the Minutemen, National Youth Alliance, and the Ku Klux Klan were con-vinced that "communist influences" were contaminating the highest levels of government. They believed that there was an international communist conspiracy seeking to establish a one-world socialistic government, and that key U.S. leaders and institutions were a part of this conspiracy (U.S. House 1974b, p. 214). Though some right-wing groups adopted fascistic tactics and engaged in sporadic terrorist activities (the Klan indulged in cross burnings, attacks on blacks, forced entries, arson, and drownings) they possessed no central guiding ideology or unified plan to bring the government down.

The leftist radical groups that have intervened against the government or the "establishment" comprised a small part of what is known as the underground, including above-ground support institutions (some civil rights organizations, women's and gay rights organizations, communist and socialist organizations, and other sympathizers); loosely-knit and often transitory radical groups advocating some form of violence (Purple Sunshine Clan, Quarter Moon Tribe, Red Willow Family); and violent revolutionary underground groups such as the Weather Underground (Sale 1975a; U.S. House 1974b, p. 101). The above-ground sympathizers and the loosely-knit radical underground provided useful services for the revolutionary cadres, including food, shelter, aliases, disguises, medical and legal aid, maildrops, hideouts, and transportation. Moreover, these sympathizers refused to cooperate with FBI agents who investigated revolutionary activities (Sale 1975a; U.S. House 1974b, p. 207; Teodori 1969).

The most significant interventions were performed by the exceedingly small revolutionary cadres. One of these groups, the street-fighting, bomb-making Weather Underground, is currently believed to consist of no more than 50 people. This organization split from the Students for a Democratic Society (estimated at 40,000 members) in 1969, and probably peaked at between 500 and 600 members. Another group, the Black Liberation Army, numbering no more than 100 members at its height in the early 1970s, evolved from the Black Panther party. Many members of this group have been captured, and the organization now derives a good deal of its support from the black prison population. The Puerto Rican Armed Forces of Liberation (F.A.C.N.), a third revolutionary group functioning in the United States since 1973, bombed public buildings in the name of oppressed Third World peoples. This organization's hard core in the United States numbers only about 20 members. Finally, the Symbionese Liberation Army, organized in the 1970s, is believed to be extinct. Though probably numbering no more than 50 at its peak in 1972, the SLA was designed by ex-inmates and leftist students as an "umbrella" organization to unite the various radical underground groups into a single militaristic body. It advocated armed guerilla warfare against the U.S. government and the corporations (Sale 1975a).

ACTION PATTERNS

The distinguishing feature of the revolutionary cadres was para-military combat group organization. Highly solidified and hierarchical, these cadres demanded of their members an unflagging devotion to social change through revolution. The major manipulations of these groups included assault and assassination, malicious bombing, and thefts or "expropriations." Because these patterns were characteristic of several radical groups over time and frequently committed by amorphous groupings, we discuss them as such rather than as separate case-study patterns within specific organizations.

Assault and Assassination

This pattern consisted of assaults as well as ambushes, gun-battles, sniper-attack assassinations, and attempted assasinations. Members of the Black Liberation Army (BLA) in the early 1970s assaulted policemen in St. Louis, Kansas City, and Canawha County, North Carolina, and killed four policemen in New York City in 1971, two in ambushes and two in gun battles. Members of the BLA frequently set up the police for attack or ambush by violating laws in the presence of policemen, thereby luring them into traps. Sometimes officers were called to investigate crimes in certain areas and then ambushed (U.S. House 1974b, pp. 124-26). In the 1960s and 1970s, several policemen were killed in sniper attacks. Twelve U.S. policemen were killed and 71 injured by members of the Black Panther party between 1969 and 1971 (U.S. House 1974b, p. 205).

Police were not the only targets of assassinations by radicals. Dr. Marcus Foster, Oakland's Superintendent of Schools, was killed by the Symbionese Liberation Army (SLA) in 1973; his deputy, Robert Blackburn, was seriously wounded. The SLA believed that the Oakland school system supported fascist tendencies in American society, and that the student identity system was "patterned after the system of apartheid" (U.S. House 1974b, p. 135). The SLA also objected to the monitoring of students' behavior by Oakland police and teachers, which it said was "patterned after fascist American tactics of genocide, murder, and imprisonment practiced by American-financed puppet governments in Vietnam, the Philippines, Chile, and South Africa" (U.S. House 1974b, p. 135).

Malicious Bombing, "Trashing," and Intimidation

The basic purpose of malicious bombing actions was police intimidation. Radicals perceived the police to be the agents of a totalitarian state, the United States, who enforced "fascist" and "racist" laws. The radicals despised the police, easy targets, and vented anger toward them and the system through malicious and imtimidating behavior, such as bombing police stations and police cars (U.S. House 1974b, p. 124). The Weather Underground bombed a number of public buildings in cities throughout the country from 1970 to 1975. They bombed the Marin County Courthouse in San Rafael, California on October 1, 1970, to protest the death of George Jackson's brother Jonathan Jackson and bombed the Reserve Officer Training Corps (R.O.T.C.) facilities at the University of Washington in Seattle on October 8, 1970, to protest against military training and the Vietnam war. They bombed the New York City police department to attack a symbol of U.S. injustice; bombed the Pentagon on May 19, 1972; and bombed the Health, Education, and Welfare Department on March 7, 1974 to protest government policies on welfare and sterilization (U.S. House 1974b, pp. 111–12). Left-wing bombs in 1974 rocked the U.S. Capitol building, Los Angeles International Airport, and several New York City banks and commercial buildings (Hancock and Gibbons 1975).

According to local U.S. law enforcement records gathered by the U.S. House of Representatives in 1974, there were 4,330 bombings, 1,475 attempts to bomb, and 35,129 threats to bomb in the United States from January 1, 1968 to April 15, 1970. Bombing and arson attacks on federal buildings alone increased from 13 (in the 12-month period ending June 30, 1969) to 38 in the following year. Property damage increased accordingly, from \$7,250 to \$612,569. Threats against federal buildings rose from 46 to 383 over this period. In the 36 percent of bombing cases where law enforcement officers were able to categorize perpetrators, 56 percent could be attributed to campus disturbances, 19 percent to black extremists, 14 percent to white extremists, 2 percent to labor disputes, and 1 percent to attacks on religious institutions. Eight percent were in aid of criminal activities such as extortion, robbery, and arson for insurance. The report claimed that these bombings were primarily the product of young radicals (U.S. House 1974b, p. 53). A systematic assessment of terrorist bombings in U.S. cities (Karber 1971) counted 1,425 politically-motivated bombings in the United States between January 1970 and March 1971.

"Trashing" includes such activities as looting, destroying property, rock throwing, and fistfighting with the police. The Weathermen staged what they called "the Days of Rage" in Chicago in October 1969, and proclaimed this event to be the domestic equivalent of the Vietnam war. Weathermen roamed through the Chicago Loop and some of Chicago's most elegant residential districts breaking windows, overturning cars, and seeking violent encounters with the police (U.S. House 1974b, p. 222).

Radicals thought to be members of leftist underground organizations harassed and threatened police during the late 1960s and early 1970s. Anonymous threatening phone calls were made to officers' homes; officers' names, home addresses, and telephone numbers were published in the radical press; false charges against officers were made to the press; obscene graffiti were chalked on police officers' homes; uncomplimentary cartoons about the police appeared in the underground papers; and police were intimidated with explosives. An example of this last tactic was the 1970 explosion of a nail-filled time bomb outside a San Francisco church while mourners gathered for the funeral of a police officer (killed during a routine robbery case). In another case, a tear-gas grenade thrown through the window of a policeman's home landed on his daughter's bed and burst into flames (U.S. House 1974b, p. 224).

Thefts or "Expropriations"

This category includes robberies, burglaries, and thefts designed to gather money, guns, explosives, and other materials needed to sustain revolutionary cadres. The thefts had both practical and symbolic significance. They were practical, because money, weapons arsenals, and explosives needed by the cadres were not easily obtainable from above-ground or underground groups. Thefts symbolized the necessity of violent tactics if the masses were to gain economic and political benefits that capitalist society denied them: only through violence could large corporate interests be "expropriated" of the power and wealth concentrated in their hands. Hence the thefts were justified by radicals as "revolutionary justice," returning wealth and power to the people. Thefts therefore were viewed as critical measures in the transformation from capitalism to socialism (U.S. House 1974b, p. 200).

Many of the thefts or rip-offs occurred during assaults, assassinations, and "trashings," when radicals, for example, stole a policeman's weapon after assaulting or killing him. However, the best example of corporation expropriation was bank robbery. Here the raw capital was stolen, rather than symbols of capital. The Symbionese Liberation Army drew attention to this kind of theft when it robbed the Hibernia National Bank in April 1974 (U.S. House 1974b, pp. 169–82). The SLA kidnapped Patricia Hearst on February 5, 1974 and extorted from her wealthy father $2 million worth of food for poor people in San Francisco.

GOAL OF THE OFFENDER

The primary goal of left-wing organizations that engaged in domestic manipulations was to change the structure of wealth and political power in the United States by bringing down the system. Secondary ends were the disruption of civil affairs and the destruction of the country's economic and political institutions. The rationale for domestic interventions was clearly articulated in the manifestos of the left-wing groups who held that the existing distribution of wealth, property, and political power (administered by the capitalist class) was oppressive, exploitative, and morally unjust. These groups believed that a violent revolution was the only way to create an economically and politically equitable social order in the United States. Memberships of these organizations had decided that the capitalists would only give way to force and violence, and that parliamentary democratic measures were counter-productive. For example, the Symbionese Liberation Army in 1973 declared a revolutionary war against what it called "The Fascist Capitalist Class, and all their agents of murder, oppression, and exploitation" (Symbionese Liberation Army 1973). Similarly, the Black Liberation Army in 1972 stipulated its commitment to revolutionary violence. In a pamphlet describing the BLA's doctrines and program, this group portrayed itself as a band of small guerilla warfare units "waging armed struggle against the agents of death—the United States government . . ." (National Committee for Defense 1972). Furthermore, BLA claimed that it was a vanguard that would eventually lead the fight for a revolutionary society. The Weather Underground advocated revolutionary social change, and the Black Panthers demanded revolution involving armed struggle. All these radical groups conceived of themselves as participating in an organized revolutionary movement against American fascism, racism, and capitalism (U.S. House 1974b, p. 118).

LEGAL STATUS OF THE OFFENSE

Interventions against government violated a number of specific federal and state statutes. The primary federal statutes broken were as follows: the Organized Crime Control Act of 1970, which prohibits the importation, manufacture, distribution, and storage of explosive devices; the federal antiriot act enacted in 1968; the Selective Service Act; laws prohibiting desecration of the American flag, harboring deserters from the armed forces, destroying national defense materials and premises, conspiracy to riot (a violation of 18 U.S.C. 2101); and laws prohibiting bombings, sabotage, mob action, possession and transportation of unregistered destructive devices, arson, kidnapping, and forgery (U.S. House 1974b, p. 212). State and local law violations included assault, murder, breaking and entering, burglary, theft, aggravated battery, vandalism, trespassing, looting, and robbery.

At times persons were arrested for the specific crimes they had committed, while at other times they were charged with legal substitutes. Many persons considered dangerous to the status quo or the state were subjected to political policing whereby an umbrella of offenses was available to criminalize conduct. For example, conspiracy laws were used as a catch-all in many cases (as in the cases against Stokely Carmichael, H. Rap Brown, and Bobby Seale). Political offenders, as Austin Turk (1975) pointed out, are persons or groups perceived to be enemies of the state because by ideology, action, or threat of action they threaten the existing political, economic, and social order. Political crime comprises the "disloyal" behavior of political criminals, whatever it might be. Members of certain radical organizations were perceived by the authorities to be political offenders by virtue of group organization, regardless of the criminality or legality of their acts. Perceived political offenders in the United States, as elsewhere, were subjected to political policing and derogated as generalized deviants. Criminal sanctions were meted out to punish, control, and deter disloyal citizens.

NATURE OF THE OFFENSE

These intervention offenses constituted organizational crime because they were committed by members of formal organizations in the course of routine membership duties, and in the behest of organizational aims. These interventions by radical groups were violent and overt, and received group support only from peer groups, members of the group committing the offenses or of other similar groups. Societal reaction (from the public, the corporate structure, and the government) was strongly negative to these offenses and offenders because the offenders' loyalty to the state was in question, and all members of any society are expected to be loyal. Persons convicted of these acts were harassed, assaulted (sometimes killed), and incarcerated for long periods of time. Even those thought to have been involved were subject to harassment, assault, arrest, conviction, and punishment. Official reaction was harsh because those in power felt more threatened than others. In short, they had more to lose should the system go under. Additionally, those in power had more to do with the legal processing and disposition of political offenders than did others.

FOREIGN INTERVENTION

Foreign governments have intervened in the domestic affairs of the United States to gain diplomatic favors, military and economic aid, and political support. Efforts to obtain these favors supposedly take place within a framework of agreed-upon rules, procedures, and international laws and standards. Lobbying by one country in that of another, for example, is supposed to operate within the legal framework of the host government. Foreign governments have breached these rules in influencing U.S. government policies (Halloran 1977b). Influence-buying in the United States from abroad marks by far the most important foreign intervention. Renata Adler (1977) points out that while the United States has been preoccupied with its own interventions abroad, the tide has started to run the other way. Foreign governments are now paying money illegally to U.S. officials for favors. A good part of the money sent abroad for foreign aid is used instead to bribe U.S. officials for favors. In the case of foreign interventions, we found earlier that bribes and kickbacks to U.S. contractors and officials were drawn in part from the huge sums of taxpayers' money that this country had spent abroad for other purposes. Therefore, whether the bribery intervention is foreign or domestic, the U.S. taxpayer is likely to foot the bill (Adler 1977).

ACTION PATTERNS

Examples of foreign bribery interventions by South Korea, Taiwan, Iran, and Vietnam follow.

South Korean Bribery

The South Korean government, from 1970 to 1975, spent about $750,000 in the United States to win sympathy and continued military and economic aid from this country (Halloran 1977a). South Korea schemed to ensure the full commitment of United States military and economic power in the defense of South Korea, and the political support of Washington for South Korean President Park. The Korean Central Intelligence Agency played a large role in this illegal scheme. The plan was initiated in 1970, when President Park's government was close to panic because it thought the United States was about to abandon its South Korean military security commitments. First, the Koreans began a drive to bring U.S. business investments into Korea to promote economic development, and to ensure U.S. military aid in protecting these investments. The Koreans succeeded in bringing American investors into Korea, and these investors are now vocal defenders of the Park regime. A joint economic council was formed in 1973, and its members (mostly businessmen from both countries) have exchanged visits and encouraged U.S. congressmen to visit Korea. The South Korean government has encouraged U.S. banks to make loans to South Korean businesses. At the end of 1975, such loans from the Bank of America, Citibank, Chase Manhattan, Morgan Guaranty, Manufacturers Hanover, and the Chemical Bank totaled $972 million (Halloran 1977b).

The South Korean government has also tried to influence the American press to pressure the Congress into granting economic and military aid. In the early 1970s, a Korean agent unsuccessfully offered an American academician $50,000 to arrange a cover story on President Park in *Time* or *Newsweek*. The Korean government in 1975 hired the public relations firm of Hill and Knowlton for $30,000 to publicize South Korean economic and political accomplishments. Korean intelligence officials planned in 1976 to invite influential journalists to Korea, to convert them to the idea that the U.S. should formulate favorable policies to Korea. Two American reporters were to be hired as collaborators in this effort. Other Korean and American reporters were commissioned to collect intelligence on the policy planning of high level U.S. officials in matters pertaining to Korea (Halloran 1977b). The South Koreans in the early 1970s attempted to buy influence with American academic institutions. South Korean intelligence agents spent $20,000 to promote seminars dealing with South Korean military security at Georgetown University, and to enlist the collaboration of this university's Research Institute for Korean Affairs. Harvard University was awarded $1 million for Korean studies, and other U.S. universities (Columbia, Pennsylvania, and American) were approached by the Koreans with similar offers (Halloran 1977b).

The Seoul government was also interested in influencing American church leaders, because missionaries in Korea had supported Korean dissidents in their resistance to Park's repression of human rights. The Koreans planned in 1976 to have the Korean CIA convert a visiting Southern Baptist minister and a 395-member evangelical group to the Korean cause. In addition, plans were made to invite leaders of the American Methodist and Presbyterian churches to Seoul (Halloran 1977b).

The most important target of South Korean influence-buying was the U.S. Congress. Tongsun Park, a purported South Korean businessman and intelligence agent, served as a middleman between the South Korean government and several U.S. rice companies. He received commissions from these companies and distributed them as gifts to congressmen and other officials, including California Representative Richard Hanna, Louisiana Representative Otto Passman, and Louisiana Governor Edwin Edwards. Hanna and Passman then influenced other congressmen to make decisions favorable to the Republic of Korea. The monetary payments by Park to Hanna and Passman (and other congressmen) were given in the form of political campaign contributions or donations to petty cash, and in some instances the cash was diverted to personal use (*Clarion-Ledger* 1977h). Such relationships violated legal and diplomatic standards concerning the conduct of foreign lobbyists and members of Congress.

Park was indicted in August 1977 on 36 counts of bribery, conspiracy, racketeering, and mail fraud. Hanna was indicted in October 1977 on charges of accepting $100,000 in bribes from Park (*Clarion-Ledger* 1977h). He confessed in March 1978 that he took more than $200,000 for using his office to assist Tongsun Park. In a plea-bargaining deal with the government, 39 of 40 counts against Hanna were dropped. He pleaded guilty in the U.S. District Count in Washington to a single count of defrauding the U.S. government, thereby avoiding a trial that was scheduled for March 1978 (*Clarion-Ledger* 1978f). Otto Passman was indicted in March 1978 on charges that he took $213,000 in bribes from Tongsun Park. The seven-count indictment charged that Passman (once a strong overseer of foreign aid allotments) misused his public office to promote rice sales for Park under the government-subsidized Food for Peace Program (*Clarion-Ledger* 1978k). Other investigations have involved former Congressmen Cornelius Gallagher of New Jersey and William Minshall of Ohio, and Governor Edwin Edwards of Louisiana (Birmingham *News* 1978).

Hancho C. Kim, a naturalized American citizen (a former Korean), was convicted in March 1978 for conspiring to corrupt congressmen and then lying about receiving $600,000 from South Korea for the plot. Kim was convicted of conspiring with a former agent of the Korean CIA, Sang Keun Kim, and with a high official of the KCIA in Seoul, General Yang Doo Wan, to defraud the United States. Sang Keun Kim, who defected to the United States, and General Yang were listed as unindicted co-conspirators. Hancho Kim was charged with receiving $600,000 from Sang Keun Kim to be spent on congressmen in order to gain favors for South Korea and to influence votes on military and economic matters. The second count charged Hancho Kim with lying to a grand jury when he denied receiving the bribe from Sang Keun Kim. Hancho Kim and his wife Soonduk were also charged with two counts of tax evasion (New York *Times* 1978c).

Interventions by Taiwan, Iran, and Vietnam

The governments of Taiwan, Iran, and Vietnam have also bought influence with the U.S. government. Adler (1977) records how the Taiwanese and the

Iranians have bought U.S. military support in the form of arms, technology, and training facilities, and how this support was purchased with bribes and kickbacks to U.S. defense contractors and government officials. The source of these bribes and kickbacks was U.S. taxpayers' money sent to these countries as foreign aid. The South Vietnamese government utilized aid money from 1965 to 1973 to buy U.S. military presence, training, and weapons. Fifty thousand American lives were also expended there. The House Banking Committee, chaired by Congressman Patman, traced kickbacks by the South Vietnamese government to U.S. defense contractors and government officials as early as 1968. The South Vietnamese goverment (immediately preceding the 1972 election) paid the Nixon administration to have U.S. soldiers fight on for a few months while the South Vietnamese officials made their last deals, stole their last money, and got out. No other country is known to have paid kickbacks to have U.S. citizens kill and die abroad in war (Adler 1977).

GOAL OF THE OFFENDER

The goal of foreign agents who lobbied and bribed the U.S. government and defense contractors was to maintain or gain for themselves and their countries American economic, political, and military aid. South Korean agents ensured U.S. military and economic support, and political support for South Korean President Park. Taiwanese and Iranian government agents bribed U.S. defense contractors and government officials to secure U.S. military training and weapons. Agents of the South Vietnamese government paid off U.S. government officials to obtain troops, training, and weapons for use in the Vietnam war.

LEGAL STATUS OF THE OFFENSE

Foreign interventions against the government violated federal statutes covering mail fraud, bribery, racketeering, tax evasion, failure to register as a foreign agent, and conspiracy, as well as U.S. State Department rules and protocols governing foreign agents' lobbying in Congress.

NATURE OF THE OFFENSE

Foreign intervention offenses were committed by agents in the course of routine work tasks performed on behalf of formal organizations (foreign governments). These bribery interventions were covert and non-violent. Cooperative U.S. congressmen, defense contractors, and other corporations supported these interventions. For the most part, the public has remained ignorant of these practices, and societal reaction to these political crimes has been weak. Many foreign and U.S. agents involved in these briberies remain unprosecuted, and it appears that those few indicted will bargain in order to receive light sanctions.

A 1978 report prepared for a House subcommittee headed by Representative John Conyers of Michigan, entitled "The Federal Cover-up of White Collar Crime," has disclosed the indifference and ineffectiveness of federal law enforcement agencies dealing with upper-class crime. The report contended that the criminal fraud section of the Justice Department had less than 50 attorneys handling the scores of huge bribery cases forwarded to this agency by the Securities and Exchange Commission. The report also indicated that neither internal revenue agents nor FBI agents were interested in prosecuting bribery offenses and other white-collar crimes (Anderson 1978c).

5

DOMESTIC SURVEILLANCE

Surveillance, defined in the broadest sense, is the accumulation of information, commonly referred to as intelligence gathering. This chapter is confined to surveillance of individuals and groups by employment of electronic mechanisms (wiretaps, micropho ne "bugs," and computers) and human agents (monitors, informers, infiltrators, and spies). Surveillance is frequently employed in conjunction with intervention tactics (the FBI utilized surveillance measures in its campaign to intimidate and control Dr. Martin Luther King). However, for heuristic and illustrative purposes, we have chosen to separate the two in this work, treating surveillance as a monitoring rather than a changing strategy. Domestic surveillance offenses by and against government are analyzed.

CRIMES BY GOVERNMENT

U.S. government agents illegally monitored and assessed the activities of individuals and groups deemed to be national security risks during the 1960s and 1970s. Under U.S. law, intelligence agencies must limit investigations to conduct that is forbidden by law, but unfortunately, the protection of criminal law procedures has not been applied to political offenders in the United States. Certainly, some form of surveillance is necessary to the security of any country, but intelligence activities, according to the general principles of U.S. law, must be held within legal bounds.

During the past two decades, the government has spied upon millions of citizens on the basis of their political beliefs, even when those beliefs posed no threat of violence or illegal acts on behalf of a hostile foreign power. Vast amounts of information about the personal lives, views, and associations of U.S. citizens have been collected. Investigations of groups deemed politically subversive (and even of groups suspected of associating with politically "dangerous" organizations) have continued for decades—investigations frequently based on vague standards permitting excessive data collection (U.S. Senate 1976). Some corporations have also utilized illegal intelligence gathering techniques to identify credit risks.

ACTION PATTERNS

Several government agencies have employed illegal surveillance patterns. For illustrative purposes, we focus upon domestic surveillance patterns utilized by agents of the following organizations: the White House, the CIA, the U.S. Army, the FBI, the IRS, the National Security Agency, and local police. We record one case of corporate surveillance.

The White House

President Nixon ordered the FBI to wiretap (in several physical locations) 17 government employees and newsmen between 1969 and 1971, to find out if any of them had leaked to the press damaging information about his policies and past campaign practices. Among these were seven members of the National Security Council, two State Department officials, four newsmen, three members of the White House staff, and one Department of Defense employee (U.S. House 1975, p. 611). The taps were initiated at about the time of a 1969 New York *Times* article that reported the bombing of Cambodia by the U.S. Air Force (U.S. House 1975, p. 213). Any person who criticized the president was subject to surveillance. Joseph Kraft, a newspaper columnist sometimes critical of the Nixon administration, was wiretapped for one week in 1969. This tap was justified by reasons of "national security," although the administration never provided any concrete evidence that Kraft's writings were subversive or damaging to the security of the United States. The attorney general did not sign an FBI authorization of the tap, and it was not authorized by court order; in short, the tap was illegal. The FBI also conducted spot physical surveillances on Kraft in Washington, D.C. in 1969, and forwarded reports on his activities to John Ehrlichman, President Nixon's domestic advisor (U.S. House 1975, p. 219).

Just how far the Nixon administration was willing to go in preventing certain groups from participating in government was shown in the Huston Plan. Chapter II demonstrated how this plan encouraged lawbreaking in the form of breaking and entering. These covert interventions were supplemented by surveillance strategies, including electronic surveillance and mail coverage. The first strategy involved intensive surveillance (with bugs and wiretaps) of individuals or organizations who supposedly threatened the national security (radical groups). The second entailed opening first-class letters legally defined as private. The targets selected for mail coverage were groups or persons believed to be either national security threats, or suspected of passing information about the U.S. to foreign intelligence agencies. In short, these mechanisms in the Huston Plan were designed to bypass the rule of law (U.S. House 1975, p. 211). Though the plan was officially disapproved by the President because of J. Edgar Hoover's opposition, a great part of it was implemented, as noted in Chapter II. Whether the activities were coordinated by the White House or several independent government agencies is a moot point; the real point is that the civil rights of millions were violated.

The CIA

The CIA violated both its legal charter and the rights of the public in a massive campaign of spying against the antiwar and other dissident movements in the late 1960s and early 1970s (Hersh 1974). Disclosure of this activity by the New York *Times* in 1974 sparked a number of official probes. When the evidence was finally released in 1975 and 1976, it was found that the CIA had prepared dossiers (during 1967-73) on the political activities of 7,200 individuals and 100 radical groups, and stored data on 300,000 individuals in a computer. The CIA also opened and photographed the contents of about 216,000 letters sent to and from the Soviet Union between 1953 and 1973. A computerized index of 1.5 million names was created from these mail openings (*Clarion-Ledger* 1975a, 1975b; New York *Times* 1976a; U.S. Senate 1976).

According to the Senate Select Committee on Intelligence, the CIA employed several hundred academics to provide leads for intelligence purposes, make recruiting introductions for intelligence purposes, and write books and other materials to be used for propaganda purposes abroad. These persons were located in over 100 American colleges, universities, and related institutions (research centers and foundations). In the majority of these institutions, no one other than the individuals involved was aware of the CIA links (Horrock 1978). Professors, graduate assistants, or members of the university administrative staff, motivated by a sense of patriotism or a felt need of money, helped the CIA identify and recruit spies from among the thousands of foreign students who study in the United States. As one expert on CIA domestic spying noted, "They have general instructions to look for foreign students who may want to work for our Government, but occasionally there are special, urgent assignments like finding Brazilian physicists" (Horrock 1978). These undercover men also recommended American students to agency recruiters, prepared background reports on spy candidates, and obtained witting or unwitting help from other professors for propaganda writing and espionage at conferences. These agents also provided the CIA with reports on student unrest and dissenters during the Vietnam war years (Horrock 1978).

The CIA, during the 1960s and early 1970s, reviewed university publications and established liaisons with local authorities in order to warn recruiters about demonstrations or possible violence. One CIA internal memo stated that agents "developed files on the universities and colleges, came to know all the

campus security people, and special units in the state and local police, etc."
(New York *Times* 1977d). This same memo stated that some of the information
gathered by agents "would indicate that they (CIA agents) attended some of the
dissident meetings" (New York *Times* 1977d).

The U.S. Army

The U.S. Army launched a campaign to gather intelligence data on political dissidents during the years 1967–70. The army systematically studied civil
disturbances within the continental United States, claiming it needed this data
to determine when and where to dispense troops and supplies. The information
the army collected concerning "predisturbance activities" included: presence of
militant outside agitators; increases in police brutality charges and resentment of
law enforcement officers; known radical leaders both overt and covert; organizational plans and activities prepared by radical leaders; friends and sympathizers
of demonstration participants, including newspapers, radio stations, television
stations, and prominent community leaders; efforts by minority groups to upset
the balance of local power and the political system; purposes and objectives of
dissident groups; sources and extent of organizational funding for dissident
groups; organizational charts and rosters of key personnel; and personnel
records and breakdowns of membership by ethnic groups, age, economic status,
and criminal record, and biographic data on key members (U.S. Senate 1974b,
p. 137).

In the course of gathering such "predisturbance activities" data, the army
spied upon groups covering the political ideological spectrum. Among these were
the Socialist Workers party, Students for a Democratic Society, Southern
Christian Leadership Conference, Congress of Racial Equality, National Association for the Advancement of Colored People (NAACP), Revolutionary Action
Movement, American Civil Liberties Union, League of Women Voters, John
Birch Society, and American Nazi party. In addition, files were kept on a large
number of private citizens and public officials, with data on their financial
affairs, sex lives, psychiatric histories, and political affiliations. Much of this
information appears to have been in the form of unverified rumor and gossip
(U.S. Senate 1974b, p. 138).

Portions of the materials collected on groups and individuals were
obtained from private institutions through covert operations. Army undercover
agents infiltrated Resurrection City during the 1968 Poor People's Campaign in
Washington, and posed as press photographers, newspaper reporters, and television newsmen (sometimes with bogus credentials) during the 1968 Democratic National Convention in Chicago. Universities were another favorite target
of army agents. Agents enrolled as students in the Black Studies program at New
York University, and kept dossiers on students and faculty at the University of
Minnesota. Army agents infiltrated innocuous gatherings, such as a coalition of

church youth groups meeting in Colorado Springs, a Halloween party for elementary school children in Washington, D.C. (because they suspected a local "dissident" might be present), a welfare mothers' organization in Milwaukee, and a priests' conference in Washington, D.C. held to discuss birth control measures (U.S. Senate 1974b, pp. 138-39; U.S. Senate 1976).

Overall, the army collected and stored an enormous amount of information on a very large number of individuals. In 1970, army intelligence had current files on the political activities of 100,000 individuals unaffiliated with the armed services. The army maintained more than 350 separate records storage centers containing files on civilian political activities. One such center, at Fort Sam Houston, Texas, reported the equivalent of over 120,000 file cards on "personalities of interest." Such data systems had the technical capacity for cross referencing according to subjects' political affiliations, specific incidents they were supposed to have been involved in, and personality profiles. Thus, the army could rapidly produce lists of citizens by name, address, ideology, political associations, and involvement in particular political activities (U.S. Senate 1974b, p. 139).

The surveillance programs of the 1967-1970 period were initiated in the absence of legislative authorization and without the knowledge or approval of senior civilian officials in the Department of Defense. In the midst of a civil crisis such as a riot, Pentagon officials issued vague, mission-type orders that gave intelligence officers a free hand in collecting whatever information they deemed necessary. Neither Pentagon officials nor members of Congress had any means by which to review the appropriateness of these orders until some former army intelligence agents came forward and "blew the whistle" in 1970. Meanwhile, the army's surveillance program grew as most government programs grow: each subordinate element in the army's chain of command expanded upon the vague orders issued from above, and the secrecy granted to army intelligence immunized each link in the hierarchy from effective review by its superiors (U.S. Senate 1974b, p. 135).

Evidence that army surveillance continued in the 1970s is contained in a civil damage action filed by the Berlin Democratic Club (BDC) against the U.S. Secretary of Defense in 1974. This action was filed by 16 American civilians and two American organizations in West Germany who were the targets of intensive surveillance by the U.S. Army from 1972 to 1974. The BDC complaint alleged four broad categories of illegal intrusive surveillance: wiretapping; infiltration of organizations and private meetings; blacklisting and political intelligence gathering; and opening of private, civilian mail. The evidence suggests that the army's attention had focused particularly on American civilians in Berlin and in the Heidelberg area. Among the former were a group of citizens who had worked for Senator George McGovern during the 1972 presidential campaign and continued to work in support of the 1972 Democratic National Convention platform. The Berlin group was formally chartered in 1973 as an affiliate of the Democratic Club. Agents of the 66th Military Intelligence Group in Berlin infiltrated this organization and filed detailed reports on its activities. This group was branded "CS" (countersubversive), and documents relating to it were placed in a "counter-subversive" file, which meant that the Berlin Democratic Club was targeted for future army counter-intelligence operations (U.S. Senate 1974b, p. 92).

The Lawyers' Military Defense Committee (LMDC) was another target of military spying on American organizations in Germany. This group of civilian attorneys regularly provided counsel to U.S. servicemen facing court-martial proceedings and other military charges. The LMDC and its clients were inter-cepted on a wiretap installed on the phone of one of the plaintiffs (an Ameri-can journalist and consultant to the lawyers' group). Conversations overheard on the wiretap included discussions about the court martial defense of a black serviceman. Several tap logs were destroyed immediately after the BDC com-plaints. By this action the army indicated that it knew the entire surveillance program was illegal (U.S. Senate 1974b, pp. 92-93).

American clergymen residing at Goessner Mission and Americans working for German underground newspapers were also targets of U.S. Army sur-veillance. The Goessner Mission is a Protestant organization jointly sponsored by the U.S. National Council of Churches, the World Council of Churches, and the German Evangelische Kirche. Two of the mission's resident ministers were the subjects of several 66th Military Intelligence Group surveillance reports. The underground newspapers kept under surveillance were *Forward*, published in Berlin, and *Fight Back*, published in Heidelberg. The intensity of this sur-veillance was demonstrated by one document from the army's files, a photo-static copy of a letter to the staff of *Forward* from a library at a South Carolina college. The letter ordered a subscription to the newspaper and requested back issues for the college library (U.S. Senate 1974b, p. 93). Yet another document appears to indicate why the army was interested in spying on *Forward*. Ac-cording to an intelligence diagram contained in army files, *Forward* was per-ceived to be the hub around which several "subversive" organizations revolved, including the U.S. Democratic party, the Berlin Democratic Club, the Lawyers' Military Defense Committee, the American Civil Liberties Union, Vietnam Veterans Against the War, various underground newspapers, and several foreign leftist organizations. The rationale for labeling all of these groups "subversive" appears to be that a few members of each were somehow involved with the *Forward* staff (U.S. Senate 1974b, p. 93).

A congressional committee concluded that the preceding spying tactics should be outlawed because many of the principals spied upon had broken no law and were engaged in legitimate political activity. The army documents (par-ticularly those relating to *Forward*) suggested a paranoid conception of politi-cally "leftist" organizations in Germany, precisely the kind of reaction exhibited in the domestic surveillance program adopted in 1970 by the Nixon White House and heads of the U.S. intelligence agencies (U.S. Senate 1974b, pp. 93-94).

The FBI

Of all federal agencies, the FBI has conducted the most far-reaching domestic intelligence campaign. From 1960 to 1964 the bureau collected 500,000 domestic intelligence files and compiled a list of 26,000 Americans who were to be jailed (because of their "subversive" political philosophies) in the event of a national emergency. Yet, not a single individual or group spied upon has been prosecuted since 1957 under the laws which prohibit planning or advocating action to overthrow the government. The FBI opened 65,000 domestic intelligence files in 1972 alone, but these dossiers do not present an accurate picture of the extent of FBI surveillance. Each file contains information on more than one individual or group, and this information is retrievable through the FBI General Name Index (U.S. Senate 1976). In addition, countless individuals during the 1960s and 1970s were the victims of buggings and wiretappings, and were spied upon from within their respective political organizations by networks of infiltrators or informers. Ironically, most persons spied upon belonged to innocuous, peaceful political groups that posed no threat to internal security. A Senate investigating committee found that none of these individuals or organizations had committed any kind of crime (New York *Times* 1976a; U.S. Senate 1976).

The FBI, on the other hand, has committed numerous crimes in the past four decades. Between 1940 and 1972 the FBI illegally opened private mail in Los Angeles, San Francisco, New York, Boston, Washington, Detroit, Seattle, and Miami for "national security" purposes. FBI agents in New York City examined 42 million pieces of mail, 1,011 of which were opened, between 1959 and 1966. From 1966 to 1972, the FBI accepted intelligence from the CIA's illegal mail interception program. In 1975, the FBI still had 79 mail covers in progress (Los Angeles *Times* 1975).

FBI documents released to the Socialist Workers party (SWP) under the Freedom of Information Act in 1977 showed that the bureau had used 316 informers against the SWP and its youth affiliate, the Young Socialist Alliance (YSA), from 1960 to 1976. The FBI acknowledged paying a total of $1.6 million to these informers, 60 of whom were still active in June 1976. At least 42 of the FBI informers held offices within the two organizations, and two ran for public offices while members of the YSA. The FBI, during this same time (1960-76), maintained an army of 1,300 "free floating" informers who traveled widely throughout the United States with little supervision, spying upon radical groups (Lubasch 1976; *Clarion-Ledger* 1977g). The SWP suit charged that the FBI informants were used as "offensive weapons" in manipulating the party political activities and sowing discord within the organization. Moreover, it was charged that the FBI broke into the party's offices on scores of occasions and sometimes stole documents. The party charged that these illegal actions affected its membership's rights to free association, free speech, and lawful political activity (Lubasch 1976). This case clearly demonstrates the concurrence of surveillance and intervention.

In another case, the FBI wiretapped the National Lawyers Guild (NLG) in the late 1940s and early 1950s, and may have burglarized guild members' offices during this time. The NLG, a national organization of lawyers and legal workers, was founded in 1937 to work for civil liberties and civil rights. The NLG was attacked as a communist-front organization during the early 1950s. In 1977 this organization filed a multimillion dollar damage suit, accusing the FBI and other government agencies of illegal harassment and disruption of legitimate guild activities. FBI documents released to the NLG in 1977 divulged that the bureau wiretapped telephones in the guild's national office in Washington from 1947 to 1951. Other evidence found in these documents showed that FBI agents in 1948 broke into the office of Thomas Emerson (then Guild president) to photograph an article he was writing for the *Yale Law Journal*. There is evidence that the FBI broke into NLG national headquarters three times in order to microfilm that organization's membership list and drafts of another article which exposed FBI wiretapping (*Clarion-Ledger* 1977e). Again we see the conjunction of surveillance and intervention.

In late 1977, the American Bar Association (ABA), generally considered to be the bastion of legal ethics, conspired with the FBI to smear the left-wing National Lawyers Guild. In early 1952, the ABA's top communist-hunter, Austin Canfield, Sr., phoned the FBI seeking information which could be used to discredit the Lawyers Guild. The FBI sent Canfield a report on the guild, and then searched its "security index" for information about guild members. Four memos based upon information from the "security index" were written and dispatched to the ABA. In the late 1960s, long after the red scare had subsided, the new president of the ABA again approached the FBI for information on the guild, and the FBI again sent the ABA a report on the NLG. The ABA also indicated to the FBI its willingness to bar NLG members from the association and to expel ABA members who associated with the Lawyers Guild or who promoted its aims (*Clarion-Ledger* 1977j).

Another example of the FBI's monitoring of harmless and peaceful groups was its program directed against the Women's Liberation Movement. The bureau used informants to keep tabs on this organization in several U.S. cities in 1969 and 1970 in order to discover its revolutionary potential. The FBI field informers reported to their superiors that the women's liberation movement "is not an organization as such but rather a cause and philosophy" interested in such issues as birth control and abortion (*Commercial Appeal* 1976a).

Just how far will the FBI go in protecting what it calls the "internal security" of the United States? A recent case may give the answer. The FBI in 1974 admitted that it had kept a "subversive" file on a 16-year-old high school girl, Lori Paton, who wrote a letter to the Socialist Workers party in 1972 as part of a social studies course concerned with various political ideologies. Miss Paton received an SWP newspaper and some printed material from the YSA. Her letter was routinely intercepted in an FBI mail cover on the party (U.S. House 1974a, p. 67). This is a type of surveillance in which all the data on the outside of first-class letters are copied and the contents of other mail are examined before being forwarded to the target of the surveillance. Miss Paton's letter aroused the curiosity of the FBI, and an FBI agent subsequently checked the Paton family's credit, the employment of the girl's father, and police records, but none of the family members had an arrest or conviction record. The agent then traveled to the high school to check into Lori Paton's background and interests (U.S. House 1974a, p. 68).

Unfortunately, FBI illegal surveillance still exists. In 1975, 110 members of the Socialist Workers party were listed in an FBI "danger index" comprised of persons believed to be threats to national security. FBI bugging of U.S. citizens in non-criminal cases continues, with more sophisticated techniques that circumvent some new legal restrictions on government surveillance (*Clarion-Ledger* 1975d). The FBI budgeted over $7 million for its fiscal 1976 domestic security informant program, more than twice the amount it spends on informants against organized crime. The aggregate budget for FBI domestic security intelligence and foreign counterintelligence is at least $80 million. In the late 1960s and early 1970s the cost was substantially greater because the Bureau was keeping tabs on the antiwar movement and black activists (U.S. Senate 1976).

"The Federal Cover-up of White-Collar Crime," a report prepared for a House subcommittee headed by Congressman John Conyers, found that in 1977 FBI resources were shifted away from the purported top three priority law enforcement areas, foreign counterintelligence, white-collar crime, and organized crime, into domestic security. The FBI has far more spies assigned to suspected U.S. subversives than the number officially acknowledged in April 1978 by director William H. Webster. Secret House testimony suggests that as many as 250 FBI informers working in this country were reclassified into foreign intelligence while continuing domestic undercover work. An undetermined number of additional informers are spying on Americans who previously were subjects of other domestic security investigations. Officials in the Justice Department and the FBI have declined to comment on this reclassification. In April 1976, the attorney general's office issued guidelines tightening the restrictions on domestic security investigations, but guidelines on foreign intelligence, if they exist, are classified. FBI and Justice Department spokesmen denied that the switch in classifications was made to sidestep the new domestic security guidelines. The bureau claims the number of pending domestic intelligence investigations decreased from 9,814 in June 1975 to 642 in mid-1977. The General Accounting Office stipulates that the FBI has transferred domestic investigations to other classifications. These Bureau actions suggest that the FBI is trying to sweep its domestic surveillance operations into the classified foreign category, where it cannot be examined by the police (Tybor 1978b; Anderson 1978c).

The Internal Revenue Service and the National Security Agency

The CIA and FBI intelligence-gathering operations are only a part of the total U.S. surveillance picture. The IRS·prepared political intelligence files on 8,000 individuals and 300 organizations during the 1960s and 1970s. This agency illegally cooperated with the FBI and CIA during this time, exchanging political intelligence information with them (New York *Times* 1976a). Further, during 1947–75, the National Security Agency (NSA) with the cooperation of U.S. telegraph companies, scanned millions of private communications between U.S. citizens and residents of foreign countries. These cables had been sent to foreign countries with the reasonable expectation that they would be kept private (New York *Times* 1976a; U.S. Senate 1976). NSA technicians, in a special project called "Minaret," intercepted the overseas cables and telephone calls of 1,650 U.S. political dissidents and suspected drug traffickers between 1967 and 1973 (Atlanta *Constitution* 1975). As of 1976, the NSA was still eavesdropping on messages sent by U.S. citizens to foreign countries (Jackson *Daily News* 1976a).

Local Police

Local police officials and agents in numerous U.S. cities kept leftist activists and organizations under surveillance during the 1960s and early 1970s. In the 1960s, undercover agents of the Madison, Wisconsin city police infiltrated perceived leftist or radical groups at the University of Wisconsin ranging from the Black Panthers to an organization of welfare mothers (*Clarion-Ledger* 1975c). The Iranian Students Association (ISA), an organization of Iranian nationals studying at U.S. universities, was spied upon by Chicago police for seven years in the 1960s. The ISA opposed the U.S.-backed government of Mohammed Reza Shah Pahlevi (*Clarion-Ledger* 1977c), which, it alleged, was brutal and oppressive. Chicago police reported on ISA meetings and discussions held as·far away as California. These talks were in the Persian language and dealt mostly with matters of interest in the Middle East. Chicago police kept names and addresses of ISA members, and other records of surveillance, passed the data on to the FBI, CIA, and SAVAK (the Iranian secret police organization).

In another case, the New Haven, Connecticut police, from the early 1960s until the summer of 1971, engaged in a massive illegal wiretapping operation, recording thousands of telephone conversations of individuals thought to belong to "subversive" political groups. The FBI was aware of this operation at all stages (Henry 1978).

Data Banks

With the proliferation of intelligence agencies, intelligence gathering has become a growth industry. Within our government the following agencies have data-gathering capabilities: the Defense Intelligence Agency; the Nuclear Regulatory Commission (formerly the Atomic Energy Commission); the State Department; the army; the air force; the FBI; the Treasury Department; the Justice Department's Internal Security, Intelligence, and Organized Crime Strike Force Divisions; the Secret Service; the narcotics control agencies; and the hundreds of proprietaries, conduits, and covers that some of these agencies maintain. The National Crime Information Center, the FBI's central data bank, is a national computer network of law enforcement data available to 40,000 public agencies at the press of a button. This data includes all U.S. citizens' arrests from 1969 to the present, regardless of case disposition; persons arrested but not formally charged with a criminal offense are included (U.S. House 1974b, p. 76). Additional federal data banks include the Department of Transportation's National Drivers Register, the registry of persons receiving treatment in federally-funded drug programs, and the Department of Health, Education, and Welfare's social security number data bank (U.S. House 1974b, p. 76).

Large, interconnected data banks enable government agencies to obtain a rapid recall of information about law-abiding citizens, should they fall under any legal or governmental suspicion. In this vein, thousands of innocent Washingtonians were corralled into Robert F. Kennedy Stadium by local police during an antiwar demonstration in 1971. Many of these people were only interested bystanders who happened to be physically close to the demonstration. Despite their innocence, many of these persons were finger-printed and photographed (mug shots) by the District of Columbia police, and thereby became subject to data bank surveillance. Individuals apprehended in similar circumstances are likely to have the personal information gathered on them by one agency passed on to a number of government agency data banks that specialize in monitoring "troublemakers." The data banks operated by the FBI and the Army Counter-Intelligence Analysis Division are cases in point. Not only do such data banks threaten the right to privacy for Americans, but they may also be vehicles for fraud and corruption. For instance, a Department of Health, Education, and Welfare computer file on 300,000 children of migrant farm workers exists for the purpose of speeding the travel of academic records from one school district to the next, but could be misused by teachers or employers (Franklin 1970).

Surveillance by Corporations

Corporations, credit bureaus, and other large organizations maintain files on U.S. citizens, and are equipped to gather and collate this information with an efficiency that was impossible a few decades ago. Modern computers hold millions of separate items of data that can be updated by the use of input terminals located throughout the United States and extracted in seconds from computer storage files thousands of miles away. As more agencies make use of computer files, more private information (much of it inaccurate and damaging) becomes available to government officials and private investigators (McKee and Robertson 1975, p. 237).

In 1964, the Retail Credit Company had 6,000 full-time inspectors operating out of 1,500 offices located in every U.S. state and Canadian province, and in Mexico and Europe. These inspectors conducted 90,000 investigations every work day, checking people's credit for merchants, their general background for prospective employers, and their credentials for insurance companies and banks. They maintained files on 42 million American citizens, with information gathered from past investigations, newspaper clippings, and public records (Packard 1964, p. 9). This organization is only one of many credit agencies operating at the national level. Thousands of local agencies gather evidence (sometimes hearsay) and exchange this data among themselves. Many persons have been denied credit or jobs as a result of an unfavorable report from agencies such as Retail Credit. A computer error in the accounting department of a large corporation can result in an individual being listed as a bad credit risk, and this information may go uncorrected and be disseminated from agency to agency for years afterward (McKee and Robertson 1975, p. 237).

In late 1973, the Federal Trade Commission (FTC) charged Retail Credit with using false and outdated information in its reports on private citizens. Under terms of the Fair Credit Reporting Act, companies are required to periodically reinvestigate the data in their credit files to safeguard against false and inaccurate reporting. Retail Credit had refused, from 1966 to 1974, to conduct reinvestigations. In addition, the FTC claimed that this company pressured its investigative agents to collect adverse credit data: Retail Credit supervisors set quotas on the number of adverse reports they expected their agents to collect, and rewarded them accordingly (U.S. House 1974a, p. 66).

The FTC further charged that Retail Credit used false pretenses in gathering information on job, credit, and insurance seekers. The company claimed that its agents visited the homes of all subjects reported upon, when in fact it often based its reports on telephone interviews with subjects. Agents also on occasion untruthfully claimed to be insurance company representatives or representatives of a prospective employer. Subjects were led to believe that the information gathered on them would be used only for the specific investigation at hand, when in fact such information often entered the files of Retail Credit and was later sold to other companies (U.S. House 1974a, p. 67). Finally, Retail Credit was charged with withholding information from persons who had been damaged by its reports (U.S. House 1974a, p. 66).

Beverly Thompson of Virginia, one of thousands of Americans subjected to Retail Credit's illegal surveillance, sued ten insurance firms in 1972 for a total of $21.6 million. She charged that these companies had refused to sell her auto insurance on the basis of a damaging credit report filed by Retail Credit. The report stated that "she was practically living with a man." Ms. Thompson also charged Retail Credit with invasion of privacy in reporting meaningless gossip, and with violating the Federal Fair Credit Reporting Act. The insurance companies could find nothing unfavorable in Ms. Thompson's 15 year accident-free driving record, and based their refusal to grant insurance on the report of her purported cohabitation with the man. As a result, Ms. Thompson was forced to pay higher auto insurance rates for less coverage (U.S. House 1974a, p. 69).

GOAL OF THE OFFENDER

The purported goal of White House surveillance was national security, that is, the protection of the United States from subversive enemies who might overthrow the government. The real aim was to provide information thought necessary to keep the Nixon administration in power, and to secure its control of the government.

The professed purpose of CIA, FBI, army, IRS, and NSA surveillance was national security, whereas the real objectives were: to gather information on the conduct and ideologies of persons and groups considered disloyal (army surveillance of antiwar organizations), and to gather data needed for current or future interventions (FBI surveillance of the Socialist Workers Party) or for political policing purposes (the Huston Plan).

Government data banks were purportedly created to increase the efficiency of government bureaucracies, but were actually used to store data on U.S. citizens to be used in national emergencies, future interventions, and political police actions. Corporations such as Retail Credit claimed that illegal surveillance allowed them to identify credit risks more efficiently, but the true objective of corporate surveillance was to make money.

LEGAL STATUS OF THE OFFENSE

These surveillance offenses by government violated the Right to Privacy Act, the National Security Act, laws proscribing disruptions of lawful political activities, postal laws, the Fourth Amendment, wiretapping laws, Supreme Court decisions requiring government agencies to get warrants prior to wiretapping, and presidential executive orders prohibiting unlawful intelligence-gathering measures. Surveillance by corporations violated the Fair Credit Reporting Act, the Right to Privacy Act, and Federal Trade Commission rules. Intelligence agencies have the power only to investigate conduct forbidden by the laws of the United States. The Senate Select Committee on Intelligence (1976) stipulated that domestic intelligence that departs from this standard entails grave risks of undermining the democratic process and harming the interests of individual citizens. According to this committee report, laws pertaining to domestic intelligence gathering should be clearly defined, and the domestic intelligence apparatus should function under effective legal oversight (U.S. Senate 1976). Credit investigators must comply with the Fair Credit Reporting Act and the Right to Privacy Act. This has not been the case.

NATURE OF THE OFFENSE

Domestic surveillance was carried out by government and corporate agents in the normal course of their everyday work as members of formal organizations, and in behest of organizational aims. Intelligence gathering by these agencies and corporations has proliferated because the constitutional system of checks and balances has not adequately controlled surveillance activities. The executive branch has neither delineated the scope of permissible intelligence activities nor established procedures for supervising the intelligence apparatus. Presidents, attorneys general, and the Congress have abdicated their constitutional responsibility to oversee and set standards for domestic intelligence practices. Senior government officials have given the intelligence agencies broad general mandates and pressed them for immediate results.

The illegal domestic surveillance patterns were non-violent and covert, concealed from victims, and were seldom described in statutes or explicit executive orders. The victims in many cases had no opportunity to challenge the data secretly collected on them. Government and corporate surveillance activities received strong support from peer groups, while the public in most cases remained ignorant. Before Watergate, the public appeared to accept government surveillance against dissident persons and groups. But some citizens who have long supported the intelligence agencies and corporations ("My country right or wrong," "What's good for General Motors is good for America") have been repulsed by surveillance crimes that interfered with their own private lives. Corporate surveillance has evoked a stronger reaction than government surveillance, but societal reaction to both has been weak. Only three government employees (FBI agents) have been indicted for illegal domestic surveillance to date, and only one court case has concerned corporate surveillance (the Retail Credit case).

CRIMES AGAINST GOVERNMENT

American citizens and agents of foreign governments have spied upon the U.S. government during the past two decades. Both electronic devices and human agents have been utilized in conventional espionage activities for the purpose of providing secret military and defense security information to a foreign country. The 1970s witnessed a new type of surveillance against government. During this period, a number of citizens privy to secret data withheld from the public released classified U.S. military and intelligence secrets and other secret policy information to the news media. These citizens were convinced that the U.S. public had a right to the data released; but the U.S. government reasoned otherwise and has utilized legal means to curb and punish such action.

ACTION PATTERNS

We record four routine spy cases involving foreign agents and domestic collaborators, and one domestic spy case that was quashed for national security reasons. The final three cases record a new and unconventional form of domestic surveillance against government, that is, surveillance by concerned citizens who decide that certain U.S. government secrets should be released to the general public regardless of whether such action is legal or illegal.

Domestic Espionage by Foreign and Domestic Agents

Four Routine Spy Cases. In October 1960, Igor Melekh and Willie Hirsch were arrested in New York City on charges of conspiring to obtain U.S. defense data and of violating the Foreign Agents Registration Act. Melekh at this time was chief of the Russian language section in the U.N. Secretariat's Office of Conference Services, and Hirsch was a German-born free-lance illustrator for several U.S. medical publications. Hirsch (according to a federal grand jury indictment brought in Chicago on the day of his arrest) made contact with an unnamed U.S. citizen in Chicago in July and October of 1958. On the day after the October contact, he introduced Melekh to this U.S. citizen for the purpose of inducing him to collect defense information for the Soviet Union. The following day, Melekh paid this individual $200. Melekh paid other agents recruited in New York City and Newark, New Jersey, in sums ranging from $200 to $700, between October 1958 and October 1960. In return for these payments, Melekh received a map and aerial photographs showing U.S. military installations in Chicago. Melekh told his agents that this information would be utilized in a Soviet military attack against the United States (New York *Times* 1960). Federal charges against Melekh and Hirsch were dropped in March 1961, on the condition that these men leave the country (Wehrwein 1961).

Four Russian nationals, John Butenko, Igor Ivanov, Gleb Pavlov, and Yuri Romashin, were seized by the FBI in Englewood, New Jersey in October 1963 on espionage charges. Butenko was an electronics engineer and a control administrator for International Electronics Corporation of Paramus, New Jersey, which was working on a highly sensitive contract for the U.S. Air Force. Ivanov was a chauffeur for Amtorg (a USSR government-sponsored organization that handles U.S.-Soviet trading relations), and Pavlov and Romashin were aides to Russian officials at the United Nations. Butenko, who had a security clearance for top secret U.S. military materials from April to September 1963, procured this classified information and transmitted it to Pavlov and Romashin (New York *Times* 1963b). In December 1963, Butenko and Ivanov were found guilty of conspiring to commit espionage. Butenko was also found guilty of failing to register as a foreign government agent (New York *Times* 1964c). Butenko was sentenced to 30 years in prison, and Ivanov received a sentence of 20 years (New York *Times* 1964d).

Air Force Lieutenant Colonel W.H. Whalen was arrested by the FBI in Alexandria, Virginia in July 1966, on charges of spying for the Soviet Union while stationed at the Pentagon with the Joint Chiefs of Staff. He was charged with conspiring with USSR embassy aides Colonel Sergei Edemski and Mikhail Shumaev to pass high-level U.S. defense data to the Soviet Union. This data included information on atomic weaponry and missiles, military plans for the defense of Europe, estimates of comparative military capabilities, military intelligence reports and analyses, retaliation plans for the Strategic Air Command, and U.S. troop movements. A federal grand jury indictment charged that Whalen was paid $5,500 by Edemski and Shumaev from December 1959 to March 1961 (Graham 1966). In December 1959, Whalen met Colonel Edemski (who was the assistant Soviet military attaché) at a shopping center in Alexandria, Virginia. Later that month, Whalen met Edemski and Shumaev (who was given the code name "Mike") at the same Alexandria location, and received an initial payment of $1,000 (Graham 1966). Over the next year and a half, Whalen met "Mike" at several shopping centers in Alexandria, and exchanged information for payments of money. Whalen gained this information from classified documents at the Pentagon, and from staff briefings and informal conversations with Pentagon colleagues (Graham 1966).

In 1961, Colonel Whalen was retired by the Pentagon because of poor health, but he told "Mike" that he would try to find a civilian job with the Defense Department that would give him access to military secrets. He was unsuccessful in this endeavor, and the conspiracy ended early in 1963, when both Edemski and Shumaev returned to Russia (Graham 1966). Whalen pleaded guilty in December 1966 to charges that he had conspired with the Russian agents to obtain U.S. defense data, and acted as a Soviet representative without registering with the U.S. Department of State (New York *Times* 1966c). He was subsequently convicted on these charges and sentenced to 15 years in prison (New York *Times* 1967a).

State Department employee Ronald L. Humphrey and Vietnamese national David Truong were charged with espionage, conspiracy, and failure to register as foreign agents in 1978 for passing State Department cables to the government of Vietnam. These cables concerned diplomatic assessments of post-Vietnam war conditions in Southeast Asia. Dinh Ba Thi, Vietnam's chief delegate to the United Nations, was cited as an unindicted co-conspirator in this case because he had relayed the diplomatic cables stolen by Humphrey to the Vietnamese government. In February 1978, Dinh Ba Thi was ordered by the Department of State to resign his U.N. post and return to Vietnam (Slavin, Wright, and Butson 1978; *Clarion-Ledger* 1978j).

A National Security Case. Occasionally foreign spies are not prosecuted because their trials would expose U.S. counterespionage activities in foreign countries. The 1964 trial of Mr. and Mrs. Robert Baltch was called off for this reason. The Baltches, along with Mr. and Mrs. Ivan Egarov, had been seized by the FBI in 1963 on charges that they had conspired to spy for the Soviet Union. According to the FBI complaint, the Baltches and the Egarovs had conspired with Russian military intelligence officers in Moscow, New York, and Washington to obtain for the Soviet government information about the locations of American military and naval installations, troop movements, and shipping and waterfront facilities. The FBI contended that they had secreted messages and information in magnetic containers left in prearranged drop-off points in Queens, and used codes, ciphers, and secret writings in order to communicate with each other (Raymond 1973). The Egarovs were eventually exchanged for two Americans held by the USSR on spy charges (New York *Times* 1963a). A year later, Attorney General Nicholas Katzenbach ordered the termination of the Baltches' trial for national security reasons, claiming that the government could not offer evidence relating to the acts specified in the indictment, and that the trial might disclose American counterespionage activities (New York *Times* 1964a). The Baltches were subsequently deported to Czechoslovakia (New York *Times* 1964b).

Release of Military, Intelligence, and Defense Secrets to the News Media

Danial Ellsberg released the Pentagon's secret history of the Vietnam war to the New York *Times* in 1971. In 1976, newsman Daniel Schorr released a confidential House of Representatives report on U.S. intelligence agencies to the *Village Voice*, a New York weekly. The House had voted in early 1976 not to publish this report. Justice Department attorneys attempted to convict Ellsberg and his co-defendant Anthony Russo of espionage, but could not prove that their actions had threatened the national security. According to the espionage statutues written in 1917, persons who pass secrets to foreign governments, especially in wartime, are "inimical to the very existence of organized government" (Packer 1962, p. 78). However, passing information to the press that does not encourage the overthrow of the government does not warrant punishment under the espionage statutes; in fact, the statutes do not cover passing secrets to the press. Therefore, conviction was out of the question for Ellsberg and Russo. Their trial was quashed by Judge Byrne for a number of reasons.

Surveillance against government has often brought to light questionable and illegal government actions. In the course of the government's court proceedings against Ellsberg and Russo, it was disclosed that Ellsberg had been overheard on an illegal wiretap planted by the FBI on the order of President Nixon. Consequently, this case was thrown out of court. In the Schorr case, Secretary of State Kissinger and CIA director Colby allegedly encouraged the congressional staff investigating U.S. intelligence agencies to leak the confidential government report to Schorr, because they feared that a subsequent airing of the official report would prove embarrassing to them. When Schorr handed over the report to the *Village Voice* (where it was subsequently published), the government knew that the published version would be an "unofficial" one, and therefore legally would not exist. Kissinger and Colby preferred this procedure because the secret official report showed how Kissinger had withheld vital intelligence data from other high-ranking officials in the intelligence establishment (Stone 1976).

Other examples of domestic surveillance against the government are the published testimonials, autobiographies, and confessions of former government employees (including disenchanted FBI and CIA agents). These materials include personal documentation of a host of dirty and illegal tricks committed by U.S. agencies on the domestic and foreign scenes. Examples include Phillip Agee's *Inside the Company: CIA Diary*, Frank Snepp's *Decent Interval*, Milton Viorst's "FBI Mayhem" (*New York Review of Books*, March 18, 1976), Robert Wall's "Special Agent for the FBI" (*New York Review of Books*, January 27, 1972), and Victor Marchetti's and John Mark's *The CIA and The Cult of Intelligence*.

GOAL OF THE OFFENDER

Surveillance against the United States by foreign agents in the 1960s was committed by patriotic spies in the best interest of their own countries. United States citizens who passed military and security data to foreign agents usually did so for money. Ellsberg's goal was to reveal the truth about the Vietnam war, while Schorr and the former FBI and CIA agents wanted to reveal the illegal machinations of U.S. intelligence agencies. In the latter cases there were concurrent moral and legal principles guiding the actors; they acted upon the dictates of their consciences. Ellsberg stated that he had released the Pentagon Papers to the New York *Times* because he thought the Vietnam war was morally wrong (Reinhold 1971). Schorr believed that as a newsman he had a moral and legal right to protect the identity of the person who gave him the confidential U.S. House report, and supported this contention by citing his First Amendment right to freedom of the press.

Ellsberg and Schorr hoped that their revelations would force changes in the pattern of governing. Ellsberg believed that American politicians might end the Vietnam war if the public knew the truth and put pressure on their congressmen. Schorr held that a free society cannot operate with a secret government. He believed that the public has the right to know how the government plans and implements policies, and that these policy matters need public input. Former CIA and FBI agents who reported on their agencies' illegal actions hoped by such revelations to curtail further illegal activities. Some even hoped that their disclosures would prompt basic changes in agency structure and function.

LEGAL STATUS OF THE OFFENSE

The foreign and domestic agents who spied on the United States violated laws against espionage, the possession of classified military and security information, and the passing on or selling of United States classified materials to foreign agents or governments, and the Foreign Agents Registration Act. Espionage laws proved inadequate against those who published government secrets. At the trial of Ellsberg and Russo, the espionage statutues were legalistic substitutes applied for the purpose of protecting government secrets and castigating opponents of the Vietnam war (and by implication, the policies of the Nixon administration). Ellsberg leaked secrets embarrassing to the administration, and in an effort to curtail such actions and to punish the "culprit," government lawyers attempted to find some new law under which Ellsberg could be convicted. The specific sections of the espionage law on which the government based its case had never before been implemented, and covered Ellsberg's actions only indirectly and tangentially. In effect, the government lawyers asked the courts to establish a precedent which would retroactively criminalize Ellsberg's and Russo's actions (*Columbia Law Review* 1973). In Daniel Schorr's case, the government did not even attempt to prosecute him for espionage. The Ford administration instead proposed a new law which would make the release of classified or confidential government information a crime.

NATURE OF THE OFFENSE

Surveillance against government was nonviolent, and both covert and overt. The surveillances uncovered in the 1960s espionage cases were confidential arrangements between the sponsoring foreign government and its employees or between foreign agents and U.S. citizens. These offenses were committed according to the rules of conventional espionage; individuals were paid to secure secret information for a foreign government. The new surveillance cases of the 1970s differed substantially from this pattern. Ellsberg, Schorr, and the disenchanted FBI and CIA employees did not spy for a foreign country, nor did they receive monetary rewards for their actions. Working on their own, they gathered data which they later passed on to the news media. The former FBI and CIA agents' revelations violated written contractual agreements with their respective agencies, and it is likely that some of these agents will be prosecuted.

Foreign and domestic spies who committed espionage were agents of formal organizations (foreign governments) who in the course of their daily work pursued the aims of their employers. Group support rested with the employing country and with small cadres of foreign and domestic spies. Foreign and domestic spies received no support from any quarter in the United States. Neither the U.S. government nor the general public supported loyal citizens' surveillance in the 1970s, although some sympathy for these disclosures was present among members of the press, a few disgruntled former FBI and CIA agents, and small groups of liberal intellectuals. Societal reaction to foreign and domestic espionage was strong. Foreign spies were tried and convicted in U.S. courts and sent to prison or deported. Domestic spies lost their jobs and were in many cases convicted and sent to prison with long sentences. Citizens who publicized government secrets were derogated and risked going to prison (Ellsberg), lost their jobs (Schorr), or risked prosecution for breach of contract (former CIA and FBI agents). Efforts are underway to make the leaking of defense or intelligence secrets a crime. On the other hand, the Supreme Court in 1973 upheld the right of the New York *Times* to print Ellsberg's purloined history of the Vietnam war. Additionally, the executive branch has drawn up new but ambiguous guidelines for U.S. intelligence agencies—particularly in the area of domestic spying (Kempster 1978).

6

DOMESTIC CONFRONTATION

Intervention and surveillance crimes were designed to change or monitor political and economic conditions within and outside the United States. Confrontation connotes a conflict between at least two groups over specific political or economic issues. The crimes of intervention and surveillance involve at least one unknowing or unwitting party; one group attempts to manipulate or monitor another's activities. In confrontation crimes there are no unknowing or unwitting parties. Confrontation offenders face one another in open conflict within a context of political or economic controversy.

Domestic confrontations are divided into two categories: crimes by government and crimes against government. This dichotomy is difficult and somewhat arbitrary, because confrontations often encompass both crimes by and crimes against government. Therefore, two additional criteria are utilized to distinguish the party that appears to have initiated the confrontation, and the party that has systematically committed unnecessary illegal acts against the other party to the conflict.

CRIMES BY GOVERNMENT

ACTION PATTERNS

Local, state, and national government officials have illegally attacked political dissenters in the past two decades. In these violent confrontations, dissenters engaging in lawful or unlawful political activities have been harassed, intimidated, arrested, assaulted, jailed, and sometimes killed. Confrontation offenses perpetrated by formal organizations in three instances follow: local police and National Guard against protesters, the National Guard against students at Kent State University, and prison guards and state troopers against inmates at Attica state prison.

Local Police and the National Guard

Local police and National Guard troops have assaulted U.S. citizens and used unrestrained force in dispersing protesters and bystanders at dissident political gatherings throughout the United States. These gatherings were defined by local community officials in each case as adverse to public order. The National Guard killed students at Jackson State University in Mississippi and at Orangeburg State College in South Carolina. Chicago city police in riot gear assaulted and sent to jail 700 antiwar demonstrators (plus some innocent by-standers) at the Democratic National Convention in 1968. Many of these demonstrators were beaten, thrown into paddy wagons and summarily dispatched to jail. Similar brutal and illegal actions have been taken by local police forces in other cities. Police in several southern cities (including Selma, Alabama and Philadelphia, Mississippi) confronted large groups of civil rights demonstrators from northern states in the early 1960s. In some of these clashes, police dogs, electric prods, and nightsticks were utilized by the police, and many of the demonstrators, both black and white, were beaten or jailed. At the Central Plaza Hotel in 1967, police assaulted and jailed black demonstrators protesting poverty in East Los Angeles ghettos. Berkeley, California city police beat University of California students and other Berkeley residents in a 1968 demonstration at People's Park. Police violently dispersed non-students and students protesting the Vietnam war at San Francisco State College, Columbia University, and New York City (the Yippie demonstration). These documented examples of illegal government confrontation were initiated by local police or National Guard troops, and involved violence which was unnecessary, illegal, and unrestrained (Stark 1972; Teodori 1969).

The National Guard at Kent State

On May 4, 1970, four Kent State University students were shot and killed by National Guard troops sent to the campus on orders of the Governor of Ohio. Three of the four students were apolitical or of conservative political persuasion, and had just returned to the campus from weekend visits to their hometowns. Most of the other students who gathered that day were curious bystanders. The circumstances at Kent State did not warrant the Guard's presence on campus or the firing on unarmed college students who were expressing legitimate griev-ances. The Kent State campus, prior to May 1970, had been mostly peaceful. The student population, drawn from the industrial towns and rural areas of eastern Ohio, was generally apolitical. However, the dispatching of U.S. troops to Cambodia in April 1970 angered the politically-oriented students and caused concern among ambivalent ones. Many students considered the invasion of Cambodia to be a shocking reversal of the officially-announced policy of withdrawal from Southeast Asia (Douglas and Johnson 1977, p. 177).

On May 1, a crowd of young people gathered at several bars in downtown Kent. At about 11:00 p.m., the assemblage began to jeer passing police cars and later started a bonfire in the middle of a downtown street. The crowd, which grew to number about 500, blocked this street and stopped motorists to ask them their opinions about the Cambodian invasion. One motorist nearly ran over a student, which angered the multitude. Shortly thereafter, a rumor circulated that black students were "trashing" on campus. This rumor ignited a downtown trashing spree after midnight in which 47 windows were broken and two policemen were slightly injured. The mayor of Kent declared a state of emergency and ordered the bars closed. Between 1:00 and 2:00 a.m., the police used tear gas to drive the students from the downtown area back to the campus. The pattern was repeated throughout the weekend. First, clusters of students engaged in disorderly incidents. Authorities could not apprehend those responsible for these disorders. Disorder grew. Police action, when it finally came, fell on innocent bystanders as well as active participants. Students in general became convinced that they were being arbitrarily harassed (Douglas and Johnson 1977, pp. 177–78).

Many turning points led up to the massacre on May 4. On Saturday, May 2, the Governor called the National Guard into Kent. That evening students set fire to the campus ROTC building, and the guardsmen used tear gas to disperse them. The next day, Governor Rhodes erroneously blamed the campus disturbances on outside troublemakers who, he claimed, had carefully planned the disruptions. On Sunday night, the authorities made another critical error. Students began to gather peacefully on the university commons and it seemed the worst had passed. Tensions eased, and some students chatted amicably with guardsmen. At 8:45 p.m., the mayor of Kent imposed an immediate curfew, read the Ohio Riot Act to the crowd, and gave the students five minutes to disperse. Police then dispersed the students with tear gas and arrested 51 for curfew violations. These actions provoked open hostility among many students. Had the authorities simply ignored the crowd on Sunday night, the assembled students would not have had any reason to cause further disturbances. Confrontation by the city police gave the students an excuse to foment more disruptions. The officials thought that Sunday evening's events made it necessary to recall the National Guard on Monday. By this time the patience of many guardsmen was wearing thin. Students returning from weekend trips were concerned about reports of these events, and many grew hostile to the presence of the guard (Douglas and Johnson 1977, pp. 180–83).

For a variety of reasons, students gathered on the campus opposite police and troops at about 11 a.m. on Monday. Some had heard a vague rumor that a protest rally would be held. Others had free time between classes. Still others stopped by to protest the presence of the National Guard. The guardsmen arrived at the campus in a single group and walked to the football field and then back to Blanket Hill on the periphery of the campus. At this point, students and guardsmen lobbed tear gas cannisters back and forth at each other, and some students threw rocks and shouted obsenities. When the guardsmen reached Blanket Hill, they turned on the crowd with loaded rifles and opened fire, killing four students and wounding nine others. Two of the students killed had been actively involved in protests against the Cambodian invasion and the presence of the guard on campus. The other two were curious onlookers who stopped by to watch the guard's movements on campus. The nine wounded students also appeared to be innocent bystanders (Douglas and Johnson 1977, pp. 184-85).

Prison Guards and State Troopers at Attica

The Attica riot of September 9-13, 1971, marks another example of unnecessary and unlawful violent confrontation by government. Inmates at this institution captured 50 hostages and took over part of the prison on September 9 in the wake of grievances about release procedures, overcrowded conditions, racial animosities, and other matters. The uprising was quelled September 13 when the prison administration gained control by force of arms. In the final assault, ten hostages and 29 inmates were killed by correctional officers and state troopers. Five hostages and 85 inmates were wounded (Wicker 1975, pp. 300-2). With the exception of the Indian massacres in the late nineteenth century, this was the bloodiest one-day confrontation between U.S. citizens since the Civil War (Douglas and Johnson 1977, p. 186).

The uprising started with a seemingly insignificant misunderstanding on September 8 when inmates and prison officers had argued in the prison exercise yard about disciplinary measures. As a result of this verbal altercation, two inmates were removed from their cell blocks and placed in special isolation cells. The next day, one of the officers involved in the exercise yard incident was attacked by several inmates and eventually died of wounds suffered (Wicker 1975, pp. 311-34). Following this incident, inmates from block A broke through a retaining gate and spread throughout the institution with little resistance, attacking officers, taking hostages, and destroying property. Prison officials were slow in responding to these disturbances, and by 10:30 a.m. on September 9 the inmates had virtual control over a great part of the institution. About 1,300 inmates gathered in Yard D with 40 hostages (Douglas and Johnson 1977, pp. 191-94).

New York Commissioner of Correctional Services Oswald and several outside observers conducted negotiations with the inmates during September 9-12. The inmates, who claimed to be political prisoners in a racist society, formed a negotiating team and presented five demands to the prison administration, including complete amnesty, transportation to a non-imperialistic country, and a list of outside persons to be invited to Attica as observers of the negotiations. Protracted bargaining ensued, in which a number of outsiders became partisan mediators for the inmates. From the beginning these intercessions were doomed to failure because of the unrealistic nature of some of the inmates' demands. Moreover, the prison guard involved in the initial altercation leading to the confrontation had died. The prison administration and the observers misread the bargaining situation. Given the penal and criminal justice system of the state of New York, negotiations should have been conducted exclusively by inmates and other members of the system—including Governor Rockefeller. The governor adamantly refused to appear on the scene. In any event, it is clear that the rioting inmates could have been subdued by unarmed personnel because the prisoners were known to have no firearms. In spite of this, when the negotiations appeared to have reached an impasse, Oswald and Rockefeller agreed to retake the prison by force (Roebuck 1976). If force was the answer, it should have been employed earlier on before the inmates' position was solidified and hardened. Anyone who knows anything about prisons and prisoners should have known better than to push an organized group of inmates to the wall. Boxed in, with no apparent alternative, inmates will make a violent stand.

The final slaughter was unnecessary, brutal, unlawful, and punishable (Roebuck 1976, p. 127). On the roofs of A and C blocks, prison and state officials assembled teams of state police marksmen qualified to shoot .270 rifles. On the third floors of these blocks, similar teams assembled. All told, four sets of marksmen provided covering fire for two more attack units of 30 troopers, each armed with 12-gauge shotguns. Additional armed units descended into Yard D. The total attack force, all wearing gas masks, numbered 211 troops. A gas drop by a state helicopter set off the attack on D Yard. The assault parties indiscriminately shot inmates seeking cover, and correctional officers selectively fired upon inmate leaders thought to have engineered the original uprising. Afterward, inmates were stripped and beaten by prison guards while prison supervisors stood idly by (Wicker 1975, pp. 196-98). Medical attention for the inmates was late in coming.

Goal of the Offender

The purported objectives of confrontation offenses by government were to maintain or restore civil order and to preserve and support basic American values and institutions. The real purpose was to stop and deter the public protests of specific groups who had overtly challenged government authority. Government agents had not worked out any effective plans for the control of large demonstrating groups and therefore dealt with them in a sporadic, punishing, and violent manner. The government viewed radicals as disloyal insurrectionaries without full legal rights. Furthermore, the officials who carried out violent actions believed (correctly) that the public would approve drastic actions against "disloyal, undesirable" citizens. Local police and National Guard confrontation offenders aimed to disperse civil rights, antiwar, and free speech groups who were disrupting local order. These officials perceived members of dissenting groups as radical, disloyal, and worthless troublemakers who deserved rough treatment and punishment. At Kent State and Attica, state officials equated the protesters and rioters with insurrectionaries bent on establishing a new sovereignty, and reasoned that giving in to the "rebels" would constitute relinquishing sovereignty over property and people they were responsible for. Governor Rhodes of Ohio stated in his May 2, 1970 speech at Kent that the campus would not be taken over by troublemakers who he alleged were burning down university buildings and Kent businesses (Douglas and Johnson 1977, p. 181). Similarly, Governor Rockefeller of New York perceived the Attica inmates as insurrectionaries mounting an attack upon the authority of his office and upon the sovereignty of New York state. Rockefeller considered the taking of hostages by Attica inmates to be a revolutionary tactic which simply could not be tolerated in a free society (Douglas and Johnson 1977, p. 193).

Legal Status of the Offense

Confrontation crimes by government included the illegal denial of citizens' rights to assemblage, civil rights, free speech, due process of law, and personal security. Other, more conventional crimes were murder, assault, battery, and false arrest. When such crimes were committed by ordinary citizens (not employed by the government), the result was felony arrest, conviction, and heavy sanction. Government officials at several levels (who planned confrontations) and police or state and federal troops (who carried them out) were rarely held accountable for their violent means of handling political protesters and dissenters. The conduct of all disloyal political dissenters has been, in the United States and elsewhere, subject to criminalization by government agents.

Nature of the Offense

Crimes of confrontation by the government have been characteristically open, violent actions in response to perceived threats to political authority. In the cases under examination, government violence succeeded in neutralizing political offenders' public protests. Many segments of the public supported government force at Kent State, Attica, and in other locales where government agents confronted public protesters. Richard J. Daley, the mentor of the Chicago police, was re-elected mayor of Chicago; Nelson Rockefeller was supported in his inaction and action at Attica, and later became vice-president of the United States; and James Rhodes was later re-elected governor of Ohio. The streets are now free of public protesters, and university students throughout the United States are quiet. Attica is under control, but it might be, as James Baldwin has suggested, "the fire next time." Top officials in local governments, state governments, and the National Guard supported, condoned, or directed confrontations, and the agents who actually exercised the confrontation offenses (policemen, state troopers, and guardsmen) in so doing fulfilled expected formal organizational work roles and carried out the aims of their employers.

Societal reaction to government agents' crimes at Kent State, Attica, and other sites has been weak, though small groups of liberal or radical academicians, some intellectuals, and members of leftist political parties have protested in the media against these transgressions. Local police and National Guard confrontation offenses against the people throughout the United States have been rarely sanctioned. Only one state trooper out of 211 participants in the Attica massacre was indicted for assault. The grand jury indicted no one for the killing of the inmates fatally shot in the retaking of the prison. No state official, state trooper (with the exception of one), or corrections officer was indicted for indiscriminate firing, carelessness, manslaughter, or any other offense during the recapture of the prison and the reprisals that followed. On the other hand, 61 of the Attica inmates were indicted for crimes ranging from murder to sodomy. The Attica Brothers Legal Defense estimated that state prosecution costs had reached at least $4 million by mid-summer of 1974 (Wicker 1975, p. 310).

Not one of the guardsmen who fired upon Kent State students was sanctioned in any way. On the other hand, 30 students and faculty members at the university were admonished by a federal judge and by university administrators for participating in protests which supposedly "provoked" the Ohio National Guard to kill the four students. Legal reaction to the Kent State confrontation remains unsettled. Ohio state officials faced a $46 million damage suit for the shootings at Kent State. A 1978 Supreme Court decision cleared the way for a new federal trial in Cleveland, Ohio by denying the appeals of Governor James Rhodes and members of the Ohio National Guard. Surviving relatives of the four students killed and the nine students wounded in the Kent State incident sued state officials for civil rights violations in the early 1970s. A 1975 trial cleared Rhodes and the guardsmen of all charges. However, one of the jurors was assaulted and threatened during the trial, and a federal appeals court judge said the effect of those incidents on the outcome of the trial should have been studied (*Clarion-Ledger* 1978g).

CRIMES AGAINST GOVERNMENT

Confrontation crimes against government have been committed by groups who believed that direct confrontation with the government was the best or only way to call attention to injustices in U.S. society. Some confrontations have been spontaneous (urban riots), while others have been organized (antiwar demonstrations). Unlike intervention against government, which is directed toward bringing the system down, confrontation against government is oriented toward the change or modification of specific economic and political policies.

Action Patterns

The action patterns representing this type of confrontation have been personal, face-to-face conflicts focusing upon specific economic and political issues. For illustrative purposes, we consider three kinds of confrontation: racial disturbances, student disturbances, and mass demonstrations. These offenses were initiated by minority, student, civil rights, and antiwar groups. Because these amorphous groups often overlapped in membership and action patterns, confrontation offenses committed by them are discussed as such rather than in terms of specific organization case studies.

Racial Disturbances

Substantial black disorders in the nation's cities began to occur with increasing frequency in the early 1960s. Relatively minor incidents at that time often touched off extensive destruction in predominantly black neighborhoods. Looting, arson, vandalism, and sniping were the normal patterns of violence. By the mid-1960s, racial disorders had become a regular feature of American life, and they escalated in size and violence. The riot in the Watts area of Los Angeles was a landmark of this period. Racial disorders reached a peak in the latter part of the 1960s, beginning with the July 1967 Detroit riot and ending with 144 riots in April 1968, following the assassination of Dr. Martin Luther King. In the Detroit riot, 43 persons were killed and hundreds wounded. Arrests numbered 7,100, and property damage totaled $40 million (U.S. Senate 1974b, pp. 45–46).

There has never been any evidence of central control or direction of the large-scale racial disorders in the 1960s; they appear to have been spontaneous confrontations. Uusually, leadership developed in an ad hoc fashion. For the most part, those with authority and prestige within the black community (public officials, churchmen, college professors, businessmen, and professionals) have opposed violent confrontations and tried to prevent them. The persons who urged violence during confrontations with the government were often lower-class street leaders of the moment who articulated deeply felt hatred against white figures of authority. They led small groups to defy public authority and destroy specific property targets, such as white businesses in the black community, considered to be external exploiters of the local residents. Black militant revolutionary groups (including the Black Liberation Army and the Black Panthers) disseminated anticapitalist propaganda providing the justification and provocation of murder of "fascist pigs" (policemen). Eventually, a small but vocal minority of residents in black ghettos was converted to a violent ideology and advocated the assassination of police, contributed to the propaganda of violence, and posed a threat to police officers. This climate of violence increased the tensions of police work, which were in turn fed back into the black community. Consequently, fear and distrust increased (U.S. Senate 1974b, p. 46).

Other racial disturbances in the past two decades have consisted of small-scale conflicts between blacks and police or other community residents. In 1966, the NAACP boycotted local merchants in Port Gibson, Mississippi who failed to comply with its demand for equal economic and political opportunities for blacks in the town. George Haynes, chancellor of Hinds County, Mississippi, ruled in 1976 that the NAACP had to pay Port Gibson merchants $1.25 million as a result of this boycott, which supposedly covered the economic losses incurred by white merchants. Hayne's ruling held that Port Gibson's blacks had no right to cause local merchants to lose money because of their conflicts with city and county officials (Tulsky 1978).

The United League of Memphis (a black civil rights organization) led a black boycott of white-owned businesses in Byhalia, Mississippi in 1974, following the shooting death of a black man there by local whites. This boycott was ruled legal because the United League had requested local merchants to hire more blacks prior to the boycott. The refusal by local businessmen to comply with this request paved the way for the boycott. In a similar case, blacks in Tupelo, Mississippi boycotted local merchants in 1978 after two local policemen were allowed to remain on the Tupelo city police force, despite their conviction on a civil rights charge for the brutal arrest and confinement of a black Memphis man in the Tupelo city jail. A U.S. district judge had ordered the two policemen to pay the victim $2,500 in punitive damages. The policemen were only demoted from the rank of captain to lieutenant by local police officials. The Tupelo boycott was ruled legal because the black protesters had distributed 1,000 flyers calling for Tupelo businesses to hire more blacks prior to the boycott, and local businessmen had refused to comply with this request (Tulsky 1978).

Occasionally, small-scale disturbances have been violent. On August 18, 1971, police and FBI agents raided a Jackson, Mississippi residence where several members of the black-separatist Republic of New Africa (RNA) were believed to be harboring a fugitive from justice. During this raid, RNA members shot and killed a Jackson policeman and wounded two other law enforcement officers. Seven RNA members were later arrested and charged with the murder of the policemen. The RNA at this time was attempting to take over Mississippi's state government and territory (by force if necessary) to establish a free and independent black nation (New York *Times* 1971a; Henderson and Ledebur 1970).

Student Disturbances

The first wave of student disorders in the 1960s was coterminous with the movement for blacks' civil rights. In one case, students at North Carolina Agricultural and Technical College in 1960 staged a sit-in at a Greensboro cafe to protest its "white-only" service policy. The next year, students staged sit-ins to protest the policy of nuclear proliferation and bomb shelter constructions in Wisconsin, Illinois, and Ohio. By 1964, students moved beyond peaceful civil disobedience confrontations to direct actions, such as occupying university buildings. At the University of California at Berkeley, 1,000 students occupied the Sproul Hall administration building to protest the university's denial of free speech, and 796 of them were arrested. Subsequent disturbances at other universities focused upon U.S. policy in Vietnam. Employment recruiters for the U.S. Navy, Dow Chemical, and the CIA were harangued by students at Chicago, Columbia, and Brown in 1966. During the 1967–68 school year, public protests occurred on 221 separate occasions at 101 campuses throughout the nation (Teodori 1969).

National attention was focused on Columbia University in the spring of 1968, when protests against the military-industrial complex organized by the Students for a Democratic Society succeeded in taking over the administration building and closing down the university. This feat was duplicated by SDS a year later at Harvard University. The spring of 1970 witnessed a sharp escalation in both the extent and severity of campus confrontations between student groups and security and local police. The decision to commit American troops to Cambodia in April 1970, coupled with the killing of four students by the Ohio National Guard the next month, produced a wave of violent disruptions at colleges and universities across the country. Over 400 campuses went "on strike" for varying lengths of time. Arson and vandalism directed at ROTC buildings and other symbols of American militarism (for example, research centers conducting studies funded by the military) became commonplace (U.S. Senate 1974b, pp. 48-49).

Mass Demonstrations

A notable development of the 1960s was the growing ability of political organizers to assemble large crowds at particular places and times for a common purpose. In 1963, over 250,000 people came to the Lincoln Memorial grounds in Washington to hear Martin Luther King's "I have a dream" speech which, in retrospect, marked a high point of early civil rights struggle. In New York City in the spring of 1967, approximately 200,000 demonstrators gathered to protest the Vietnam war, and close to 70,000 persons demonstrated at the Pentagon in October. The Democratic National Convention attracted 10,000 antiwar protesters to Chicago in August of 1968. In October and November of 1969, the largest antiwar demonstrations yet to occur took place in cities across the nation; a quarter of a million protesters came to Washington, D.C. during this period.

The overwhelming majority of political protesters remained peaceful in their expressions of dissent at such gatherings, although the number of violent demonstrations escalated in the later 1960s. The Pentagon demonstration in 1967 involved police-demonstrator confrontations and a substantial number of arrests for acts of civil disobedience. The 1968 Democratic National Convention in Chicago was the scene of even greater confrontations between the antiwar demonstrators and the police and National Guardsmen. The so-called "Counter-Inaugural" demonstration in Washington in January 1969, organized by antiwar protesters, resulted in police confrontations with small bands of roving demonstrators. The November 1969 Vietnam Mobilization gathering in Washington saw vandalism, street violence, and demonstrator confrontations with police and National Guardsmen. New Haven, Connecticut experienced minor confrontations between local police and persons protesting the trial of black revolutionaries there in May 1970. Similar confrontations occurred in May 1970 at the conclusion of a demonstration in Washington which attracted 60,000 persons opposed to the intervention of U.S. troops in Cambodia (U.S. Senate 1974b, p. 52). On May Day, 1971, thousands of antiwar demonstrators from throughout the United States descended upon Washington in an attempt to shut down the government (Quinney 1975, p. 63). The Washington, D.C. police arrested and criminally processed 13,000 of these people, most of whom were young college students.

Thousands of human rights demonstrators organized by the National Alliance against Racist and Political Repression massed in Washington in March 1978 to persuade President Carter to seek freedom for nine members of the Wilmington 10 (jailed for political reasons in the 1960s) who remained imprisoned. U.S. Park Police estimated that 8,000 persons gathered for the peaceful demonstration and protest march at Lafayette Park, just across Pennsylvania Avenue from the White House. The marchers, carrying placards and chanting slogans, exhorted Carter to play an active role in seeing that the nine men still imprisoned in North Carolina be released immediately.

Mass demonstrations from the early 1960s to the early 1970s comprised large gatherings of persons at a given time in support of a specific cause. The patterns taken by these demonstrations were similar. The coming event was first publicized by the mass media (the legitimate press, television, campus press, and the underground press). Television press conferences were common. Generally, an agenda was announced which called for an assembly of participants at a particular spot to attend a rally and listen to speeches. The most notable examples of political demonstrations involving government confrontation with protesting groups were the 1967 march on the Pentagon and the October and November 1969 Vietnam Moratorium and Mobilization demonstrations in Washington, D.C. (U.S. Senate 1974b, p. 53). Most demonstrations resulted in direct physical confrontations with the police. Several legal subterfuges (parading without a permit, violation of fire ordinances, curfew violations, violations of municipal health and safety laws, disturbing the peace, blocking traffic, disorderly conduct, loitering and trespassing) were employed to deter and disperse these mass demonstrations. Demonstrators confronting the police also committed a series of conventional offenses, such as assault, vandalism, and possession of weapons.

Goal of the Offender

Confrontation offenses against government were efforts to establish racial equality, full civil rights, and free speech, and to stop the Vietnam war. Racial disturbances and riots were geared toward the first and second objectives, student confrontations were oriented to all of them, and mass demonstrations were directed toward the second and fourth aims. The Vietnam war was the catalyst which united a number of protesting groups concerned with a wide range of social problems. Many groups agreed and proclaimed that the war was pursued for profit, and tied this in with many other social problems attributed to an insensitive government allied with a selfish corporate structure, for example, pollution, racism, sexism, poverty, and militarism (Clinard and Quinney 1973, p. 163).

Legal Status of the Offense

In confrontations against government, legal violations included disorderly conduct, rioting, civil disobedience, assault, vandalism, possession of weapons, blocking streets, occupying buildings, and boycotting businesses. However, most of the confrontations involved surrogate-illegal offenses. That is, participants in many confrontations were actually arrested because they were engaging in "dangerous" political activity; the substitute crimes they were charged with were relatively insignificant offenses such as parading without a permit, violation of fire ordinances, disturbing the peace, and unlawful assembly. For example, 208 protesters at the 1967 Pentagon march were not arrested for protesting as such, but for failing to honor the parade permit expiration deadline (Franklin 1967). Antiwar protesters in Chicago, Oakland, Harrisburg, Boston, and Gainesville were prosecuted in accord with the conspiracy provisions in the 1968 federal antiriot act (Quinney 1975, p. 63).

Nature of the Offense

Confrontations against government were violent in some cases and nonviolent in others. All were overt offenses. Persons committed confrontation offenses as part of their everyday activities within formal organizational structures in support of organizational goals. Confrontations, however, did not mesh well with the U.S. political and economic system. In the United States, adequate legal provisions are avowedly provided for individuals and groups who wish to air their political or economic grievances in a peaceful and orderly fashion. On the other hand, confrontation offenses which appear to threaten the system or disrupt normal business activities are unacceptable, regardless of their legal status. The government eventually responded to the confrontation violations of the 1960s by passing certain placating legislation (civil rights laws, pollution laws, and the War Powers Act). The government and the corporate structure were threatened and frightened by the confrontations, and initially responded to them with countervailing violent measures. The general public was also frightened, and gave little support to racial disturbances, student protests, and mass demonstrations. Strong support for confrontation against government was found only among self-defined disenfranchised groups and small revolutionary cadres.

Societal reaction to confrontations against government was initially harsh. Persons confronting the government often had their civil rights violated by local, state, and federal law enforcement officials. Some were beaten and assaulted, and many were illegally arrested. Many others were subsequently subjected to political policing and surveillance. Societal reaction to confrontation against government appears to have been less severe in recent years than in the past. Fewer confrontations occur. Former radicals, now coopted, are part of the establishment and have been exonerated of crimes they committed in the late 1960s and early 1970s. Current protest groups rarely resort to violence or civil disruptions when confronting the government, and it may be that peaceful confrontations against the government will be more tolerated in the future than in the past. Should massive demonstrations resembling some of those of the 1960s recur, however, societal reaction would probably be harsh again. In turn, the counterreaction remains problematic.

7

EVASION AND COLLUSION
BY GOVERNMENT

In the three types of political crime thus far analyzed (intervention, surveillance, confrontation), crimes by government were perpetrated by government and corporate agents who directly (overtly or covertly) and wittingly broke laws in order to preserve and enhance the existing U.S. economic and political power structure. These offense types were targeted toward specific individuals and groups. On the other hand, evasion and collusion offenses of government or corporate agents embrace secret deliberations and acts designed to circumvent or inhibit the full implementation of the government's administrative, civil, or criminal law. Offenses within this type target the general public rather than any set of individuals or groups. In contrast, criminal evasion and collusion offenses are committed by the people against the government to avoid compliance with federal, state, or local statutes. Some have contended that corporations commit crimes against the government, just as do ordinary citizens. However, we rule out this argument because we consider the government to be an instrument of the corporate class. Certainly, corporations are occasionally brought before regulatory, civil, and sometimes (though rarely) criminal courts for legal violations, but the resulting sanctions are weak, ineffective, or non-existent. Therefore, we consider these cases to mark a sham battle between two strong allies: government agents and corporate agents. No attempt is made to cover the entire spectrum of offenses entailing evasion and collusion. We present a few significant forms of the offense type illustrating crimes by government in this chapter, and against government in Chapter 8.

ACTION PATTERNS

High level government officials have often denied responsibility and accountability for their illegal organizational acts and those committed by their underlings. Government regulatory agents at the federal and state levels and capitalist agents, through acts of omission or commission (usually in concert), have evaded the legal oversight of big business. Special prosecuting officials have repeatedly failed to carry out the legal duties officially charged to them. Corrupt public officials, including the police, have deliberately failed to enforce the law for personal financial gain, or for the maintenance of illegal operations economically and politically beneficial to other public officials and criminals.

Official Denials of Responsibility and Accountability

High government officials, especially presidents, have denied complicity in and responsibility for past and current illegal official activities, as in President Eisenhower's handling of the U-2 incident, President Kennedy's initial denial of CIA activities in the Bay of Pigs invasion, President Johnson's actions in the Tonkin Gulf episode, and President Nixon's cover-up of the Watergate scandal. Eisenhower and Kennedy later confessed evasive and collusive illegal behavior. Johnson and Nixon did not admit wrongdoing, despite substantial evidence to the contrary. Nixon, for example, has for five years repeatedly denied any involvement in the Watergate break-in and cover-up, though evidence indicates he knew about the caper from the conception to resurrection. What's more, he orchestrated (after March 21, 1973) a cover-up plan to protect many of his aides involved in the Watergate scandal (U.S. House of Representatives 1975, pp. 39, 60-69, 120-23, 134-40, 151-68, 174-75, 177-78, 182-97).

In addition to presidents, high level officials of the executive branch have denied past and current official illegal activities. L. Patrick Gray, FBI director during the latter years of the Nixon administration, lied to Senator Ervin's committee (the Senate Select Committee on Campaign Practices) about his role in the Watergate cover-up. He denied obstructing the FBI probe of the Watergate break-in, when in fact he had burned pertinent and sensitive political documents removed from the safe of E. Howard Hunt only a few days after the break-in (U.S. Senate 1974a, p. 94). During the same administration, Secretary of State Henry Kissinger allegedly committed perjury before the Senate Subcommittee on Multinational Corporations, which was investigating his role in the CIA-ITT interventions in Chile (Petras and Morley 1975, pp. xi, 131-37). Former CIA director Richard Helms was convicted in 1977 of lying to this same committee about his actions in the Chilean intervention (Marro 1977).

Regulatory Agency Failures

Introduction. In our opinion, the evasion and collusion of government officials and agents of big business to help big business avoid government regulation constitutes the most significant and insidious form of political crime. The bulk of these offenses have entailed the deliberate actions or non-actions of federal departments, regulatory commissions and agencies, and corporations. As business and industry began to abuse their powers under the laissez-faire philosophy that prevailed in the second half of the nineteenth century, Congress created regulatory and administrative commissions to regulate big business in lieu of criminal court procedures. The regulatory agencies have come to perform some police, legislative, and judicial functions; however, regulatory authority is limited to civil action. Moreover, these so-called regulators of big business in the public interest have come to be dominated by those who are supposed to be regulated (the big corporations).*

In fact, some scholars have argued that the agencies and commissions formulated to "regulate" big business were established by government and capitalist agents in order to obviate the legal processing of corporations in courts of law (especially criminal courts). Likewise, scholars have maintained that regulatory agencies were initially structured in the best interests of big business. C. Wright Mills, for example, has pointed out that the large corporations became the "raison d'être" of the business world and the core of our national economy in the second half of the nineteenth century, beginning with the growth of the railroads and the expansion of the banks and other financial institutions. Simultaneously, corporations recognized the necessity to control any form of government regulation (Mills 1967, Chapter 7). Marver Bernstein claims that social movements (such as the Grange) developed to overcome abuses by big business. Such political groups first sought relief from local and state governments, but when these efforts failed, their demands for protection against exploitations were shifted to the federal government. He argues that the regulatory agencies established by the federal government, ostensibly to protect the public from big business, served large corporate interests from the very beginning, and that through time government power utilized through these agencies has further enhanced the private interests of big business (Bernstein 1955, pp. 17-18).

Gabriel Kolko has shown with massive documentary evidence that the establishment of the Federal Trade Commission, the Federal Reserve Board, the Interstate Commerce Commission, and the food and drug laws during the Progressive era (1900-1917) was not opposed, but instead supported, by large corporate interests (Kolko 1963). The regulatory commissions set up by big business and government agents in answer to public complaints did not meet public demands for the application of criminal laws against socially injurious business activities, that is, for the adjudication of big business offenses and offenders in criminal courts of law. Indeed, administrative regulatory procedures helped to rationalize markets for big corporations and limited competitition from smaller businesses. The establishment of the first regulatory commission, the Interstate Commerce Commission (ICC), in 1887 served as a prototype. In

---

*For a discussion of the development of government regulatory agencies and bureaucracies see Sherrill (1972, pp. 162-85).

the 1870s and 1880s, small businessmen and farmers joined forces to demand government action outlawing abuses practiced by the large railroads, for example, high transportation and storage rates and poor service (Bernstein 1955, pp. 17-37). The Grange movement opposed railroad rates that favored big business and drove small businessmen and farmers under. When state legislation proved inadequate, the Grange turned to the federal government for help. The Grange wanted a set of criminal laws to cover the railroads' illegal activities, and it demanded that railroad company offenders be tried in criminal courts. What the Grange received, 20 years and 150 bills later, was an independent tribunal (ICC) which regarded its mission as the adjudication of disputes between private parties. The first chairman of the ICC, Judge Cobley, was a strong spokesman for the right of private property against any government interference. Thus, at the outset, an advocate of big business was selected to chair a regulatory commission, a selection that became a future pattern. The ICC has provided "regulated groups" with privileged access to the government's rules, procedures, and regulatory plans of action. Corporation lawyer Richard Olney (to be appointed attorney general in 1887), in a letter to the president of the Chicago, Burlington, and Quincy Railroad, summed up how the ICC could be beneficial to the railroad industry. He held that the ICC would satisfy the popular clamor for government supervision of the railroads, while actually providing only nominal oversight of their activities. Olney contended that the longer the ICC functioned, the more it would adopt the ideology of the railroad owners, eventually becoming a barrier between the railroad corporations and the people, and a protection against hasty congressional legislation hostile to railroad interests (Adams 1973). Bernstein stipulates that the case of the ICC marks a recurrent pattern in the so-called government regulation of big business. Norman Denzin (1977), an eminent research sociologist, strongly supports Bernstein's thesis in a five-tier (manufacturers, distributors, retailers, the legal order, and drinkers) case study of the American liquor industry. He clearly demonstrates the organizational nature of regulatory and corporate violations entailing systematic evasive and collusive acts.

"The Federal Cover-up of White-Collar Crime" report prepared by congressional investigators (1977), bears out Bernstein's claims. The report charges that there is an on-going, massive cover-up of white-collar crime which is cleverly built into the design of the federal enforcement model and the policies and postures of the Justice Department and federal regulatory agencies. The report notes that desperate hoodlums steal only a pittance compared to the loot that dishonest businessmen and corporate executives plunder each year. The investigators found a disturbing pattern of indifference and ineffectiveness among many law enforcement agencies dealing with upper-class crime. The FBI, for example, though possessing accountancy-trained investigators assigned to its white-collar crime force, displays little interest in white-collar crime. Internal Revenue agents are not allowed to assist the Justice Department in white-collar investigations, though they are acknowledged to be the only government agents expert enough to analyze the complex financial transactions and bookkeeping often involved in business crimes. This situation has all but crippled the Justice Department's white-collar crime enforcement efforts. Further, the report discloses bitter enmity existing between the Securities and Exchange Commission's enforcement division and the Justice Department's criminal division, both of which are grossly under-funded and under-staffed. The report also shows how corporations violating Securities and Exchange Commission laws are provided with an easy escape hatch; the corporations are allowed to sign "consent decrees which spare them from admitting guilt" (Anderson 1978c). Under this standard operating procedure, the corporation is simply made to promise that it will not engage in the illegalities again. Sometimes a mild fine is imposed, which the corporation writes off as a cost of doing business. A supplementary report from the Library of Congress argues that some of the failure at white-collar crime enforcement is due to political pressures on the executive branch from powerful and influential business leaders (Anderson 1978c).

Though the House report on white-collar crime does not deal exclusively with regulatory agency violations, most of it does. Moreover, law enforcement agencies such as the FBI and the Justice Department have regulatory as well as enforcement functions, and government law enforcement agencies have something to say about the cases they are willing to receive from the regulatory agencies and to prosecute. A series of cases documenting evasion and collusion offenses of government agents (regulatory agencies and commissions) and capitalist agents follows. We conclude with a brief case study of the oil industry, which succinctly demonstrates evasion and collusion offenses as a types of political crime committed by teams of government and capitalist agents.

Banks

The Office of the Comptroller of the Currency is responsible for regulating competition among the 4,700 national banks in the Federal Reserve System. This agency's functions include the supervision of bank mergers and determination of the scope of permissible banking practices. The Office of the Comptroller also develops policies that are supposed to protect small banks from being abused by larger banks and small depositors from large ones. In other words, this agency is supposed to protect the interests of ordinary citizens. Actually, important policies of the Office of the Comptroller are formulated by the National Advisory Committee to the Comptroller, a group comprised of representatives from the largest national banks. In the 1960s, the comptroller, with help from the advisory committee, was unusually lenient in policing bank mergers. Therefore, big banks diversified their holdings and expanded into international markets far beyond normal banking practice, and invested in manufacturing and business enterprises much like the multinational conglomerates. When the international economic crises of the 1970s arrived, the banks suffered, as did other big corporations. One of the nation's largest banks, Chase Manhattan of

New York, was labeled a "problem bank" by the Federal Reserve Board, because the depositors had lost confidence in it. Of 56 banks that failed in the mid-1970s, 34 had passed the latest governmental examination with a "no problem" rating. The Office of the Comptroller, in collusion with the National Advisory Committee to the Comptroller, was responsible for this negligent performance (Leinsdorf and Etra 1973, p. 280).

In another instance, the Senate Banking Committee reported in 1976 that four federal banking regulatory agencies were failing to enforce laws that prohibit discrimination in the granting of home-mortgage credit. The four agencies (the Federal Home Loan Bank Board, the Federal Reserve Board, the Federal Deposit Insurance Corporation, and the Office of the Comptroller of the Currency) had never found racial discrimination in any supervised bank, though evidence of such discrimination was wide-spread. Eight years after the enactment of fair-lending legislation, three of the four agencies had not even issued antidiscrimination regulations. As a result of this negligence, credit-worthy minority loan applicants were frequently refused loans. The four agencies regulate lending institutions holding $125 billion worth of mortgages on family homes built for one to four persons (*Clarion-Ledger* 1976b, 1976f).

Federal Communications Commission

The public suffers in an economic sense when regulatory agencies fail to fulfill their responsibilities. This is illustrated by the Federal Communication Commission's (FCC) regulation of long distance telephone rates. In 1953, the FCC determined that utility companies could establish charges on interstate calls yielding no more than a 6.5 percent rate of profit. Despite this ruling, American Telephone and Telegraph (ATT) proceeded to charge its customers more than it was allowed by the FCC, at times yielding as much as a 7.9 percent profit rate. Between 1955 and 1961, ATT reaped $985 million in unauthorized profits due to these overcharges. When the FCC finally investigated the overcharges, it ruled in ATT's favor by raising the acceptable rate of profit from 6.5 percent to 7.5 percent retroactively. This action preserved most of ATT's illegal profits (Mintz and Cohen 1971, pp. 249-50).

The FCC continues to favor the giant telecommunications industries. For example, in 1977 this agency ruled that ATT would not have to divest itself of its subsidiary, Western Electric, a large equipment supply company that sells mostly to telephone companies owned by ATT (Chattanooga *Times* 1977). A further example shows how the FCC's close relationship with the industries is encouraged by Congress. In 1977, a congressman from Wyoming submitted a bill protecting ATT from smaller completitors. An ATT lobbyist remarked that, should this bill fail, Congress should inform the FCC to do nothing about telephone industry competition until another similar bill was submitted (Chattanooga *News–Free Press* 1977).

Environmental Protection Agency

Some of the following examples were mentioned in Chapter 2 in connection with corporate intervention. At this juncture we discuss these cases and others in terms of regulatory agency failures. About 100 cancer-causing pesticides remain in use because of inaction by the Environmental Protection Agency (EPA). The EPA is charged with making sure that agricultural chemicals present no danger to man or environment, and must decide whether or not a chemical is safe. However, it often depends upon the chemical industry for data. Pressure placed upon the EPA by the pesticide industry frequently checks the EPA's scientists' evaluation procedures. As long as the EPA bows to such pressures and fails to enforce the laws, carcinogens will continue to be spread through pesticides and other chemicals (*Clarion-Ledger* 1976a). Many of these chemicals have been known to bring sickness and death to stoop laborers in the South who come into direct contact with them (Anderson and Whitten 1976b).

The EPA has done nothing to ban production of nitrosamines, a group of chemical carcinogens that pollute the air when used in industrial production, and it refuses to properly monitor them in the air above U.S. cities. In a similar case, the Energy Research and Development Administration is rapidly developing new energy sources without considering their harmful by-products. New synthetic gases, for example, use nickel as a catalyst, though this process could produce cancer-causing nickel compounds. Other compounds that are produced in the new energy technologies (for example, the coal conversion process) can cause leukemia, brain damage, and pneumonia (Anderson 1976c).

It was the EPA's responsibility to protect the public from radioactive clouds blowing out of China late in 1976, but its warning system broke down when the first fallout drifted across North America in late September 1976. The monitors failed to detect the first traces of radioactivity that were washed to the ground by heavy rains. The fallout was discovered almost by accident, when workers at the Peach Bottom, Pennsylvania nuclear reactor plant picked up radiation on their wet feet. The EPA knew that cows could eat wet, contaminated grass, and that there was danger that the radioactive poison from China would find its way into the milk supply within a matter of hours. Yet the EPA neither sought out available weather forecasts nor warned farmers of the possible threat to their milk. Two states, Connecticut and Massachusetts, reported in the fall of 1976 that radiation levels had reached the dangerous level and ordered that cows be taken off outdoor grass and put on stored feeds. The EPA also neglected to notify the Nuclear Regulatory Commission that the Chinese fallout was on the way. As a result, NRC mistakenly concluded that the radioactivity at the Peach Bottom Reactor had been caused by airborne effluent from building vents. EPA kept the public uninformed about the radiation until October 5, 1976, a full week after it learned of the impending fallout.

In yet another case, the EPA admitted in 1976 that, because of its own negligence, federal and local agencies were inadequately prepared for a serious air pollution incident occurring from November 16 to November 20, 1975, which contributed to the deaths of 14 persons in the vicinity of Clairton, Pennsylvania, just outside Pittsburgh. The polluted air came from a huge U.S. Steel coke plant located nearby. Neither Allegheny County, the state of Pennsylvania, nor U.S. Steel had any adequate plans on file to reduce pollution should it reach dangerous levels. The plant was never shut down. EPA has legal authority to impose curtailments of industrial operations when and where imminent danger to human health exists, and it approves all state plans for preventing severe pollution incidents. The EPA in this case obviously failed to do its job (*Clarion-Ledger* 1976c).

Despite such incidents, EPA administrator Russell Train in 1975 ordered his assistants to reduce the number and complexity of regulations they were writing to combat pollution. Train expressed the view that many EPA regulations were excessively complex, burdensome, unnecessary, and unessential to the implementation of EPA programs. David G. Hawkins, an attorney in the Washington office of the Natural Resources Defense Council, disagreed with Train, arguing that any retraction of EPA pollution regulations would be illegal. He said that this policy "will produce delay and inaction in environmental programs and will frustrate citizen participation by creating a body of secret agency decision-making" (*Commercial Appeal* 1975c).

In 1973, William Ruckelshaus, then administrator of the EPA, granted the auto industry a one-year delay in meeting the 1975 auto emission standards for hydrocarbons and carbon monoxide stipulated by the Clean Air Act of 1970. This delay was approved because of political pressures by the auto industry's lobbyists. In one notable case, Lynn Townsend, chairman of the Chrysler corporation, lobbied presidential aide John Ehrlichman, who later told reporters in Detroit that the 1970 Clean Air Act made no sense to him. A few days later, the EPA gave the E. I. DuPont Company and the city of Philadelphia emergency permits to continue dumping millions of gallons of industrial and municipal wastes off the Delaware coast as they had done for years. Within the same year, the EPA asked Congress to give the city of Los Angeles and its suburbs an additional two to four years to meet 1977 federal clean air standards. Adding insult to injury, the EPA, in the summer of 1973, acquiesced to the aircraft industry's request for an extension of exhaust emission standards until 1979, and 1981 in some cases, at which time they would have to cut back on the tons of carbon monoxide, hydrocarbons, smoke, and nitrogen oxides that company airplanes dump on settled areas (Sherrill 1974, pp. 249-50).

Interstate Commerce Commission

In 1970, Interstate Commerce Commission inspectors were discovered to be checking fewer than 400 of the 5,000 commercial buses they were required to inspect by law. Of the 400 checked, 300 were allowed to operate despite serious defects in equipment. The ICC also admitted in the same year that some interstate bus lines operated illegally, without an ICC certificate, and without meeting bus safety standards. In 1969, the Senate Commerce Committee, which supposedly oversees the ICC, requested that this agency supply it with a copy of a study that was critical of the commission's merger policies. The ICC refused. Only after prolonged negotiations did the ICC (by a one-vote margin) consent to show the House Commerce Committee a portion of its documents relating to some key mergers, including the disastrous merger between the Pennsylvania and New York Central Railroads (Penn Central), the largest business merger in the nation's history (Sherrill 1974, pp. 209-10).

Bureau of Mines

Through the years, this agency has been remiss in enforcing safety regulations in mines, regulations that the mine owners have fought consistently. In 1970, when there were 260 fatalities and 10,575 injuries in American mines, the bureau made only 31 percent of its required safety inspections and 1 percent of its required health inspections (Sherrill 1972, pp. 176-77; Lieberman 1972, p. 195). In 1971, the Health and Safety Office of the bureau installed a telephone "hot line" that coal miners anywhere in the country could call, collect, to report any mine safety violation. The phone was unmanned, but incoming calls were allegedly taped and played later by bureau officials. On December 22, 1971, a young reporter discovered that the tape hadn't been checked by Bureau of Mines officials for two months, and that the messages had all been erased (Sherill 1974, p. 213).

Department of Agriculture

The U.S. Forest Service under the U.S. Department of Agriculture (USDA) allows lumber companies to destroy public lands by "clear-cutting" all trees in a given forest area, thereby scalping the forest rather than selectively cutting mature trees. Clear-cutting can cause erosion, which inhibits reseeding or replanting and speeds up bacterial actions which render soil so sterile that it takes 50,000 years to regain is normal fertility (Sherrill 1972, p. 198). In 1975, a Virginia court ruled that clear-cutting violates the Organic Act of 1897, which prohibits harvesting trees from federal lands unless the trees are dead, physiologically mature, large growth trees, or individually marked for cutting. This ruling has caused consternation in both the Forest Service and the timber companies. Subsequently, new government regulations were written, supposedly restricting clear-cutting; however, clear-cutting is still permitted in specified conditions (Jabs 1976).

As another example, a little-known but very important branch of the USDA, the Pesticides Regulation Division of the Agricultural Research Service (now a part of the Environmental Protection Agency) was supposed to enforce the Insecticide, Fungicide, and Rodenticide Act of 1947. This division was directed to register pesticides prior to their shipment in interstate commerce, and to certify that they were safe and effective when used as directed. In its 22-

year history at USDA, the division has allowed 60,000 pesticides to appear on the market, but prosecuted only two corporations for marketing unsafe pesticides. In the meantime, evidence of massive violations of the Insecticide Act accumulated. In 1966, there were 242 known violations, including two blatant ones. A certain brand of vaporizer emitting the pesticide lindane, and the Shell Chemical Company's No Pest Strip, both emitted poisonous pesticides and clearly violated the Insecticide Act (Mintz and Cohen 1971, pp. 232-33).

Department of Labor

An office in the Labor Department is supposed to police the employment practices of more than 100,000 companies which do business with the U.S. government. A report of the U.S. Civil Rights Commission claimed in 1976 that this office has not wiped out racial and sexual discrimination in the nation's building trades and trucking unions. The Labor Department office has the power to withhold federal contracts from companies that discriminate against minority and female workers, but has done so in only six instances since its inception (*Clarion-Ledger* 1976e).

In another Labor Department case, Dr. Martin Corn, assistant secretary of labor for occupational health and safety, told a Senate agricultural subcommittee in 1976 that his department could not prevent such incidents as that in Virginia where several chemical workers at the Life Sciences Corporation were exposed to the pesticide Kepone. He acknowledged the failure of the department's health and safety inspectors to take seriously a Life Sciences chemical worker's complaint that his health was endangered by his exposure to Kepone dust. Dr. Corn admitted that the lack of action by the department probably contributed to the severe Kepone poisoning symptoms later suffered by other workers at the company. The former Life Sciences Corporation employee had filed a complaint, alleging unhealthful working conditions at the Hopewell, Virginia plant, with the Richmond, Virginia office of the Federal Occupational Safety and Health Administration (OSHA) in September 1974. This complaint did not bring an immediate OSHA inspection of the Life Sciences plant. Ten months later, Virginia health officials discovered Kepone in the bloodstream of one of several sick Life Sciences employees, and found the plant so heavily contaminated with Kepone dust that it had to be shut down. Dr. Corn claimed that the complaint had been given low priority because little was known about the harmful side effects of Kepone at the time. He said no immediate inspection was made of the plant following the worker's complaint, because the industrial hygienist who worked on the case was transferred from Richmond to another OSHA office. This was a very weak excuse.

OSHA officials were still not convinced that an immediate on-site inspection of the Life Sciences plant was necessary, even after Kepone poisoning was found to be the cause of severe tremors among many of the chemical workers. In response to this finding, OSHA officials claimed that they thought the Life Sciences Kepone production line had already been shut down, and that they obviously did not fully appreciate the dangerous nature of Kepone. Virginia health officials eventually found that "visible and considerable Kepone surface contamination existed throughout the plant."

The Food and Drug Administration

Congress in 1963 directed the Food and Drug Administration (FDA) to draw up regulations for the enforcement of laws concerning what drug manufacturers must tell doctors about prescription drugs. The laws stated that drug companies must inform doctors about both the positive and negative aspects of a drug, and assess its usefulness as a therapeutic device. The FDA regulations provided three sanctions for false drug advertisements: private letters of reprimand, seizures of interstate shipments of midadvertised drugs, and criminal prosecutions. All three of these strategies have been weak in protecting the public from harmful drugs falsely advertised to physicians. The regulations, in fact, have been more beneficial to the drug companies than to the public. The private letters and the seizures of falsely advertised drugs were handled without fanfare, and were essentially a private matter between the guilty company and the FDA. Until the mid-1970s, doctors who bought falsely advertised drugs were not informed of these regulatory actions, and thus could not pass this information along to their patients. Criminal prosecutions have been rare, and have resulted in inadequate and weak penalties. Only six drug firms have been prosecuted since 1964 under these regulations; four of the companies pleaded no contest, one was acquitted, and one had its case dismissed (Mintz 1976). The profits to be gained from falsely advertised drugs are so great, and the penalties so uncertain and weak, that some drug companies have openly and willfully decided to ignore FDA regulations. For example, American Cyanamid Corporation has violated the FDA rules on three separate occasions since 1969 (Mintz 1976).

In yet another case, the FDA in 1972 disclosed how much mold, insect parts, rat feces, rot, worms, hair, and other filth it allows in the nation's food supply following commercial processing: one roden pellet in each pint of wheat; insect damage or mold in 10 percent of all coffee beans; up to 10 million bacteria per gram in dried eggs; and mold in 20 to 40 percent of most tomato products. The General Accounting Office found in 1972 that the FDA did not live up to its own minimum standards. In fact, the GAO found in a random sampling study that 40 percent of all food processing plants allow "serious potential or actual food adulterations" (Sherill 1974, p. 212).

Internal Revenue Service

The Internal Revenue Service (IRS), according to official government statistics, is decreasing the number of its tax audits on large corporations and increasing the number of audits on small firms. Statistics on audits have shown that the audits of large companies decreased from 52,005 in 1972, to 44,194 in

1975. Small firms were audited 83,888 times in 1972, and 110,695 times in 1975 (Jackson *Daily News* 1976c). This lack of action aids large corporations to escape taxes. Another measure helps large firms escape IRS scrutiny. IRS commissioner Donald Alexander in 1975 struck a key question off the federal income tax forms: "Do you maintain a foreign bank account?" This query was intended to catch corporate tax evaders who hid their money in foreign accounts in order to escape U.S. taxes and cover up foreign kickback schemes. Alexander succeeded in dropping this key question, despite protests from his own IRS enforcement officials. What's more, he did not consult officials at the Treasury and Justice Departments prior to taking this action (Jackson 1976).

Nuclear Regulatory Agency

The Atomic Energy Commission (AEC), now the Nuclear Regulatory Agency, has licensed nuclear electric-generating plants without considering their potential for thermal pollution. At some of the plants, the discharges from the cooling system have raised river temperatures by as much as 28 degrees, and many conservationists believe that this has caused massive fish kills in numerous rivers. The AEC, wholly oriented toward the private atomic industry, has claimed that the licensing law confines it to the question of radiological health and safety, despite the fact that the National Environment Policy Act has enjoined all government agencies to weigh other environmental factors in nuclear pollution control decisions.

The new Nuclear Regulatory Agency (NRA) has not only failed to weigh environmental factors in regulatory decisions, but has become a full-fledged advocate of nuclear power. The NRA is supposed to regulate nuclear energy use, not promote it. According to Ralph Nader, the NRA has stepped beyond its charter. Nader cites correspondence between ranking NRA administrators showing that they have recommended tax breaks and subsidies to private companies to encourage these firms to develop nuclear energy (Jackson *Daily News* 1976b).

National Highway Traffic Safety Administration

The motor vehicle industry annually turns out about 9 million cars and trucks comprising 500 different makes and models. The National Highway Traffic Safety Administration (NHTSA), which is supposed to check autos for minimum safety standards, tests only about 55 vehicles each year for compliance with some of the safety standards. Most of its money is used to test tires, not autos. U.S. auto makers recall millions of vehicles each year for various safety reasons, but only about 100,000 of these vehicles are recalled because of NHTSA testing (Sherrill 1974, p. 212). In many cases auto companies recall certain models only if a particular defect has resulted in severe injury or damage (New York *Times* 1978b). In fact, the cars are never actually recalled; the companies ship new parts to local auto dealers for complaining customers. Oftentimes after long delays, the new parts are substituted for the defective ones by local mechanics who may lack the technological knowledge to effect the necessary replacements. The defective car is never moved to a city or locale where effective replacement could be made. Under this arrangement, the customer is usually a loser with no legal recourse. The local auto dealer tells the complaining customer that his hands are tied, and direct complaints to the company are referred back to the local dealer. Factory representatives, who are supposed to inspect the autos of complaining customers when local mechanics cannot eliminate mechanical weaknesses, act as public relations men rather than effective troubleshooters. In the meantime the customer is stuck with the car and its payments, no matter how defective the product, and he is never awarded a new car as a replacement.

The Renegotiation Board

This obscure regulatory board within the executive branch was supposed to determine when U.S. defense contractors retained illegal excess profits from the Defense Department, and to penalize these contractors. It was the only government body that regulated defense companies. The board was so overworked and undermanned that each of its accountants had to evaluate $15 million in defense spending every hour. Consequently, corporate defense contractors have been able to cover up and retain billions of dollars in illegal excess profits. Ninety percent of the large defense contractors avoided the Board's regulation. In 1966, of the 100 largest defense contractors, none was regulated by the Renegotiation Board. Between 1967 and 1974, an average of three large defense firms per year came under the Board's scrutiny. One board member has estimated that the addition of 95 new staff members would have retrieved $8 million for the government from excessive defense payments in 1977. However, President Ford's budget office in 1976 refused to assign any more auditors to the Board, and it was discontinued in September 1976 (Anderson and Whitten 1976c).

Antitrust Division in the Department of Justice

Professional organizations and individual professionals have been guilty of price-fixing and thus of violating antitrust laws. The Antitrust Division in the Department of Justice is primarily a law enforcement agency rather than a regulatory commission. However, failure to enforce antitrust statutes pertaining to professional price-fixing schemes amounts to collusion between the division and powerful professional organizations, and prevents competitive pricing for professional services. What's more, the division is a regulatory as well as an enforcing agency. The lack of antitrust action against professionals who operate as businessmen allows them to give a higher priority to profits than to professional services. The following cases indicate this lack of regulation and control.

A 1975 Supreme Court ruling held that the collusive price-fixing schemes of lawyers, doctors, pharmacists, architects, accountants, and other professional persons are not exempt from prosecution under the Sherman Antitrust Act. Lawyers who argued the case on behalf of consumers before the Supreme Court have demonstrated that this ruling defines price-fixing by professionals as illegal. Despite the Supreme Court ruling, standard fee-setting has remained an established practice in the professions. Lawyers, for example, have devised fee schedules throughout the nation that set floor prices for various standard legal services (divorce cases, estate planning, adoption, bankruptcy, debt collection). This practice was in effect as early as 1975. Legal and medical associations negatively sanction the advertisement of professional fees. Following the court's ruling in 1975, however, the Justice Department, the Federal Trade Commission (FTC), and consumers' groups appeared to be chipping way at professional price-fixing. In November 1975, the Justice Department sued the American Society of Anesthesiologists over "relative value guides" which its 11,000 members used to determine fees. Then in 1976, the FTC brought an antitrust complaint against the American Medical Association's ban on advertising by physicians. Later, the Consumers Union challenged in a federal court the composition of the Pennsylvania State Board of Optometrical Examiners. The consumers group complained that this board has collusively increased the prices paid by consumers for eyeglasses, and has reduced competition in the profession (Kohlmeier 1976).

Physicians and medical associations routinely evade the antitrust statutes by failing to allow alternative health care delivery systems. The prevailing system of health care delivery, based upon the fee-for-service charge, amounts to a separate fee for each service. This concept is protected by medical associations which consider it unethical (or rater, unremunerative) to promote any other system. The American Medical Association (AMA) upholds the present system, whereby doctors may not advertise or solicit patients, and consumers do not know when to visit a physician or which kind of specialist to consult; nor do they know which doctors are competent and how much they charge. An alternative to this trial and error system would consist of prepaid, fixed payments to physicians, in return for which patients would receive treatment for all illnesses occurring within a specified time period, and would also be entitled to preventive check-ups. Group health programs would provide an alternative to the current fee-for-service arrangement which permits doctors to reap higher incomes than they would receive from fixed payments. Payments under the alternative plan would also be more susceptible to consumer evaluation. Subsequent competitive pressures would probably lead to salaried positions for doctors within a group practice situation, rather than profits in an individualistic business situation (Green 1972, p. 268).

The Ralph Nader report on the current quality of medical care reviewed evidence of startling incompetence among highly paid doctors, which it attributed to the fee-for-service system. Many doctors perform unnecessary surgery. For example, a survey conducted in one state found that almost 31 percent of all women given hysterectomies had no pathology of the organs removed. The fee-for-service arrangement provides financial incentives for such unnecessary operations. Because consumers are unable to separate the competent doctor from the incompetent, there is little inducement for doctors to keep abreast in their fields after they leave medical school (Green 1972, p. 268).

Prepaid group medical practice would eliminate some of these abuses associated with fee-for-service arrangements. Placing a team of doctors on fixed salaries would facilitate "peer review," a practice known to encourage dramatic improvements in the quality of medical care. In one experiment, the introduction of peer review increased the proportion of "justifiable" operations from 30 percent to 80 percent in two years, while the overall number of operations declined by 65 percent. Comprehensive prepaid group health programs offer preventive check-ups without additional charge, increase efficiency through the use of specialists, and spread the lower cost of medical care evenly among consumers (Green 1972, p. 269). Prepaid programs would remove control over the delivery of medical services from doctors and place it in the hands of consumers exercising free market choice. For this reason, organized medicine (the AMA) vehemently opposes any such new program, thereby violating the antitrust laws and the principles of a 1943 Supreme Court decision.

The 75 prepaid group programs now in existence throughout the U.S. serve only about 4 percent of the population. Health coverage provided by such programs would be greater, and the nation's health would be better, if the Justice Department's antitrust laws had been enforced following the 1943 Supreme Court decision. By failing to act, the Justice Department has allowed medical societies to block the development of prepaid group programs. In fact, the only judicial precedents established since 1943 have resulted from private suits brought when the antitrust division declined to act (Green 1972, p. 269). This situation reflects the power of the lobbying bloc which enables the medical profession to operate as a lucrative business organization.

A Case Study of Evasion and Collusion in the Oil Industry

Oil is a slippery business. Inquiries into the operations of the major companies that control the flow of this valuable energy resource disclose a corporate monopoly shored up by the U.S. government. This vertical monopoly escapes anti-trust laws, equitable taxation, supervision by several regulatory agencies, including the Federal Trade Commission (FTC) and the Federal Energy Administration (FEA), and adequate control by any government body. The major international oil companies, in a collusive, symbiotic relationship with local, state, and federal government agencies, maintain a monopoly over the crude oil industry.

Control of International Oil. Several sources document the fact that the big international oil companies (British Petroleum, Shell, Exxon, Mobil, SoCal,

Texaco, and Gulf) control the discovery, recovery, transport, refining, and marketing of the bulk of the free world's crude petroleum. This control results in an absence of free markets, free enterprise, and political accountability. The dominance of the petroleum majors rests on mergers, exchanges, agreements relating to competitive areas of energy, and vertical control over crude production, refining, marketing, and transportation. The majors enjoy multinational tie-ins with exporting countries as the producers, refiners, transporters, and marketing agents for these host nations. The international giants share joint interests through patents and banking ties, common capital underwriters and accountants, territorial agreements related to drilling operations, crude oil exchange agreements, and price-fixing (Blair 1976; Engler 1977).

A 1973 Federal Trade Commission staff report suggested that the major oil companies (the Seven Sisters mentioned above) operated much like a cartel (U.S. Senate 1973c). By 1972, these seven integrated majors were producing 91 percent of the Middle East's crude oil and 77 percent of the free world's supply outside the United States. Control over supply has been effected through jointly-owned operating companies and restrictive long-term contracts. The major international oil companies receive the cooperation and assistance of government bodies and agencies (within both the producing and the consuming countries) in establishing and controlling a vertical monopoly (Blair 1976, pp. 52-76).

The majors have secured control over most of the world's markets by means of cartel arrangements instituted in most of the world's consuming countries. Employing boycotts, intimidation, and the support of government agencies (including the State Department), they kept independent oil companies out of the cartel system. Utilizing foreign and domestic control systems, they have been able to limit the world output of crude petroleum to a predetermined growth rate. Furthermore, they have been able to eliminate significant differences in delivered prices at any given destination throughout the world. These control systems have enabled the majors to monopolize the supply and distribution of oil (Blair 1976, pp. 27-120).

The Control of Domestic Oil. It has been estimated that Big Oil is spending upward of $100 million a year to create a favorable but misleading image of the industry. In addition to a $4 million annual budget for television, Mobil alone is spending $5 million on print advertising defending Big Oil's business operations. Big Oil reasons that should it be able to continue to palm itself off to the public as a group of competing companies, vertical divestiture would be averted, and the deregulation of natural gas prices could be achieved. Big Oil became frightened when some senators introduced legislation in 1973 to invoke divestiture, in response to the supply shortages and climbing prices that characterized the market in that year (Sherrill 1976, p. 88). The oil cartel has so far been able to block diverstiture by means of a monumental advertising program that appears to have convinced the public that competition exists in the oil industry, and an awesome exercise of influence in the Congress.

Since 1956, the oil industry has pushed for deregulation of the price of natural gas, which for many years has been set by the Federal Power Commission, mandated by Congress to give the industry a fair profit and no more. In the past five years, the FPC has stretched the law to give the oil companies much more than a fair profit, and should deregulation occur, many billions of extra dollars in profits would accrue to the oil companies (Sherrill 1976, p. 88). So far, the industry has prevented divestiture. The cartel has threatened not to build refineries in states whose members of Congress support divestiture. Further, small and independent oil companies that form a constituency in several oil states have been threatened with oil cut-offs should they support candidates who promote divestiture (Sherrill 1976, p. 42).

To support the claim that competition exists in the oil industry, Big Oil points to 10,000 different companies that produce oil and natural gas, 131 different companies that refine oil products, 100 companies that transport oil and natural gas by pipelines, 15,000 wholesale oil distributing companies, and 300,000 retailers. The industry contends that no one company controls more than 11 percent of any part of the industry (crude production, refining, transportation, or retailing), and that the top eight oil companies do not control more than 57 percent of any one of these fields. On this basis, the industry argues that there is less vertical integration in oil than in at least 25 other major U.S. industries. Additionally, the cartel argues that only large companies can lay out the enormous amounts of capital necessary to operate the industry, and absorb the monetary risks involved (Sherrill 1976, p. 92). This averred efficiency is based on a monopoly over raw materials. Vertical integration guarantees a supply of oil to sell at both the wholesale and retail levels. When there is a shortage of oil, as in 1973, the first companies to feel the crunch are the independent companies that have no control over the crude oil supply. If the oil cartel's production was divorced from its refineries, and if every company had the same chance to buy, the independent companies could operate as efficiently as (if not more efficiently than) the majors (Sherrill 1976, pp. 92-99).

The problem is that the control of domestic oil is concentrated in the hands of the major oil companies. Of the nation's proved reserves of crude oil, 93.6 percent is held by 20 major oil companies. Nearly two-thirds of these reserves are held by the eight largest firms—over one-third by the four largest companies. In control of reserves, crude production, refining capacity, and retail sales, the top eight are Exxon, Texaco, Gulf, SoCal, Standard (Indiana), Atlantic-Richfield (Arco), Shell, and Mobil. The majors own or have interests in 70 percent of domestic pipelines, and own or lease half the world's tanker tonnage. Natural gas is also a part of the oil industry. Integrated oil companies control over 70 percent of natural gas reserves and production (Engler 1977, pp. 20-47).

A network of intercorporate relationships is effected through joint ventures involving foreign oil reserves, pipelines, offshore leases, joint biddings, corporate stockholdings, and interlocking directorates. This is documented in several Federal Trade Commission studies (Blair 1976, pp. 125-50). Therefore, any discussion of individual oil companies in reference to competition and monopoly is misleading. The Seven Sisters and about a dozen other big oil companies do not operate independently, but rather through a complex web of crisscrossing business relationships that tie them together at many junctures. They exchange oil and tankers, share pipeline space, swap refined products, and are partners with one another throughout the production, transportation, and marketing processes. Sixty-eight of the major oil companies operate wells in partnership. This kind of cooperation and joint ownership has nullified competition. The big companies have split up the retail market they have dominated since 1911. Standard (Indiana) is the leading retailer in 15 Midwest and Plains states; Exxon (until 1972, Standard Oil of New Jersey) is the leading retailer in 14 states in the East and South; Standard Oil of California is the leading seller in six states in the Northeast. These oil companies have developed indirect interlocks which circumvent the Clayton Act of 1914, forbidding directors to sit on the boards of competing oil companies. Mr. X may sit on the boards of Texaco and Chase Manhattan Bank, and Mr. Y may sit simultaneously on the boards of Exxon and Chase Manhattan Bank. Senator Haskell found that 16 Citibank (New York) directors were affiliated with seven oil companies (Sherrill 1976, pp. 94-95).

The history of the oil industry shows that it controls its so-called controllers (the regulatory agencies) as well as production, prices, and competition. The Seven Sisters' (Exxon, Shell, Gulf, British Petroleum, Mobil, SoCal, Texaco—all great international companies) operations extend throughout all the stages involved in the supply of petroleum products, from the recovery of crude to the operation of service stations. Beneath these giants are a group of smaller, integrated companies (big in comparison with most corporations) that are less secure either in source of supply or outlets for their products. Their operations are confined to one or a few countries. Dominated by the Seven Sisters, these companies live and let live, and exchange thoughts on common policy and the control of prices with the major companies. The majors exert control over the independent companies' supply of crude oil and market outlets, and therefore control them (Blair 1976; Engler 1977).

The domestic oil policies in the United States are formulated by a series of state and federal statutes, recommendations of committees made up of oil company economists, and recommendations made by the Bureau of Mines of the Department of the Interior. Together these policies permit a pattern of monopolistic control over oil production, distribution (among refiners and distributors), and the price paid by the public (U.S. Senate 1962, p. 13). The major forms of government assistance have been directed toward the limitation of domestic production and the restriction of imports (import quotas). The first was achieved through prorationing procedures for each oil producing state, and the second by presidential directives (Blair 1976). Prorationing has inflated oil prices by restricting production to or below demand. Costs have been inflated by reducing the output of the more productive, inexpensive wells, and keeping in operation costly, inefficient ones. The import quota established March 11, 1959 remained in effect for 14 years; it raised the price to U.S. buyers and seriously depleted U.S. oil reserves (Blair 1976, pp. 168-86).

Adjustments by the Seven Sisters to the OPEC Cartel. The international and domestic market controls attained by the oil companies following World War II proved successful until the mid-sixties, when oil began to flow around and beyond the control of the majors. Smaller oil companies gained valuable concessions in Libya, and began forcing their way into world markets by offering lower prices. The majors offset the Libyan oil expansion by a reduction of production in Middle East countries. Additionally, private brand operators began selling gas at discounts of four to six cents a gallon during this period. Furthermore, the concession system of the majors was challenged by members of the Organization of Petroleum Exporting Countries (OPEC), who demanded participation and nationalization programs. Crude oil prices were raised sharply, and payments to the oil producing countries by the majors were now purchases, not royalties disguised as taxes. Purchases did not qualify for tax credits charged on foreign income. The former practice of maximizing the value of preferential tax advantages by making after-tax profits primarily at the stage of crude production and using refinging and marketing merely as conduits for the disposal of crude oil needed to be replaced (Blair 1976, pp. 207-8).

Over a five-year period, the majors found solutions to their problems. They effected a reduction of competition in international and domestic markets, developed a new site of profits (downstream operations gained emphasis), and established a higher rate of profit return. The eight vertically-integrated oil companies weakened the competition of the private branders by denying them supplies, limiting their access to markets, and by price squeezes. This was made possible by the majors' ownership and control of most pipelines, oil refineries, and crude oil. The OPEC countries increased the price of oil sold and reduced production, but they left the drilling, refining, transportation, marketing, and foreign pricing of oil in the hands of the Seven Sisters. The oil companies had control over the distribution of crude oil; therefore they charged more downstream. Thus, OPEC and the major oil companies, in combination, control oil production and the world price of oil (Blair 1976, pp. 242-93). OPEC nations are not concerned with the price of oil downstream as long as they get a share; and the major oil companies are not too much concerned with the crude oil prices charged by OPEC countries, as long as they are able to pass the increased price along to the consumer. Ultimately, this policy of both the OPEC nations and the oil cartel can only weaken the economic structure upon which both depend. But then corporate capitalism is not necessarily rational.

Following the oil embargo in the fall of 1973, oil prices quadrupled. The international oil companies accepted no responsibility for this increase and claimed to be victims along with the consuming public. The oil cartel transferred the higher price of crude oil to the public through increased gasoline and fuel prices charged to consumers. Soaring prices actually meant soaring profits. For example, Exxon's 1974 profits were 24 percent over 1973 profits; Standard Oil's (Indiana) profits went up 90 percent; Mobil's went up 22 percent, and Texaco's went up 23 percent. The General Accounting Office estimated in 1974 that the oil companies may have overcharged customers by $1 billion to $2 billion by sidestepping government regulations. In this same year (1974), Senator Jackson's Permanent Investigation Subcommittee staff accused the nation's ten largest oil companies of deliberately slowing down refinery output. The Federal Trade Commission, not known as a zealot in the control of big business, accused the eight largest U.S. oil companies of conspiring to reduce gasoline supplies and monopolize refining and marketing (Sherrill 1976, p. 89). This accusation probably was prompted by the public's outrage over the high price of gas and oil.

To more than offset the increase in the cost of OPEC oil, the companies charged more for downstream operations and achieved a higher target rate of return. The majors justified a higher profit rate by claiming that the additional funds were required to expand supplies of oil. This claim was (and is) spurious, as we will see. The major have also monopolized alternate energy sources through mergers and the acquisition of competing sources of energy, such as coal, uranium, and oil shale (Blair 1976, pp. 318-20).

Preferential Taxation. Congressman Charles Vanik of Ohio has claimed, on the basis of his detailed study of the 1975 federal income taxes paid by 148 companies (a representative cross-section of America's largest corporations and conglomerates), that oil profits largely go untaxed. He found that 18 companies paid taxes on between 0 and 10 percent of their adjusted net income, despite the fact that the corporate tax rate (unlike the progressively scaled individual tax rates), was a statutory 48 percent. Mobil Oil paid 1.8 percent; Standard Oil of Ohio paid 2.2 percent; Occidental Petroleum, 3.7; Gulf Oil, 6.0; and Texaco, 9.2. Of those paying above 10 percent, Exxon paid 22.7; Standard Oil of California, 28.4; Standard Oil of Indiana, 29.8; and Shell Oil, 36.0. Five multinational oil companies paid $107 million in corporate federal income taxes on pretax profits of more than $2.2 billion, for an effective average tax rate of 4.8 percent. In a larger, five-year tax study, Vanik found that corporate America's income tax contributions to the federal treasury have continued to decline. Protected corporations are currently paying twice as much in taxes to foreign governments as they pay to the federal treasury in income tax. Small business has not been able to participate in the tax relief that is the province of big business. The tax code has develped into a lawyer's paradise of exemptions, exceptions, special provisions, and benefits applicable primarily to corporate taxpayers, while the exemptions available to individuals and small businesses remain relatively insignificant (Vanik 1976).

Tax advantages provided by the U.S. Congress have contributed to the structural integration of the oil industry. In 1948, when the corporate tax rate was 48 percent, taxes paid by the 19 largest oil companies came to only 7.6 percent of their income before taxes (*Oil Week*, June 30, 1957, p. 187). The oil industry's lawyers and congressional allies have secured preferential taxation for the industry for 50 years through percentage depletion, the deduction of tangible drilling costs, and the foreign tax credit (Blair 1976, pp. 187-204). In 1972, percentage depletion and deductions for exploration and development cost the U.S. Treasury $2.35 billion (U.S. Senate 1974c, Part 4, p. 19). These revenue losses were shifted to individual taxpayers and other industries. Tax favoritism for the oil industry has proven to be a greater advantage to the major companies than to the nonintegrated refiners and marketers; for example, the foreign tax credit is worth more to the larger, integrated Seven Sisters than to the independent companies. Since 1975, tax loopholes have been declining in importance, but this has been more than offset by the increase in the after-profit margin resulting from a sharp rise in the price of oil (Blair 1976, p. 204).

Antitrust Violations. John Blair (1976, pp. 171-80) has documented evidence that the major oil companies have violated antitrust laws in three ways: 1) The concerted restriction of crude oil supplies, by tailoring their yearly output of crude outside the United States to achieve a predetermined industry growth rate, controlling production in the oil producing countries to meet marketing needs, and the reduction of oil output during 1974-75 to maintain the sharply increased OPEC prices; 2) Failing to share crude oil with independent refineries; 3) Concentration of ownership in the hands of the majors' vertically-integrated structures. In support of the first contention, Blair shows that during 1950-72 the majors geared foreign production to a predetermined industry growth rate. The Justice Department, with powers under Section I of the Sherman Act, and the Federal Trade Commission, under Section 5 of the Federal Trade Commission Act, failed to restrict this violation. In support of the second contention, Blair shows how the major oil companies purposefully and collusively withheld foreign crude from independent refiners in the 1970s in order to drive them out of the foreign and domestic oil markets, thus raising the price of oil to the consumer. Finally, Blair and others clearly demonstrate that the major oil companies are vertically integrated, and thereby control the production, distribution, marketing, and price of oil throughout the world.

Despite evidence that the major oil companies transgress antitrust laws, movements against these companies have repeatedly failed (Blair 1976, p. 394). A classic oil antitrust case follows. On June 23, 1952, President Truman wrote a memorandum to the secretaries of State, Defense, Interior, and Commerce, and to the FTC, stating that he had requested the attorney general to institute appropriate legal proceedings against the operations of the international oil companies. He requested that these officials cooperate with him in gathering evidence for antitrust proceedings. Subsequently, a special grand jury was convened and 21 oil companies, including the seven international majors, were served with subpoenas. The grand jury's specific objectives, based on an FTC investigation, were to bring to an end: 1) The monopolistic control of foreign production; 2) The curtailment of domestic production necessary to maintain the level of domestic and world prices; 3) The use of quotas to limit sales in foreign markets; 4) The limitation of U.S. imports and exports; and 5) The exclusion of U.S. independents from foreign sources of supply (U.S. Senate 1974c).

The oil companies' attorneys objected to these goals, arguing that their documents were sensitive (involving national security), and that the court did not have the jurisdictional power to require documents from foreign subsidiaries of U.S. companies. These objections were denied. The companies then shifted their efforts from the judicial to the executive branch, where they were more successful. On January 12, 1953, Truman directed the attorney general to change the criminal suit to a civil case. This action removed the possibility of jail sentences for company leaders, and more importantly, made more difficult the introduction of documentary evidence. President Truman invoked national security as the reason for his action—in reality, lack of action.

Fifteen years later the civil case was closed with a number of meaningless consent decrees. After President Eisenhower was inaugurated, a special assistant to the president informed Secretary of State John Foster Dulles in writing that the enforcement of the antitrust laws against oil companies in the Near East was secondary to the interests of national security. In 1953, the National Security Council (NSC) transferred primary responsibility over the case from Justice to the Department of State, and then policy makers at State, Defense, and NSC scuttled the case. The National Security Council effected the most telling blows by directing the Justice Department not to challenge the legality of joint operations (production, refining, storage, and transportation) among the seven international majors. The NSC prohibited the Justice Department from using the one most effective measure of antitrust enforcement, namely, dissolution and divestiture. The result was a series of consent decrees which did not prevent the major companies from achieving the five goals mentioned in the original indictment— goals inconsistent with economic competition. Participation in cartel arrangements was to be pursuant to the requirements of law in the foreign nations where the operations were to take place. By 1968, all of the weak consent cases were dropped (Engler 1977, p. 75; Blair 1976, pp. 71-76).

The Lack of Regulation. The ineffectiveness of public regulation of the oil industry inheres in the fact that a symbiotic relationship exists between a monopolistic industry and a compliant government. Economic dominance enables the oil industry to draw support from the federal bureaucracy, a bureaucracy that is either sympathetic, captive, innocent, or incompetent. In the main, government efforts support the major oil companies: risks are shifted to the taxpayers; costs are shifted to ecologists and to the producing nations. Government policy functions to help keep supply down and prices up at levels whereby a maximum gain in profits accrues to the big oil companies.

The federal government receives its notions about regulatory practices from a network of energy advisory bodies comprising leaders of the major oil corporations and trade associations. For decorative purposes, a few representatives of independent oil companies complete this entourage. These advisors define the boundaries of policy alternatives and supervise policy implementation. In short, they block legislation unfavorable to the control of oil, and obstruct the implementation of legislative and public agency controls of oil. The National Petroleum Council within the Department of Interior is the largest and most active advisory body and is treated as a "partner" of the Office of Oil and Gas. It serves as the official pipeline between government and the oil industry. The council claims to operate on a private budget, but it also receives financial support from the American Petroleum Institute, an official organ of the oil companies, and the private source of most petroleum data (Engler 1977, pp. 173–215).

Much of what exists in the oil industry remains under the "private government" of oil. Banks are vehicles for circumventing the antitrust laws which prohibit interlocking directorates. A Senate investigating committee attempting to identify the leading stockholders in the major corporations found that banks served as centers for circumventing antitrust prohibitions against interlocking directorships. The big oil companies, including Exxon, Mobil, Texaco, Gulf, and Standard, either refused on grounds of confidentiality to give this committee information on stock ownership, or they submitted incomplete, camouflaged reports that did not identify the actual owners (U.S. Senate 1973b, pp. 29–33).

Over a period of years, there have been efforts by the staffs of the Federal Power Commission, the Federal Trade Commission, the Antitrust Subcommittee in the Senate, and the Commerce Committee in the House of Representatives to penetrate the mystery of oil and gas accounts. Since 1968, studies of oil company records have demonstrated that the major companies have been withholding supplies of gas, rigging their books, and formulating false reserve estimates which were passed on through trade associations and used for policy making (Cockburn and Ridgeway 1977). Federal Power Commission (FPC) records show that gas producers have not been making necessary efforts to fulfill the nation's gas needs since 1971. Producers have not made the investments needed to maintain the producing wells at the maximum rate. Withholding such investments is an illegal act if there are outstanding contracts that demand the delivery of a certain quantity of gas. In the last six years, the gas under contract has not been delivered, but the FPC has failed to enforce existing contracts. In other words, the FPC has assisted the natural gas producers in breaking the law. Gulf Oil and Texaco withheld gas from the market during the severe winter of 1977 (New York *Times* 1975c; *Clarion-Ledger* 1977a, 1977b).

Companies that are drilling for oil off U.S. shores are also holding back production in an effort to increase profits and encourage deregulation (which would increase profits further). Senator Jackson's Interior Committee study of oil production off the Gulf of Mexico disclosed in 1975 that many oil wells in the Gulf were not operating. The 300 leases studied (85 percent of the leases for drilling off the Gulf Coast) should have been producing twice as much oil as they were at the time of the investigation (Kraft 1975).

A recent case illustrates the rigging of books. The Federal Energy Administration in the spring of 1977 claimed that 20 oil companies overcharged the public $336 million for oil transferred from foreign affiliates. The issue involved oil transactions from October 1973, the start of the Arab oil embargo, through May 1975, more than a year after the embargo ended. During this period the U.S. government kept price controls on oil produced within this country, while foreign oil prices tripled. A company could circumvent the domestic price controls by paying more than necessary for imported oil, a cost legally passed on the the U.S. consumers. If an American-based company made such overpayments to one of its own foreign affiliates, the extra money paid by consumers would remain within the company, boosting its profits. Since 1974, the FEA has been auditing such "transfer payments" to see whether U.S. companies were paying their own affiliates more for foreign oil than companies in general were paying non-affiliates on the open world market. FEA has concluded that some oil companies were crediting their own affiliates with prices higher than the so-called "arms-length" price expected in an independent transaction. In 1975, FEA assessed these overpayments at $275 million, but the companies objected. FEA reviewed their accounting once more, and then reaffirmed the original finding that companies "inflated" their payments to foreign affiliates—and increased the estimate of overpayments to $336 million. The highest overpayment and resulting overcharge was attributed to Gulf Oil, at $79.6 million, some 23 percent of the total estimate (Rattner 1977).

Government "regulators" of the oil industry are often lawyers who have previously represented the industry. A recent case in point is that of Lynn R. Coleman, nominated by President Carter in 1977 to be the Department of Energy's general counsel (the top attorney's position). Coleman declined to divulge to a Senate confirmation committee a full list of oil and gas companies represented by his Houston-based law firm, Vinson and Elkins, which has 240 partners and members, including former Texas governor and Secretary of the Treasury John Connally. Big John, as everybody knows, was made by Texas oil companies, and he takes care of his makers. The Vinson and Elkins firm represents numerous companies that have cases pending before the energy agency. Coleman admitted to the Senate committee that his law firm had represented a number of major oil companies in the past, including Texaco, Exxon, Mobil, Shell, and Union Oil. One senator accused him of siding against the public interest in some of his legal cases. Despite this apparent conflict of interests, Coleman was confirmed by the Senate by a 75–20 vote (*Clarion-Ledger* 1977o, 1978l).

The Case of the Interior Department. The U.S. Department of Interior is the federal agency with basic responsibility for managing energy and natural resources for the public. A brief look at this department's relationship with the oil industry confirms that the U.S. government leaves the control of oil to the "private government" of oil (Engler 1977, pp. 3–12). Interior is responsible for securing basic energy data, supervising the public land and energy leasing policy, administering oil import policies, stimulating research for alternate sources of energy, managing publicly owned mineral resources, and protecting the environment. It holds public lands (amounting to one-third of the land area of the United States and the continental shelf) for disposal to private claimants or lessees. This department has not maintained the public interest regarding the development, use, and conservation of energy resources, but rather has served as a partner of private industry in keeping prices up, profits secure, and the control of energy in private hands (Engler 1977, pp. 146–47). Interior's leasing policy favors joint bidding by the big oil companies, grants them development time extensions (permitting large sections of public lands to be tied up by big oil companies), and contributes to the oil companies' control over alternate sources of energy, such as coal, oil shale, tarsands, uranium, natural gas, and geothermal and solar sources. Privileges granted to these large companies include water rights necessary for the newer process of recovery and conversion of alternate energy sources, as well as land leases (Engler 1977, pp. 40–50; Blair 1976, pp. 325–47). As of 1976, oil companies controlled between 26 and 40 percent of coal production; seven of the 15 largest coal companies were subsidiaries of oil companies. In 1978, two of the four largest coal producing firms, Consolidated Coal and Island Creek Coal, were owned by Continental Oil and Occidental Petroleum, respectively. The nuclear energy industry is also being monopolized by the oil industry, which owned about 30 percent of our uranium reserves in 1966, and between 50 and 55 percent in 1976. A 1978 Federal Trade Commission staff report disclosed that 12 U.S. oil and gas companies owned more than 50 percent of all U.S. uranium reserves in 1975. According to this report, the United States' biggest oil companies owned $100 billion worth of coal and uranium reserves in 1978. Virtually all the shale and geothermal lands leased to date have gone to oil companies (Sherrill 1976, p. 98; Starkville *Daily News* 1978).

The Interior Department acts as an administrator of offshore leasing activities, and in this capacity has opposed the internationalization of seaboard resources. Interior backs the oil companies' demands to conduct offshore leasing arrangements through bilateral negotiations with individual governments. Interior's leasing policy is also geared to the best interests of big oil and gas lessees. Few questions are asked as long as the government gets a percentage of the revenues from the leased public lands. The Treasury and Interior Departments receive payments accruing from public leases and land sales; in fact, the Interior Department is an avid promoter of public land leases (Engler 1977, pp. 146-48).

The Interior Department not only supports Big Oil in its leasing policies, but simultaneously fails to protect the environment. Prior to the oil blowout in the Santa Barbara channel in 1969, there was much local and state opposition to offshore drilling because of ecological, aesthetic, and conservation concerns. Interior permitted this offshore drilling without first attempting to appraise potential ecological implications. The prime concern was the revenue to the federal treasury from the successful joint bids by Gulf, Texaco, Mobil, and Union. Interior assured the people in Santa Barbara that there was no need to fear because foolproof shutoff devices were in operation. Furthermore, Interior insisted that oil drilling not be postponed, because the companies had already obtained federal leasing rights.

To appease the anger of environmentalists following the blowout, the Western Oil and Gas Association gave a grant of $240,000 to the Allen Hancock Foundation of the University of Southern California. Findings from a study released by this foundation upheld the oil companies' claims that the blowout was an exceptional happening, and that there was no irreparable damage to sea life on the beach (Engler 1977, p. 149). The Santa Barbara claims for the oil spill ran into the billions. Union, Gulf, Texaco, and Mobil terminated a long legal battle by giving the city of Carpinteria a $9 million out-of-court settlement. In a separate settlement, these companies paid $4.5 million to beachfront property owners who had filed a class action suit against them. Each of the companies was also fined $500 after pleading guilty to one count of criminal pollution—hardly a formidable sanction. Three hundred and forty-two other counts stemming from the Santa Barbara blowout were dismissed by the municipal court, which explained that the companies had suffered enough from the civil judgments filed against them (New York *Times* 1974c, 1971b; *Wall Street Journal* 1972).

Even when the Interior Department moves against erring oil companies, the results are ineffectual. For example, in 1970, because of negligence, a Chevron platform in the Gulf of Mexico caught fire, resulting in a sizeable oil slick. Subsequent investigations demonstrated that many other offshore wells were also defective, and Secretary of the Interior Hickel moved to prosecute. Criminal indictments were handed down for 1,500 "willful" offenses. All nine companies pleaded *nolo contendere* ("no contest") and paid fines. Hickel's actions against Big Oil were unwelcomed by the White House, and he was soon replaced by Rogers C. B. Morton, a faithful spokesman for private industry, inclusive of the big oil companies (Engler 1977, pp. 197-98).

Interior does not have adequate knowledge concerning the extent and value of oil and gas reserves. Instead of developing its own surveying methods, it relies extensively upon geophysical data compiled by the oil industry and the

U.S. Geological Survey (an agency within the Department of Interior). In fact, corporations generally indicate the regions they desire the department to open up, and suggest the tracts which should be publicly leased. The U.S. Geological Survey purchases seismic data from oil corporations that gather their information jointly and make it available to the government on a proprietary basis, as well as from private seismic research companies. Presale underevaluation by Interior is often startling (Engler 1977, p. 158). A report of the General Accounting Office raised questions about conflicts of interest when 1974 financial disclosure statements showed that 22 percent of the U.S. Geological Survey staff held stock in or received pensions from the private oil and mining companies holding leases supervised by this agency (New York *Times* 1975a).

Interior has permitted oil companies to divide production and jointly bid for rights to operate lands in the state domain, such as the joint ventures in the Santa Barbara Channel (Engler 1977, p. 160). This appears to violate antitrust laws. Interior plays a reactive rather than an active role in leasing policy: Interior leases when the oil industry suggests property auctions. The government rarely decides which offshore or onshore areas should be opened first for bids. Studies have shown that 90 percent of all leases on public and Indian lands are inactive, and that most have never been put into production. Some of these leases have been bought for speculation or are being held for the future plans of the energy industry; thus public resources are being banked in private industry accounts. The Bureau of Land Management in the Interior Department has never moved to cancel a lease (Engler 1977, pp. 160–63).

Interior's leasing policies stem from the view that energy is a commodity rather than a resource, and that the oil industry rather than the public is its client. In 1968, for example, the deputy administrator of the department's Oil Import Administration wrote to the major oil companies and trade associations asking for support for his promotion to head that agency. The deputy administrator described how he had favored the major companies' position on strict control over imports, and had opposed the exemptions granted to the new oil companies (Washington *Post* 1968). Another factor underlying Interior's policies is the "revolving door" tradition, which ensures a steady interchange of personnel between industry, industry-oriented universities, oil law firms, and the government (Engler 1977, p. 171). Biographies of members of the department's Oil and Gas Office continue to show that most have had oil ties (U.S. House 1971, pp. 467–71). The case of oil clearly shows the symbiotic relationship between capitalistic and corporate agents in the commission of political crimes. Though from time to time there appear to be clashes between government agencies over the control of oil, the results are the same—little control.

Watergate Special Prosecution Force

Special investigative offices created under unusual circumstances or "national crises" have often failed to perform the duties expected of them, and have at times committed crimes (of omission) in this failure. The Watergate Special Prosecution Force released its final report on the Watergate scandal to the public in 1975, after 28 months of investigation at a cost of at least $7.7 million dollars. It had been ordered to provide the public with a full statement of all the criminal acts pertaining to the Watergate scandal. In actuality, the report reflects the failure of the Prosecution Force to fulfill its official obligation. The report was deceptive, misleading, and incomplete. Like the Warren Report, it appears to have been based on the notion that the public must retain confidence in the economic and political system as it now exists. Therefore, the offenses connected with Watergate had to be treated as merely passing aberrations not demanding fundamental change in the economic and political structure. Only 48 pages of the 888-page report described the main work of the special prosecutor, that is, the investigation, the charges, and the dispositions. The remaining 840 pages dealt with window-dressing in the form of observations and recommendations. Little information was presented about what the investigation uncovered, the offenders involved, what the evidence showed, how the evidence was evaluated, and the reasons why many were not indicted. Throughout the report it is stated that the prosecutors did not obtain sufficient evidence to bring criminal charges, but the report provided few details about "sufficient evidence." Richard Nixon's crimes were not recorded and there was neither any listing of the charges made against him nor details about his culpability in the cases under investigation. Such negligence was uncalled for because the prosecution's office has listened to 64 of the specially subpoenaed tapes, including 15 never published. The Special Prosecutor claimed, without legal basis, that he could not release any information in these cases where people were not indicted for specific crimes. This position was untenable and probably criminal, because the idea of full disclosure was specifically built into the prosecutor's office from the beginning. The prosecutor was, in fact, supposed to release full information on those not indicted or prosecuted as well as those indicted or prosecuted, along with the reasons for such action or nonaction. The Watergate Special Prosecution Force was authorized to provide the country with a full and reliable account of the Nixon administration's crimes, not to target a few high-placed offenders for trial. The prosecution force not only covered up important information but failed to perform its investigative duties. The Force did not employ investigators, but instead relied on the FBI and the IRS for all interviews and inquiries, despite the fact that both of these agencies were involved in the Nixon Administration's crimes. Furthermore, the prosecutors did not bring any charges against those who sought to thwart the force's investigations, even though witnesses often withheld information and perjured themselves. The force failed to bring charges against some of those involved in criminal conspiracy who were supposed to be ill or whose defense attorneys had talked them out of an indictment. The Special Prosecutor did not bring any multiple charges against people involved in more than one crime. For example, John Mitchell was charged only with the Watergate cover-up, but not for his probable perjury in the ITT case, his extra-legal authorizations of the White House wiretaps, his presumed services on behalf of various corporate campaign donors, campaign trickery, and his obvious connections with the Gemstone project, which designed and directed the Watergate burglary (Sale 1975b).

The Special Prosecutor failed to bring any charges in 60 percent of the investigations initiated by his office. He found no defendants in the crime of erasing the eighteen and one-half minutes from the June 26, 1972 White House tape. With the exception of the Fielding break-in, he found no one responsible for the White House plumbers' crimes. He failed to charge anyone for the abuses by the Internal Revenue Service, the Incumbency Responsiveness Program, the campaign sabotage by 26 Segretti agents in 18 states, the assaults by federal law enforcement agents on antiwar protesters, the Rebozo-Hughes slush fund (used for campaign contributions to Richard Nixon's 1972 campaign), the pardon of Nixon by Ford, or the planning and execution of the original Watergate burglaries. Many of those involved in the Watergate cover-up were not mentioned in the report, including Earl Silbert, the original Watergate prosecutor, Assistant Attorney General Henry Peterson, L. Patrick Gray, and Attorney General Kleindienst (who probably was guilty of obstruction of justice for not disclosing information he had from the beginning about the involvement of the White House in the Waterbugging). Neither the CIA's nor the FBI's offenses in limiting the Watergate investigations were recorded. Finally, the Special Prosecutor failed to prosecute either former Justice Department officials Richard McLaren and Erwin Griswold for allegedly lying to Congress in the ITT case, or the Associated Milk Producers for influencing President Nixon's decision to raise dairy price supports in 1972 (Jackson 1978; Sale 1975b).

Police Corruption

Police corruption has frequently entailed crimes of evasion and collusion. The police have often failed to enforce many laws for personal and political reasons, and have often broken laws that they were supposed to enforce. When confronted by the public or investigators of police departments for wrongdoing, police officers respond with several defensive claims: they have not done anything wrong; they had to bend the law in order to enforce it; the goodies, graft, or illegal largesse they received was due them for maintaining and negotiating social order; and the public did not want certain laws enforced (Roebuck and Barker 1974).

Police corruption may be defined as any type of proscribed behavior engaged in by a law enforcement officer who receives or expects to receive, by virtue of his official position, an actual or potential unauthorized material reward or gain. The following behaviors by police officers constitute police corruption: violations of formal (written) police departmental administrative rules, laws, regulations, and policies, violations of informal (general operating) rules, and violations of criminal laws (Barker and Roebuck 1973, pp. 8-9). Writings on police corruption have been generally descriptive and piecemeal accounts by muckraking journalists and exposed corrupt officers. Scholars in the social and behavioral sciences have usually ignored such corruption, although a few sketchy participant accounts about deviant police behavior are available. Writers on police corruption have tended to view police crime and misconduct as the illegal behavior of corrupt individuals ("rotten apples") operating within an otherwise lawful and orderly police organization. Such a naive view neglects the linkages between the individual transgressors and the police organization of which these individuals are a part; in short, the structural and organizational elements of police corruption (Barker and Roebuck 1973, pp. 4-6).

The law enforcement system of the United States engenders built-in corrupt practices endemic to bureaucratic police organization in a democracy. Law enforcement is a subsystem within the legal system which includes the public prosecutor, legal counsel, the judiciary, and corrections. There is nowhere within this legal system a formal provision for the organizational subordination of one subsystem to the others. There is no way that decisions in any one subsystem can be directly and effectively enforced in others by administrative or other organizational sanctions. Those subsystems are loosely articulated units in the legal system and possess divergent ends. Therefore, in both internal structure and external relationships, conflicts between subsystems often arise as to the means which each may use to achieve its immediate organizational ends; for example, the police and judges may hold conflicting views in matters of arrest and due process procedures. Because no subsystem in the legal system is subordinate to another, wide discretion is granted to participants in each subsystem in order to insure that the law is enforced and adjudicated fairly. Given the conflicts among subsystems within the legal system, the police (as well as other officials in the criminal justice system) may abuse this discretion as a matter of policy (Reiss and Black 1967).

Further, the recent increase of bureaucratic enabling regulations and the increased efforts to professionalize police organizations in the United States have logically led to further discretionary innovations as well as administrative efficiency. Bureaucratization and professionalization frequently do not mesh with due process of law. The police may violate the law to enforce the law—for example, break into businesses and private dwellings to install electronic surveillance devices, make illegal harassment arrests, allow fences and bootleggers to operate, tap phones, pay off informers, reduce charges to insure convictions, and underenforce or not enforce certain laws. Ample evidence exists pointing to such violations by the police (Barker and Roebuck 1973; Skolnick 1967, pp. 230-45). These acts, when routinized in police practices, are readily convertible to personal gain or corrupt practices. In short, the personal transgressions of individual corrupt policemen are engendered by the structure of the legal system.

Police departments are often labeled deviant organizations as a consequence of the discovered and labeled behavior of some of their members. Whenever police officers are exposed for engaging in corrupt acts, they receive extensive coverage in the news media. Frequently, this exposure sullies the reputation of the whole organization in that the deviant label is applied to the total membership. Police organizations may support corrupt activities of their memberships through the use of cover-up tactics. For several reasons, some police organizations are reluctant to expose, label, and publicly punish their own members for violations which result in automatic sanction for non-members. Personally honest police chiefs will go to extraordinary lengths to shield corrupt officers within the ranks of their organizations. Sanctioned officers may be secretly tried, warned, punished, transferred to another departmental unit or assignment, or permitted to resign in lieu of dismissal or prosecution. These procedures support corrupt behavior because an officer, after weighing the risk and gain involved in a contemplated proscribed act, might decide that the gain would outweigh the risk of being caught and mildly sanctioned.

The norms and values of the police organization may covertly support or condone selected deviant or criminal police practices. Policemen may witness corrupt practices on the part of fellow officers (acts they condemn), but fail to report because of a sense of comradeship with the erring policeman, or because of the organization's norm of secrecy about squealing or reporting fellow officers for misconduct. Often, in these circumstances, officers will either lie or equivocate about the deviant transaction or claim a lack of knowledge about it. The consistent norms of secrecy inhering in police organizations therefore support police solidarity and, simultaneously, corruption (Barker and Roebuck 1973, pp. 10–20; Reiss 1972, p. 213).

Forms of Police Corruption

Barker and Roebuck (1973, pp. 21–42), in a participant-observation research project, found eight types of police corruption in one large southern city: corruption of authority; kickbacks; opportunistic thefts from arrestees, victims, crime scenes, and unprotected property; shakedowns; protection of illegal activities; the fix; direct criminal activities; and internal payoffs. This typology was supported by secondary evidence that these eight kinds of corrupt offenses exist in other cities throughout the United States. In this study, the peer group was considered a microcosm of the police organization, and peer group support for corrupt and illegal acts was assumed to reflect organizational support. The police peer group was defined as all working policemen within a specific police organization.

Police departments have been described by scholars as closed societies jealous of their rights and prerogatives, resentful of criticism and outside meddling, and anchored in tradition. Moreover, police departments function as closed societies with the help of the following enabling characteristics: clannishness on and off duty; strong social identity within an occupational milieu, including a particular argot and a conception of themselves as socially isolated; internal promotion from top to bottom positions which insures that all police personnel at one time or another experience similar occupational situations; local recruitment from the same social stratum (generally lower-middle class); and familial and ethnic ties in many departments. The assumed organizational support does not mean that all police organizations approve of all corrupt police practices, although most police administrators privately admit that the eradication of all types of corrupt police practices is not feasible. Police administrators are really concerned with how much and what types of corrupt police behavior should be permitted (Niederhoffer 1969, p. 176). It was assumed that peer group acceptance of, indifference to, or concern with corrupt police practices reflects the prevailing political and economic norms of the communities in which policemen work. A general description of Barker and Roebuck's (1973, pp. 21-41) abstracted types follows.

Corruption of Authority. The officer's authority is corrupted when he receives officially unauthorized, unearned material gain by virtue of his position as a police officer without violating the criminal law *per se*. Ostensibly, the officer receives free meals, liquor, commercial sex, free admissions to entertainment, police discounts on merchandise, services or other material inducements because the corruptors supposedly like the police.

In other studies conducted in Boston, Chicago, and Washington, D.C., 31 percent of all businessmen surveyed in wholesale or retail trade or business and repair services openly acknowledged favors to the police. Of these, 43 percent gave free merchandise, food, or services to all policemen, and the remainder did so at discount. Presentation of self in uniform was all that was necessary to secure these benefits (Reiss 1972, pp. 161-62). Other rewards which violated departmental rules and regulations included payments by businessmen to police for property protection beyond routine duties, secret payments by property owners to police for arresting robbers and burglars at their establishments, and finders fee payments by bondsmen bounty hunters to police for the arrest and notification of bond jumpers.

In the preceding cases some remunerations were directly solicited, some were suggested, and some were unsolicited. The corruptors, for the most part, were respectable citizens showing their gratitude for efficient police work. Even when the intentions of the corruptor appear honorable, the officer's authority is corrupted because the acceptance of unauthorized goods and services obligates him to the corruptor. Most officers are aware that acceptance compromises their authority. Within the department, corrupt acts of this sort are defined as violations of departmental regulations, but not as criminal violations. Most police peer groups accept these gratuities (goodies), which they do not define as corrupt when received from noncriminals of high status. Many officers believe that they are entitled to these informal remunerations as fringe benefits. In departments where the acceptance of gratuities is a routinized custom, the officer who refuses to accept them is frequently considered a deviant by his peer group. Many police departments, though publicly disavowing this behavior, accept it as a system of informal rewards, particularly if the officers receiving the gratuities are otherwise acceptable to the department, and if the corruptors are respectable citizens and adept at smoothly and surreptitiously rendering the awards. It was found that informal police organizational policy usually condones these gratuitous practices.

Kickbacks. In many communities police officers receive goods and services or money for referring business to towing companies, ambulances, garages, lawyers, doctors, bondsmen, undertakers, taxi-cabs, service stations, moving companies, and others anxious to sell services or goods to persons with whom the police interact during their routine patrol (President's Commission on Law Enforcement and Administration of Justice 1967). Corruptors are usually legitimate businessmen and professionals who stand to gain through a good working relationship with the police. Within some departments, officers seek and compete for certain work assignments because of the availability of kickbacks in such details as traffic accident investigation (especially those units that investigate serious injuries and fatalities, which almost always result in civil litigation encouraging a lawyer-police conspiracy); complaint desk assignments (lawyers-bondsmen-police conspiracy); and bond details (bondsmen-police conspiracy). Kickbacks violate departmental norms and sometimes criminal laws, but are not generally defined, processed, or acted upon as criminal violations.

The peer group may support kickbacks from legitimate businessmen as clean fringe benefits earned by virtue of their position. Many officers who refuse all kickbacks are labeled deviant by peer groups. The degree of peer group support depends on the following contingencies: trustworthiness, reputation, status, and affluence of the corruptor; adeptness of the corruptor in presenting his rewards as clean money; and the secrecy of the situation between the corruptor and corruptee. Many departments condone or overlook kickbacks so long as the corruptor is a legitimate businessman or professional, the corrupted officer is otherwise acceptable to the department, and the value of the goods and services is held to a minimum. However, some departments react negatively to kickbacks in cash. A department's condonation of kickbacks is based on the following situational contingencies: informal definition of clean money, discretionary measures utilized by corruptors and corrupted, and the status and reputation of the corruptor. In communities where such working arrangements are traditional among policemen, businessmen, and professionals, the police establishment may offend the legitimate business and professional community by strong, overt reaction.

Opportunistic Theft. Thefts from arrestees, victims, crime scenes, and unprotected property do not involve any corruptor; only the corrupt officer and unsuspecting victims. Rolled arrestees, traffic accident victims, and unconscious or dead citizens are unaware of the act. Officers investigating burglaries may take merchandise or money left behind by the original thief. Officers may also take items from unprotected property sites discovered during routine security patrol; for example, merchandise or money from unlocked businesses, building supplies from construction locations, and unguarded items from businesses or industrial establishments. Finally, policemen may keep a portion of the confiscated evidence they discover during raids, such as money, liquor, narcotics, and property. All of these behaviors violate departmental and criminal norms. Peer group support rests on an informal policy of accepting or rejecting clean money, the definition of clean money (the smaller the amount of money and the smaller the worth of the article taken, the cleaner the money) and dirty money, and the umbrella of secrecy within the situation.

Shakedowns. Shakedowns arise opportunistically when an officer inadvertantly witnesses or gains knowledge of a criminal violation and violator, and subsequently accepts a bribe for not making an arrest. The corruptor may be a respectable citizen who offers a bribe to an officer to avoid a traffic charge, or a criminal adventitiously caught in the commission of an illegal act who induces the officer to free him. Many professional criminals carry what is known in the criminal argot as "fall money," a sum carried on the person that can be used to bribe an officer should they be apprehended while committing a crime. For example, professional burglars frequently carry one or two thousand dollars in their pockets to pay off police at the scene of the criminal act should they be arrested. The burglar drops the stolen merchandise, pays off the police and walks away. Shakedowns are engaged in with relative impunity because the victim is unlikely to complain when he is apprehended in some kind of illegal activity. Shakedowns violate both departmental and criminal norms and are punishable under bribery statutes. The corruptor and the officer are equally guilty of a crime.

Officers who take bribes from transports of contraband such as gambling paraphernalia, gambling money found at the scene of the infraction, bootleg liquor, soft drugs, and money from traffic violators are not considered deviant among peer groups who make distinctions between clean and dirty money. Even officers who do not engage in any forms of corruption are likely to maintain a code of silence when learning of these acts. On the other hand, taking bribes from certain kinds of felons (narcotic pushers and robbers) is considered deviant by many police peer groups because the money is dirty.

Protection of Illegal Activities. In this type corruptors are organized criminals actively engaged in systematic illegal activities who seek to operate without police harassment by bribing members of the police organization. So-called victimless crimes (frequently in violation of unenforceable laws), including vice operations (pertaining to gambling, illegal drug sales, prostitution, liqur violations, abortion rings, pornography rings, homosexual establishments, after-hours clubs), frequently designate police-protected enterprises. Officers in some departments also receive protection payoffs from professional criminals, including robbers, burglars, jewel thieves, confidence men, fences, and forgers. Legitimate businesses operating illegally often pay for protection; for example, some cab companies and individual cab drivers pay police officers for illegal permission to operate outside prescribed routes and areas, to pick up and discharge fares at unauthorized sites, to operate cabs that do not meet safety and cleanliness standards, or to operate without proper licensing procedures. Trucking firms pay for the privilege of hauling overloaded cargoes and driving off prescribed truck routes. Legitimate businesses may pay police officers to avoid Sunday blue laws. Construction companies in some cities pay police officers to overlook violations of city regulations, such as trucks blocking traffic, violating pollution guidelines (burning trash, creating dust), destroying city property, and blocking sidewalks. Regular operation of all of the above enterprises exemplifies police collusion with illegal corruptors. Many police departments are corrupted by organized criminals' organizations. Police collusions and conspiracies with illegal and legal enterprises, organized criminals, and professional criminals break both formal departmental and criminal norms.

Peer group support is dependent on the peer group's policy of accepting or rejecting clean money, the informal definition of clean and dirty money, the trustworthiness, status (position, respectability, influence, prestige, authority and power in the underworld and/or upperworld) and affluence of the corruptor, and the situational facility of secret and secure transactions. Police who receive protection money as well as many community members view some forms of this type of corruption as a necessary, regulated, patterned evasion; that is, a publicly accepted norm is covertly violated on a large scale with the tacit acceptance or approval of the same society or group, as long as such corruption is concealed (Reiss 1968). Although the community may desire the illegal services and goods regulated by protection money, officers (even those not on the take) who fail to enforce the law in this type are compromised and corrupted by inaction. Those officers who attempt to enforce unsupported laws may be thwarted. For example, arrestees are freed because of insufficient evidence, small fines or sentences are dispensed, judges and prosecuting attorneys chastise and discourage officers for overzealousness in this area, and cases are quashed (or "nolle prossed").

Protection of vice operators may be so complete in some departments that officers who inadvertantly arrest protected operators must pay a fine to the corrupt officers who have illegally licensed the vice operators. Protection money also requires illegal, routinized, departmental sanctions against uncooperating operators. Such sanctions vary from harassment and arrest to assault. There is usually a distribution of payoffs, with all members of vice details receiving pro-rated shares of the action. Protection money organization may resemble an interlocking bureaucracy as a suborganization representing the police and organized crime. The degree and extent of organization may (and often does) penetrate other municipal government institutions (Smith 1965; Messick 1968; Gardiner 1970).

Another study of policemen on the take (receiving pay-offs from organized criminals engaged in vice operations) indicates that such policemen have completely rationalized away being on the take as a necessary regulatory service. These policemen were law and order men down the line when dealing with shoplifting, robbery, assault, homicide, public drunkenness, and political crime (parades, sit-ins, demonstrations, public protests, and marches). A typical quote from one of these respondents illustrates selective law breaking and support for the established political system:

> If the courts and the civil liberty boys would leave the city fathers and the police alone, we could clean up crime off the streets. We could even make it safe for women and little children to come and go as they please. But these damned due process people. They don't realize that you got to play rough with the scum. So you bend a rule here and there. So you beat up a few now and then. You got to forget about legal rights sometime. Scum have no legal rights anyway. Take these agitators and demonstrators, they're a bunch of dirty pinko slobs. If we could shoot a few down, we wouldn't have any more trouble. Those bums get in the way and make it hard for us to run an orderly city (Roebuck and Frese 1976, p. 196).

An official, strict law and order policy frequently results in crime.

These men on the take proclaimed that certain aspects of the underworld and its services (prostitution, gambling, illegal liquor, illegal after-hours clubs, and so on) were necessary evils that had to be regulated rather than eliminated. Viewing themselves as realistic regulators of vice in their city (a northeastern city of more than two million people), they felt entitled to certain rewards, over and above those conferred by official status, from both the upperworld and underworld. These policemen drew a clear-cut distinction between clean money (free services and goods, kickbacks, and protection money received from prestigious legitimate and illegitimate businessmen) and dirty money (gained from direct criminal activities such as theft, burglary, robbery, extortion, and shakedowns). As one corrupt policeman stated:

> We're honest civil servants. We don't take any dirty money. If we caught policemen robbing and stealing, we'd turn them in in a minute. I never stole a dime on the beat. Clean money is a different matter. I was five years an altar boy and never stole a candle (Roebuck and Frese 1976, p. 197).

Departmental reaction to the protection of illegal activities hinges on the degree of its involvement with criminal organizations or legitimate businesses that operate illegally, its informal definition of clean money, the identity of the corruptor, and whether or not there is public disclosure of flagrant violations. If department involvement is deep and widespread, exposed and publicly identified officers will usually be allowed to resign as quietly as possible in order to prevent any large-scale outside investigations. On the other hand, should strong pressure for sanctions be exerted by legal systems and community organizations without the police establishment (local district attorneys, investigating commissions, county and state police agencies, chambers of commerce, or news media), the disclosed officers are usually dismissed and criminally charged. The few that are charged are rarely convicted, and those convicted rarely do time. Those sanctioned usually accept their fate as an occupational hazard. Furthermore, those few who wish to testify and implicate others are rarely able to support sufficient evidence to invoke indictments of their peers or supervisors who are also on the take. The code of silence helps here. Few yellow canaries sing, and for those who do there are few around to support the song.

Police deparments with informal policies that condone the acceptance of protection money attempt to block investigations, at times with the aid of criminals and other corrupt legal systems (corrupt district attorneys, mayors, political bosses, and city, county, and state officials) within the administration of justice. Aid in this direction may take the form of physical violence against persons or property, or devious legal and administrative procedures within or without the police organization (Messick 1968).

The Fix. Two sub-types constitute the fix: the quashing of prosecution proceedings following the offender's arrest, and the taking up (disposal of record) of traffic tickets. Corruptors are arrestees attempting to avoid blemished driving records. The fixer in criminal cases is often a detective or some other designated police officer who conducts or controls the investigation upon which the prosecution proceedings are based. The optimum period to fix a criminal case is prior to the preliminary hearing. Should the case proceed to the grand jury or trial court stage, it becomes more difficult and more expensive to effect. Therefore, investigating police officers are in the most advantageous position to effect the fix, though district attorneys and judges may be involved at later stages. The investigating officer usually agrees to "sell" the case, that is, withdraw prosecution in return for some material reward. He either fails to request prosecution, tampers with existing evidence, or gives perjured testimony. The case may be sold directly to the criminal by the investigating officer or negotiated by a go-between—jailer, lawyer, police officer, or bail bondsman. For example, William Chambliss (1969, p. 94) reports the case of a professional safecracker who was able to avoid prosecution in all but five of 300 arrests spanning a 40-year period. In some police departments it is even possible to fix homicide cases and felonious aggravated assaults against police officers (*New York Times Magazine* 1971, p. 44).

The traffic fixer is usually the ticketing officer who subsequently agrees to dispose of the ticket for a fee. Other police officers who have control of the traffic ticketing process at any time after the original citation (supervisory officers or desk sergeants who have access to ticket records) may also fix tickets. Contact with the fixer may be made directly by the citizen or by a designated middleman, such as another police officer. The fix (both sub-types) violates departmental and criminal norms.

Peer groups overtly oppose the sale of felony cases; however, a conspiracy of silence in some police departments lends covert support to individual officers who might engage in this activity. The selling of misdemeanor cases and the fixing of traffic tickets is not as seriously frowned upon in those peer groups that accept clean money.

Direct Criminal Activities. This type involves no corruptor. Policemen directly commit crimes against the persons or property of another for material gain—acts which are clear violations of both departmental and criminal norms. These actions usually receive little or no support from most police peer groups, not even those engaged in other types of corruption. Direct criminal activities (burglary and robbery) are defined as extreme forms of dirty money crimes, and those who commit them do so at great peril from uninvolved colleagues on the force. Generally, a small peer-group organization commits this type. Groups of police officers operate (as burglars and robbers) in small working groups similar to the *modus operandi* of professional criminals. Since 1960, a number of police burglary rings have been uncovered in several police departments throughout the United States (Cook 1966, p. 243; Wilson 1970). Departments that tolerate other forms of corruption usually prosecute and send to prison officers discovered engaging in direct criminal activities. Direct criminal activities are just too highly visible. Morality doesn't seem to be the case of point, because many policemen pay their "regular snitches" (informers) whom they know to be engaging in criminal activity—usually criminal behavior other than that immediately under investigation.

Internal Payoffs. Internal payoffs regulate a market where police officers' prerogatives may be bought, bartered, or sold (Burnham 1970, p. 18). Actors in this type, both corruptors and corrupted, are exclusively police officers. Prerogatives negotiated encompass work assignments, off-days, holidays, vacation periods, control of evidence, and promotion. Officers who administer the distribution of assignments and personnel may collect fees for assigning officers to certain divisions, precincts, units, details, shifts, and beats, and for insuring that certain personnel are retained in, transferred from, or excluded from certain work assignments. In some departments where members receive protection money from vice operations, officers contact command personnel and bid for lucrative assignments. Usually, everything else being equal, the profitable assignments go to the highest bidder. Certain off-days and selected vacation periods are sometimes sold by supervisory personnel; an officer who wishes to be off on the weekend, who wishes to avoid split off-days, or who desires a vacation during peak summer months may pay a supervisor for these privileges. Members of a police department whose prerogatives include the control of criminal evidence (investigating officers, detectives, evidence technicians, and desk sergeants) may sell wiretaps, fingerprints, forged documents, contraband, and other physical evidence or instrumentalities of a crime to an officer, who in turn uses it in a shakedown or fix (*Newsweek* 1971).

Most peer groups do not support this blatant and criminal activity which exploits and victimizes them. On the other hand, some peer groups engaged in other types of illegal corruption (protection money, shakedowns, and fixes) accept internal payoffs as necessary and inevitable. Internal payoffs, when found, are highly organized activities within departments engaged in other illegal types of corruption. This final type of police corruption marks the last step in the progression to a thoroughly deviant and criminal police organization.

These eight types of police corruption are arranged in a hierarchical fashion from rule breaking to lawless behavior, and suggest a progressive process in dynamics, accretion, and gravity—a process that might be checked or altered at any one or more levels of progression according to the tolerance limits of the police organization or the community. In departments where several types of corrupt behavior exist, the police department operates in a systematically lawless manner (Berker and Roebuck 1973, p. 38). Evidence shows that police corruption constitutes a form of organizational crime. Chambliss (1976, pp. 162–63) found police corruption in a West Coast city to be a portion of a larger system of relationships that were pursued for profit. These vices, he points out, were organized around, run by, and created in the interests of economic, legal, and political elites. The cabal that managed the vices was composed of important businessmen, law enforcement officers, political leaders, and a member of a major trade union. Working for and with this cabal of respectable community members was a staff which coordinated the daily activities of prostitution, book making, the sale and distribution of drugs, and other vices. Representatives from each of these groups met regularly to distribute profits, discuss problems, and to make the necessary organizational and policy decisions essential to the mainte- nance of a profitable, trouble-free business. Finally, it appears that city police throughout the United States are primarily concerned with public order crimes, violent crimes, crimes that interfere with propriety or civil order, property rights, everyday citizen activities on the street, and any public demonstration, marches, boycotts (legal or illegal), sit-ins, or protests which appear to disrupt the established economic and political order. In short, they function as centurions for the upper class.

Official Corruption

Legislative and Executive Corruption

Corruption by public officials parallels that of the police in many ways, though there are differences. Police in the main receive bribes and payoffs from members of the underworld, whereas public officials receive such illegal pay- ments from corporate organizations. Illegal payments to police are miniscule in comparison to those made to public officials. Public officials, by virtue of their position and contacts, are in a position to trade favors for illegal personal gain. Bobby Baker and Thomas Dodd were among those convicted in the 1960s for using their public offices to gain unauthorized profits and perquisites. Baker, who was secretary to Lyndon Johnson when Johnson was Senate majority leader, was indicted for fraud, larceny, and tax evasion. The major charge was that he collected $100,000 from a group of California savings and loan executives to be used as campaign contributions, and then kept $80,000 of this sum for his own use (Green et al. 1975, pp. 176-78). Baker was finally convicted on seven counts of income tax evasion, theft, and conspiracy to defraud the United States in 1967 (New York *Times* 1967b).

U.S. Senator Thomas Dodd engaged openly in corrupt behavior. He pocketed for private use at least $160,000 raised at campaign dinners, supposedly for campaign expenses; he double-billed the government for his travel expenses, keeping the surplus; he took repeated private vacations at the government expense; he used his office to promote the career of a retired major general who was a propagandist for German right-wingers; and he accepted money from private firms and then pressured government agencies to give these firms special treatment. Dodd was eventually convicted of conspiracy, perjury, and bribery for accepting a $25,000 payment to thwart an investigation of Monarch Construction Corporation, a firm which had swindled Washington, D.C. residents for hundreds of home repair jobs between 1963 and 1965 (Green et al. 1975, pp. 180-84).

In 1973, Vice-President Spiro Agnew acknowledged that he awarded government contracts to Baltimore County engineers in return for $87,500 in kickbacks from 1962 to 1972. He resigned October 10, 1973, pleading no contest to one count of tax evasion stemming from his acceptance of these kickbacks while governor of Maryland. Agnew was placed on three years unsupervised probation and fined $10,000, despite the fact that Justice Department officials had the evidence to convict him on several counts of bribery, conspiracy, and extortion. In the end, they settled for Agnew's no contest plea coupled with his resignation (Ripley 1973; Goeller 1978).

Richard Nixon unlawfully received compensation in the form of government expenditures exceeding $2 million at his privately-owned properties near San Clemente, California and Key Biscayne, Florida. Further, he failed to report certain income, and incorrectly claimed federal income tax deductions for a gift of personal papers to the United States valued at $576,000 (U.S. House 1975, pp. 17-18, 316-20, 462-63). He still owes the Treasury for part of these back taxes.

Though the House of Representatives and the Senate have established ethics committees to crack down on corrupt, illegal, and unethical conduct, these committees have proven ineffective. Congress has proven unwilling to regulate itself and its ethics committees have refused to investigate crimes committed by congressmen. Congress has left to the press and prosecuting attorneys the job of digging up evidence that has resulted in criminal charges against a dozen senators and representatives. Half of this number have been found guilty, two are awaiting trial, and at least four were under investigation in 1976 (Anderson 1976e). Representative Andrew Hinshaw of California was convicted on two bribery counts, and in 1976 faced a second trial on conspiracy charges. Hinshaw arranged government raises for staff aides who, in turn, contributed to his legal defense fund. He used his congressional power to badger witnesses for information helpful to his defense. When members of the Justice Department, FBI, and Postal Service testified before his committee, he cross-examined them for information that he might use later at his trial. At least three members of Congress have been convicted by the courts of trading favors for cash, but have been overlooked by the ethics committees: Senator Daniel Brewster of Maryland, Representative John Dowdy of Texas, and Representative Hinshaw. Representative Henry Helstoski has been indicted on charges of extorting money from aliens residing in the United States illegally, in exchange for sponsoring immigration legislation on their behalf (Anderson 1976e).

Corporations are not permitted under law to make direct campaign contributions to congressmen. However, Jack Anderson claims that his staff has counted 45 members of Congress (some of the biggest congressional names) who have received corporate contributions. According to him, many senators and representatives also engage in the pursuit of capital gains whose profits are affected by legislation. Others trade on the stock market, and buy and sell shares of companies whose profits they influence. Some members of Congress have become rich through their influence over the government regulatory commissions; for example, some own broadcasting stations that are regulated by the Federal Communications Commission. Still others have holdings in gas and electric companies, which are regulated by the Federal Power Commission. Many congressmen own large shares of stock in savings and loan companies, an industry that has benefited from special congressional legislation. The records at the Federal Reserve Board list the names of a dozen congressmen and their relatives who own large shares of stock in the banking business. More than 100 House members collect payments, law fees, or dividends from financial institutions, and there is a concentration of interest-free federal deposits in banks affiliated with congressmen. Congressmen vote appropriations for federal agencies, and these agencies deposit money, interest free, in commercial banks. Henry Reuss of Wisconsin, House Banking Committee chairman, for example, owned a substantial interest in the Marshall and Isley Bank Stock Corporation, a holding company which controls 14 banks. Prior to Reuss's power over banking legislation, Marshall and Isley attracted few interest-free deposits (Anderson 1976e).

Large landowners in Congress use their power to keep the living conditions of migratory farm workers at a low level, while insuring large profits for themselves through high crop price supports, which were intended to save small farms but now serve to subsidize big landholdings. Congressmen also engage in nepotism by hiring one another's relatives and friends. Yet another payroll padding scheme has been outlawed but still persists. It is illegal for members of Congress to demand or receive kickbacks from their employees, though from time to time a congressman is caught receiving them. For example, Representative J. Irving Whalley of Pennsylvania, guilty of this misconduct, was convicted in 1973, technically for obstructing justice (Anderson 1976e).

These corrupt practices, much like police corruption, are linked to a larger system of organized corruption that is pursued for profit—organizational crime. Evidence shows, for example, that the profitable exploits of Nixon and Agnew were not simply blotches on the records of these individuals, but rather were integral to a larger system of lucrative official favors and back-scratchings (Sale 1973; Quinney 1975, pp. 159-61). As another example, Maryland governor Marvin Mandel was convicted in 1978 by a federal grand jury and sentenced to four years in prison for his part in a mail fraud scheme in his home state. Mandel and five co-defendents were convicted of conspiring to enhance the value of a racetrack owned by some of the defendants. The governor received $350,000 in gifts for his political help (Hoenig 1977). Criminal political corruption cases of recent years extend well beyond the old-style, cash-on-the-barrelhead bribes that used to be given in exchange for a government contract. Instead, they often involve a complex relationship between special favors and gifts, campaign contributions, or investment shares. In order to bring these cases into federal court, prosecutors must use mail fraud statutes and laws designed to prevent labor racketeering. These complex cases require thousands of government documents to prove that gifts or payoffs to politicians are illegally exchanged for political favors (*Clarion-Ledger* 1977i).

Bureaucratic Corruption

Employees of the General Services Administration (GSA), during the period 1972-78, awarded hundreds of thousands of dollars for the repair and alteration of federal buildings to non-existent companies and companies that do not perform the work paid for. This information was revealed in a GSA and FBI investigation, which has yet to trace any bribe or kickback money received by GSA employees in the fraud scheme. GSA and FBI investigators believe that anyone connected with the paying or receiving of GSA money for work not performed is liable to criminal prosecution. A federal grand jury in Washington issued subpoenas for GSA contracts and other documents, and the FBI broadened its investigation to federal contracts awarded by other federal agencies and in other U.S. cities. The General Services Administration awards contracts for the construction, leasing, and repairing of U.S. government offices. GSA spends $4.5 billion a year for government supplies, including nearly $250 million to repair, alter, and operate federal buildings in the Washington area. Managers of these buildings have authority to award the individual repair and alteration contracts, often without competitive bidding, in amounts of $10,000 or less. A number of the suspected fraudulent contracts are of this type, although others involve larger amounts (Kessler 1978).

This fraud has taken a number of forms. One scheme involved awarding and paying for a contract for two coats of paint when only one was needed and applied; another involved contracting to install 20,000 square feet of tile on a 10,000 square-foot floor. In some cases, contracts have been awarded to private firms when the work has actually been performed by GSA employees. In other cases, several contracts have been awarded to perform a single job. In one instance, GSA contracted to paint a wall seven times in five years. Laboratory tests on the layers of paint determined that most of the coats contracted for had never been applied. GSA contracts have been awarded both to legitimate contracting firms and to "shell" companies with private residences as addresses. One "company" receiving contracts consisted of two former GSA employees. Some companies have received hundreds of contracts over several years to perform work on a single building. Such fraudulent contracting practices were uncovered when a GSA employee in Chicago was convicted in 1976 for awarding fraudulent repair contracts. Several other cases are under investigation (Kessler 1978).

A confidential internal audit of the Nuclear Regulatory Commission (NRC) has shown that this agency manipulated personnel and pay records in an effort to conceal the existence of a large force of outside consultants. On June 30, 1976, the NRC had a personnel ceiling of 300, but also had 469 non-permanent employees (including consultants) who could have been counted against this ceiling. To avoid going over the ceiling, only ten of the 75 consultants who submitted expense vouchers for the month of June were actually paid that month. The other consultants had to wait until the next month to be paid, because it began a new fiscal year. Holding consultants' vouchers to avoid exceeding the ceiling violated federal regulations established by the Office of Management and Budget, which sets limits on the staffs of all federal agencies. In March 1977, NRC was heading toward the same situation. This agency had 209 consultants in addition to 400 other employees who counted against a personnel ceiling of 300. Two NRC consultants were paid $465 a day, though a consultant's pay at this time was limited by law to $152 a day. This was arranged by hiring the consultants through regular channels without pay while contracting with the regular employers to reimburse them. The NRC also paid former Congressmen William Cole and Alfred Westland a total of $186,000 over a period of two and one-half years, though neither had a personnel file at the commission. The NRC's legal director had ruled that these two consultants' duties were more promotional than regulatory, and that their jobs should have been transferred elsewhere. Mr. Cole, a Republican congressman from New York for 22 years, and a director of the International Atomic Energy Agency, was appointed by President Nixon to the Western Interstate Nuclear Board in 1970. Both boards were organizations of state officials, and they were originally designed to promote the use of nuclear energy. Cole and Westland served as federal liaisons with state governments, reporting to the president through the chairman of the Atomic Energy Commission (Thomas 1978).

In another case of bureaucratic corruption, a Justice Department report released in 1978 disclosed that FBI employees painted former director J. Edgar Hoover's house yearly, replaced his lawn sod twice a year, gave him tax advice, and prepared his annual return. The Justice Department also reported that several FBI officials were provided with goods and services by the bureau; that the FBI's substantial electronic business was improperly funneled to one firm; and that various FBI funds were misused. FBI employees called upon to perform extra services often did not think them to be proper, but felt compelled to follow orders for fear of losing their jobs or receiving arbitrary transfers. One employee who complained about the suspect relationship between the FBI and its major electronics supplier was denied promotion and transferred to the Tampa office. The special agent in charge there was told that the employee was not a good "team player" and that he did not get along well with co-workers. These FBI activities violated several criminal statutes, but will not be prosecuted because the five-year statute of limitations has run out (*Clarion-Ledger* 1978a).

GOAL OF THE OFFENDER

The common aim of the five sub-types of corruption discussed in this chapter was to circumvent or inhibit the full implementation of regulatory or criminal law in order to make money or to secure protection from public exposure and possible prosecutions. All of these offender groups utilized collusive techniques. Unlike offenders engaging in intervention, surveillance, and confrontation offenses, this offender group sought to receive officiallly unauthorized, unearned material gain, or to escape from regulation and prosecution, by virtue of official position or economic power.

The confessed aim of officials' denial of responsibility has been to protect national security by keeping U.S. state secrets secure from hostile foreign nations. The real purpose for the denial of responsibility has been to keep the truth about official blunders from the U.S. public. The proclaimed objective of government regulatory agencies and commissions has been to regulate big business in the public interest without endangering the U.S. economy. In response to criticisms about failures to regulate, these agencies have issued a series of spurious and contradictory disclaimers: present regulatory procedures are adequate; overregulation hurts the corporations who in turn employ less people; overregulation thwarts competition in an open economy; overregulation amounts to socialistic economic planning; overzealous regulation impairs the essential friendly relationship between big business and government; overregulation disrupts corporate efficiency; small staffs and inadequate funding stymy the efforts to regulate. The real goal of so-called government regulators has been to aid big business escape government regulation. As a case in point, the various government bodies reponsible for regulating the oil industry claim that oil is regulated in the best interests of the American people, the oil industry, and the U.S. government. Corporate agents wholeheartedly agree. Nevertheless, the object lesson of oil clearly shows that government department and regulatory agency policies and procedures are formulated and implemented by teams of government and corporate agents in such a manner as to perpetuate a vertically integrated oil industry—a monopoly beneficial to the oil cartel but detrimental to the consumer.

The professed intentions of the Watergate Special Prosecutor's Office were to file a complete report on the Watergate complexus, and to investigate, charge, and convict key principal actors in the scandal. The true aim of this office was to heal the wounds of Watergate in support of the existing economic and political system. Efforts geared toward this objective covered up illegal, evasive, and collusive tactics by several government departments and allowed several guilty parties to escape investigation, prosecution, or conviction. The rationalizations of corrupt police included two major claims: as underpaid and unappreciated public servants they deserve gratuities ("goodies") in exchange for protecting the public from conventional criminals (robbers, burglars, assaulters, and rapists) and subversive (political offenders); and as even-handed and necessary regulators of social vices mandated by the people (prostitution and gambling) they deserved protection payments from proprietors and employees in vice businesses. Corrupt officers' actual purpose was to collect as much money as possible for themselves and for other cooperative public officials who participated in corruption enterprises. The professed aims of high public officials engaged in political corruption were to perform routine favors for constituents, and to reap deserved gratuities in exchange for the rigorous job of representing a constituency. The actual intention of these agents was to make money for themselves and others involved in political corruption.

All social actors who engaged in evasion and collusion offenses were, by all outward appearances, respectable people employed in honorable occupations—occupations that offered them a secure cover within an insulated opportunity structure for the commission of crimes. This "Mr. Clean" appearance of respectability disguised these actors' economic and political ends—ends contrary to the interests of most Americans.

LEGAL STATUS OF THE OFFENSE

Evasive and collusive actions by teams of government or capitalist agents, with one exception (the Watergate Special Prosecution Force), violated specific international, criminal, regulatory, or civil laws. Government officials' denials of responsibility for past unlawful official conduct violated international laws, and laws proscribing high crimes and misdemeanors, perjury, conspiracy, obstruction of justice, and defraud of the United States. The evasion and collusion between regulatory commision agents and agents of big business at times violated regulatory agency rules, laws, and procedures, civil law statutes, and criminal laws (for example, antitrust laws). The Watergate Special Prosecution Force committed para-legal offenses by failing to carry out its public obligation to provide the public with a full account of the crimes involved in the Watergate scandal. Different forms of police corruption entailed varied offenses ranging from violation of police administrative rules to criminal conduct (sale of and falsification of evidence, kickbacks, extortion, case fixing, perjury, bribery, theft, burglary, robbery, and assault). The most prevalent and lucrative offense was bribery. Corrupt public officials, in misusing their offices for personal financial gain, committed a variety of offenses: mail fraud, bribery, conspiracy, racketeering, income tax evasion, theft, and conspiracy to defraud the United States. They also broke internal bureaucratic rules and regulations banning political corruption.

NATURE OF THE OFFENSE

Evasive and collusive actions by government or corporate agents comprised nonviolent, covert offenses committed by organizational agents in the normal course of daily work tasks as employees of government or corporate organizations. These agents pursued personal as well as organizational aims. The general public was the target of these actions and suffered the consequences through the loss of input into government decisions because of ignorance about present and past actions by high government officials, economic loss, and some loss of faith in the system.

High government officials who denied responsibility for past illegal acts (which negatively influenced their later decisions and actions) and kept these acts and the action plans on which they were based secret from the public for extended periods of time, did so with the collusive aid of staff members and inner circle confidants. The extended secrecy of these acts served to cover up high-level official blunders. The official position of these social actors enabled them to make crucial but arbitrary decisions with impunity—decisions that were inaccessible to the average citizen and circumvented the democratic process. The Watergate Special Prosecutor, in partnership with some of his staff, thwarted the prosecution of key principles in the Watergate scandal. The Prosecution Force's final report was a cover-up document, deceptive in nature, inept, evasive, and incomplete. It clearly demonstrated the prosecutors' evasion and collusive techniques undertaken in support of the economic and political system, the deliberate nonenforcement of the law, and the secreting of information from the public. The chief detrimental aspect of such a cover-up is the perpetuation of false consciousness among the citizenry, that is, a belief that all is well in a corrupt political and economic system.

Police corruption was found to be a form of organizational crime endemic to many police departments throughout the United States—widespread to the extent that many people have come to expect, accept, and even desire certain

certain forms of it. Police corruption functioned to direct police attention to street crime and political policing rather than to organized crime or white-collar crime. Obviously police corruption has cost the public vast sums of money and the lack of adequate police protection. Policemen have been able to violate the very laws they are expected to enforce because of the authority and opportunity structure of criminal behavior that inheres in their position. Corrupt high public officials engaged in collusion with other executive officials and some business-men to gain unauthorized financial rewards. The official roles of these offenders allowed them to build up a network of contacts with constituents eager to buy influence with the government. The legislative process in the United States operates on the basis of interest-group representation; therefore, Congressmen frequently work on behalf of specific constituencies rather than on the behalf of the whole.

Evasive and collusive tactics engaged in by teams of government and corporate agents to protect big business from government regulation clearly mark the most significant offense pattern with this type of political crime. The partnership or symbiotic relationship existing between government and big busi-ness is clearly demonstrated in this offense pattern and makes clear that the government is an agent of the corporate structure.

Group support for government officials' denials of responsibility and for the failure of the Watergate Special Prosecutor's office to investigate Watergate scandal participants has been strong among peer groups, the government, the corporate structure, and the public. The failure of government agents to regulate big business has received strong support among these sectors. The majority of U.S. citizens are erroneously convinced that big business is overregulated and that less regulation would be beneficial to consumers—an excellent example of false consciousness. For instance, the public has bought the big companies' claim that higher oil and gas prices are necessary for increasing future oil supplies and for pro-viding better services to consumers, and that the cause of these high prices is scarcity and the OPEC nations. Moreover, the public appears to be satisfied with what little it knows about the vertical integration of oil. The bigger things are, the better things are. Group support for certain forms of police corruption is high among police peer groups, the public, the government, and the corporate structure. The U.S. government, the corporate structure, and the citizens want police to have control of lower-class crime and criminals. The police are expected by all of these groups to regulate rather than eradicate vice. There could be no organized crime without the public's strong demand for the goods and services provided by such organizational crime. Any kind of police activities directed toward white-collar crime are frowned upon. Group support for corrupt public officials has come from peer groups and constituents eager to buy government influence.

Societal reaction to crimes of evasion and collusion has been mild to weak in all cases considered in this chapter. It was mild in the cases of official denials of responsibility, the Watergate Special Prosecution Force's failure to prosecute Watergate offenders, police corruption, and political corruption. Only a minimal number of individuals are criminally prosecuted within each sub-type. Those prosecuted and convicted have received weak sanctions, such as dismissal from office, suspended sentences, unsupervised probation, and light jail or prison terms.

Societal reaction to government agents' failure to regulate big business (involving crimes by government agents and corporate agents) has been extremely weak. Offenders in this category have been rarely discovered, indicted, or convicted. The oil cartel, for example, has been able to violate regulatory, civil, and some criminal laws with impunity. In the present economic and political system, where power and wealth are highly concentrated in the hands of a few corporate actors, this weak societal reaction will probably prevail because members of the corporate class have convinced the public that corporations are not involved in unlawful conduct.

What's more, when some honest government agent regulators fail to participate or go along with the evasive and collusive relationship existing between government and the corporate structure, they are frequently fired or demoted. Dr. Herbert Ley, commissioner of the Food and Drug Administration from 1966 until 1969, was fired because his agency was becoming too consumer-oriented in the eyes of the Nixon administration and the drug industry. Lobbyists for the drug industry (which did a $100 billion a year business in the 1960s) tied up six hours of Dr. Ley's time each day while he headed the FDA. Dr. Stanley Mazaleski, a Public Health Service scientist, was fired by his superiors at the Public Health Service in the early 1970s for complaining that his agency was slow in setting safety standards for workers exposed to dangerous chemicals. Ernest Fitzgerald, a cost analyst for the Defense Department, met the same fate in 1972, when he was fired after correctly testifying before Congress that Lockheed cargo planes would cost $2 billion more than the amount stipulated in the government contract (Dudar 1977, p. 41). A top-level Department of Agriculture official who complained about corruption in his department was stuck in a room by himself and given the job of organizing departmental beauty contests. Similarly, a National Institutes of Health scientist who legitimately complained to his superiors in the early 1970s about the safety of certain vaccines lost his secretary and telephone and was put in a small room by himself (Sherrill 1974, p. 213).

A regulatory bureaucrat who complains before Congress about his agency is supposed to be legally protected from agency reprisals, but this is seldom the case. For instance, when Ernest Fitzgerald testified before Congress and eventually lost his job, the Defense Department literally committed a crime. Unfortunately however, the bureaucratic system is structured to serve the corporations that it conducts business with, not the public. Bureaucrats who complain about their agencies have little recourse to any means of self-protection. Fitzgerald's firing and his fight to regain his job cost him $400,000 in legal fees, an amount he had to pay out of his own pocket (Dudar 1977, pp. 41–43). One wonders how such an honest man ever accumulated $400,000.

Furthermore, collusion between government and corporate agents is encouraged by the interchange of personnel between the corporate structure and government regulatory agencies. Personnel shuttle between government jobs and industry jobs so often that demarcation of the two groups is difficult. William H. Tucker, for example, who rules in·favor of cutbacks in service for Penn Central while chairman of the ICC, later became a vice-president of Penn Central (Sherill 1974, p. 214). Similarly, when Clifford Hardin left the Agriculture secretaryship in 1971, he became vice-chairman of the board of Ralston Purina, one of the largest agribusiness corporations in the country. He was replaced at USDA by Earl Butz, a stockholder and director of Ralston Purina and two other large agribusiness corporations, International Mineral and Chemical Corporation and Stokely-Van Camp Company. Butz helped swing the sale of $750 million worth of grain to the Soviet Union in 1972, a disaster for U.S. consumers. The taxpayers paid $130 million to subsidize this deal, and because of the resulting shortage of wheat in this country, paid an estimated $400 million extra in the price of wheat products. Big grain exporting companies (who may have been secretly tipped off about the forthcoming grain deal) made windfall profits exceeding $100 million. Clifford Pulvermacher and Clarence Palmby, two high-ranking Agriculture Department officials who helped Butz arrange the Russian wheat deal, later were employed by grain exporting companies. Pulvermacher became vice president of the Continental Corporation, and Palmby became a Washington lobbyist for the Bunge Corporation (Sherill 1974, p. 214).

Large corporations are the ultimate beneficiaries of weak government regulatory agencies because they are allowed to operate in a systematically lawless manner. Regulatory action, when and if it comes, is usually imposed upon small industries and small businessmen. For example, regulators have charged small grain and dairy cooperatives and the breakfast cereals industry with violating antitrust laws, while neglecting the more obvious antitrust violators such as the automobile and telephone industries (Baker 1975). The ICC sanctions small trucking firms for violating ICC regulations, but ignores violations by large trucking firms. Furthermore, small businessmen are intimidated by a bevy of federal ·agencies who descend upon their premises annually, requiring unnecessary paperwork and punishing them for insignificant federal regulation violations (Aug 1976). The big corporations evade regulation, while the smaller concerns serve as sacrificial lambs toward the perpetuation of the regulatory charade.

8

EVASION AND COLLUSION
AGAINST GOVERNMENT

Evasion and collusion against the government consist of conduct designed to avoid compliance with specific laws considered to be immoral or unjust by the offenders. Violators are usually loyal law-abiding citizens who believe in and support the economic and political system; however, they vigorously object to specific laws which they feel certain groups of citizens have a right to break, for example, refusal to send children to public schools, refusal to submit relatives to medical attention, refusal to salute the flag in public schools or pledge allegiance to the United States, refusal to support or accept scientific knowledge based on vivisection (anti-vivisectionists), refusal to retain only one wife (religious bigamy), refusal to pay taxes, and refusal to accept military conscription.

ACTION PATTERNS

We comment on two kinds of tax evasions, and objection to military conscription.

Military Taxation Avoidance

A small minority of Americans (the precise number is unknown) have refused to pay the portion of their federal income taxes which goes to maintain past, present, and future wars. As conscientious objectors to military taxation, these persons argue that their tax monies should not be used to buy guns, napalm, and other military equipment used in warfare which destroys human life. Such persons have tried for years to persuade the government to provide means by which their income tax could be channeled into peace-keeping rather than war-making activities. These offenders have utilized a number of means to avoid paying the share of their taxes which go to support the military: listing all the wounded children in the Vietnam War as dependents on the federal income tax form; refusing to accept the portion of a regular salary which normally would be converted into military taxes; stashing savings in obscure places in private homes (under mattresses) rather than in bank accounts; and allowing IRS officials to seize items of personal property rather than paying military taxes.

An important step forward in the long struggle for the principle of conscientious objection to military taxes was achieved on January 3, 1974. On this date, a federal judge in Philadelphia ruled that the American Friends Service Committee (AFSC), a pacifist organization, could not be compelled to collect from two of its employees (through the withholding procedure) that portion of their income tax (51.6 percent) which would go for war purposes. The Internal Revenue Service asked for a stay of execution of the judge's ruling, pending an appeal. The ruling marked the first judicial recognition of conscientious objection to war taxes. Should this case reach the Supreme Court, a high court decision to uphold the Philadelphia judge's ruling could open the door to similar suits and thereby establish some rights for conscientious objectors to military taxation (Christian Century 1974, pp. 371-72).

Because the Philadelphia case was not a class action suit, it applied only to the AFSC and to the two individuals (Lorraine Cleveland of Newtown, Pennsylvania and Leonard Cadwallader of Germantown, Pennsylvania) who brought suit against the U.S. government. Lorraine Cleveland has been a tax evader since 1950. She and her husband, in 1949, sent a letter of protest to the IRS along with their federal income tax payments. They had been shocked by the dropping of the atomic bomb on Japan in 1945, and sobered by the doctrine of individual responsibility upheld by the Nuremburg trials in 1948. Their tax protests began in earnest the next year when, after calculating the amount they owed the IRS, they sent a check for double that amount to the Children's Bureau rather than the Internal Revenue Service. This action resulted in a great deal of correspondence between the Clevelands and IRS officials which highlighted conscientious objection to military taxation. Finally, the IRS entered a levy against Bill Cleveland's salary as a teacher and collected the tax due, plus penalty and interest. This pattern was repeated year after year as the Clevelands sent their tax monies to the Bureau of Indian Affairs, the Department of Health, Education, and Welfare, the special assistant on disarmament, and the Peace Corps, rather than to the IRS. The government always collected the Clevelands' taxes by a levy against Mr. Cleveland's salary or against the couple's bank account. Nevertheless, going through this process permitted the Clevelands to make a protest which Lorraine described as contributing "to my own integrity, my sense of wholeness—by bringing my actions into harmony with my deeply held beliefs and with the guidance of my conscience" (*Christian Century* 1974, p. 372).

The American Friends Service Committee as an organization was not allowed to protest military taxes as the Clevelands had done. The AFSC employees who had paid (through withholding) all the taxes they owed were denied an opportunity to make a protest. As the war in Indochina continued, tensions increased with the AFSC, and many of its employees within this organization believed that they should not pay military taxes. They expected the AFSC (as a pacifist organization) to help them in their efforts to block government levies against their salaries. One employee felt so strongly about this matter that he resigned. In 1969, the AFSC, after a committeewide consultation process, decided to honor the request of five of its employees (including Lorraine Cleveland and Leonard Cadwallader) to withhold only 48.8 percent of their taxes. The other 51.6 percent (which they contended contributed to war making) was disbursed directly by AFSC to its employees along with their regular take-home pay. AFSC then sent the government the full amount of tax due (employees' withholding taxes) for 1969, taking the difference ($579.09) from the organization's general fund. In May 1970, the AFSC entered a suit in federal court for the return of these funds, on the grounds that the government had no right to compel it to withhold taxes from those employees conscientiously opposed to war. Lorraine Cleveland and Leonard Cadwallader also entered the suit as plaintiffs. The suit dragged on until July 1973 because the government entered two motions for the suit's dismissal. The AFSC argued that it had established its organization in 1917 to provide a means for young conscientious objectors, who opposed war on the basis of their religion, to perform alternative service in wartime. As such, this organization holds a commitment to religious conviction and personal consciences. Additionally, the AFSC averred that it strives to obey American laws fully, but that when the law conflicts with religious principles and conscience, conscience must be top priority (*Christian Century* 1974, p. 372).

The government presented no evidence to refute AFSC's position, but based its case instead on the constitutionality of the Internal Revenue Code. Part of the government's argument held that it would be cumbersome for IRS officials to collect taxes from pacifists by levying against their salaries or bank accounts (even though it had done this for years in dealing with the Clevelands). The Philadelphia judge presiding over the case sided with the AFSC, stating that the method of collecting federal taxes from the plaintiffs violated their First Amendment rights to free exercise of their religion. Since the AFSC case, there have been some efforts to meet the goal of conscientious objector status for some taxpayers. Congressman Ronald Dellums of California introduced bills for this purpose in several sessions of Congress. A bill he presented in 1974 would permit citizens who are morally opposed to war to divert a part of their taxes into a World Peace Tax Fund. This would modify the IRS code, obviating illegal actions by those who refuse to pay military taxes (*Christian Century* 1974, p. 372).

Avoidance of Property Taxation

Recent protests against taxes at all levels of government have shifted to mass refusals to pay local property taxes, and requests for abatements on assessments. There are also movements under way in several states for referenda that would establish legal limits on taxes and on the growth of government spending. The mass actions which appear to violate criminal laws are noted briefly in three states.

In California in the mid-1970s, some citizens refused to pay property taxes. In one notable case, a Los Angeles woman whose property taxes doubled during 1976 refused to pay her local property tax bill at the end of that year. She claimed that a person who is not making monthly payments on a home can skip paying taxes for five or six years without facing eviction. This woman was a member of a taxpayer protest group in the Los Angeles area, and is apparently encouraging other members of this group to follow her lead (*U.S. News and World Report* 1977). In Massachusetts, where the property tax is a sore point with many taxpayers, taxpayer protest associations such as the one in Los Angeles are rapidly proliferating. In late 1976 and early 1977, five local taxpayer groups were formed in this state. There have been massive protests by Massachusetts taxpayers in the form of 16,000 requests for abatements on assessments.

Wisconsin came close to witnessing a genuine tax revolt in 1977. When the state legislature was considering a bill that would have resulted in a large increase in property taxes for Washington Island (a vacation area where land values have soared), the islanders authorized the town board to look into the possibility of seceding from Wisconsin and joining the state of Michigan. This bill was defeated (*U.S. News and World Report* 1977).

Military Conscription Avoidance

Objection to military service and to conscription has had a long, uneven history in the North American colonies and in the United States. The 1960s witnessed the beginning of an antiwar and anticonscription movement unparalleled in U.S. history (Schlissel 1969). In this period, the acts of objectors to military conscription passed beyond the original grounds of protest against military service to a more militant stance, and an increasing number of men (more than ever before) refused or failed to show up for induction. The federal government has been compelled over time to drastically reformulate conscription laws, and to reassess and modify the application of these laws to various classifications of men. In turn, objectors to conscription at different historical stages have utilized diverse methods to avoid military service. Pressures from both private and political sources regarding the Vietnam War and conscription were great. Henry Steele Commager (1972) presented what he labeled "The Case for Amnesty," in which he cited a vast array of amnesty instances and methods of avoiding military conscription throughout the history of the United States. Obviously, over time, conscription rules and sanctions as well as societal reactions thereto are relative and problematic (Roebuck and Fiery 1975, pp. 1–2).

ACTION PATTERNS

Four types of objectors to military conscription are delineated on the basis of action patterns utilized to avoid military conscription during the Vietnam war: averters, draft evaders, draft resisters, and noncombattants. The classification hierarchy used by the Selection Service System (1970) in classifying registrants served as the basis for the analysis of action patterns.

Averters. All individuals included in this category undertook action to avert conscription utilizing one or more of the following options:

1. Conscientious objector status for religious or non-religious reasons (I-O).

2. Deferment as a full-time high-school student under age 20 (I-S), or deferment as a full-time undergraduate college student (II-S).

3. Deferment as an apprentice or full-time student in an "approved" trade, business, or vocational school, or junior college (II-A).

4. Deferment for essential agricultural employment (II-C).

5. Deferment as a full-time student of medicine, dentistry, veterinary medicine, osteopathy, podiatry, or optometry (II-S).

6. Deferment as a government official (IV-S).

7. Deferment as a minister or divinity student (IV-D).

8. Deferment because of dependents—either a fatherhood or a hardship deferment (III-A).

9. Deferment as medically unfit (I-Y or IV-F).

10. Intentional incapacitation, permanent or temporary, to gain a I-Y or IV-F classification. This type of action is legal as far as the enforcement of the draft laws are concerned, but is considered unethical.

11. Stalling for time, through the effective use of deferments or other devices, hoping to avert the draft until age 26.

12. Enlistment in other branches of the armed services in order to avoid being drafted (Reserves, National Guard, Coast Guard, and so on).

Evaders. Evaders utilized the following options:

1. Fraudulently or illegally attempt disqualification for medical or mental reasons (feigning mental illness; pretending to be homosexual; producing fraudulent medical records; lying on questionnaires concerning health).

2. Changing, damaging, or multilating Selective Service files for purposes of personal evasion.

3. Theft of Selective Service files in order to be "lost" to the Selective Service System.

4. Going "underground."

5. Emigrating to another country to evade conscription.

Resisters. Resisters employed the following options:

1. Noncooperation. Refusal to register; failure to show up for required physical; refusal of induction; refusal of alternative civilian work service after receiving I-O (conscientious objector) status, but not going underground.

2. Showing up for induction, but refusing to step forward (usually having been denied conscientious objector claim).

3. Refusing or voluntarily giving up a deferment or exemption and refusing induction.

4. Changing, damaging, or mutilating Selective Service files for purposes of mass evasion.

Noncombatants. Noncombatants chose one of the following options:

1. Refusal to carry weapons for formal religious reasons.
2. Refusal to carry weapons for ethical reasons.

Averters

Averters attempted to legitimately avert the draft by applying for deferments or exemptions that would permanently obviate induction. One was exempt from induction at age 26 unless one had received a prior deferment. In this case one was liable for induction until age 35. However, if induction was postponed until age 26, one was unlikely to be drafted. Averters could join other branches of the service, find physical conditions rendering them medically unfit for the service, or intentionally incapacitate themselves in order to gain a physical deferment or exemption.

Pentagon computers separated millions of Americans into various groups based on the means they used to escape the draft. One group of 1.4 million men avoided military service by utilizing loopholes in draft laws. Another group of 1.8 million undergraduates was granted college deferments during the height of the manpower build-up, between 1965 and 1969 (*U.S. News and World Report* 1971). The Selective Service System (1970) reported a great increase in persons attempting to avoid the draft between 1965 and 1971. For example, Selective Service classification appeals increased from 9,904 appeals during the fiscal year of 1965, to 168,138 in 1969.

Vocational and Dependency Averters

From 1965 to 1969, the number of Americans holding various occupational deferments as school teachers, graduate students, members of the Peace Corps, and apprentices in certain job areas jumped from 220,012 to 491,998, representing an increase of 124 percent (*U.S. News and World Report* 1971). Within the year (1969) that draft laws were modified enabling teachers to receive draft exemptions, the New York City Board of Education received 20,000 more applications for teacher's licenses than the year before. The vast majority of these were from men under age 26 (then the cut-off age). In 1969, of the thousands of participants in short-term teacher-training programs, 85 percent were male college graduates under 26. Eight times as many men as formerly were taking teacher education courses in one city college alone (New York *Times* 1969). Those holding dependency deferments from 1965 to 1969 climbed from 3,766,117 to 4,194,756, representing a gain of 11 percent. For the most part, the dependency deferments went to men who married and quickly became fathers (*U.S. News and World Report* 1971).

Reserve Averters

In 1965, when it became clear that there would be no general mobilization of the reserve forces and that membership carried an automatic draft deferment, 810,000 draft eligible men (1965–69) joined various branches of the reserves. A study made for the army found that 83 percent of those joining the army reserve did so, by their own admission, to avoid being drafted. Of those who enlisted in the air force reserves, 86.5 percent said they wanted to "beat the draft." Half of those who entered the marine reserve and 75 percent of those who selected the navy said they did so to escape full-time military service (*U.S. News and World Report* 1971).

Medical Averters

Changes in the draft regulations after 1971 abolished deferments for graduate study and essential jobs. Subsequently, rejection for medical reasons became a widely used escape avenue. Two types of classifications were given to those found medically unfit: Class I-Y, draft exempt except in time of declared war or national emergency; and Class IV-F, total immunity from military service. A I-Y classification was an unconditional release that served to prevent induction in times of peace or undeclared war. Because the Vietnam conflict was undeclared, I-Ys were exempt. David Suttler (1970) analyzed physical exemptions that enabled medical averters to avoid conscription. He found the odds were four to one that any given person would not fail the preinduction examination on medical grounds. The youth who underwent his induction physical ignorant of the standards on which he was examined was likely to find himself in uniform. The odds against obtaining a medical exemption could be improved dramatically by utilizing knowledge pertaining to medical exemption. Persons did not have to be unhealthy to be militarily unfit; in fact, professional athletes were often draft rejects. The Army, by law, was required to make public its *Standards of Medical Fitness*, which became a bible of the draft resistance movement. It listed some 400 defects and disabilities that could lead to a classification of I-Y or IV-F. Many medical problems mildly annoying in civilian life were interpreted as grounds for military service exemption.

Thousands of men, vigorously healthy by their own admission, were disqualified for military service because they once were sick (past allergies, reaction to insect bites, bronchial asthma, and so on) (Suttler 1970). Averters frequently engaged cooperative physicians who "found" and reported disqualifying physical and mental disabilities for them. Many of these problematic disabilities would have otherwise gone undetected at the preinduction physical examination. In short, many medical averters negotiated problematic medical disabilities with doctors and their draft boards. The medical escape route proved remarkably effective. In Boston and New York in 1970, nearly two-thirds of all men given preinduction physicals were rejected. Nationally, from 1968 to 1970, there were perceptible increases in medical rejections (*Newsweek* 1970).

Conscientious Objector (I-O)

A conscientious objector was defined by law as a man who was opposed to participation in war because of religious, moral, ethical, or other deeply held beliefs that were central to his life. Selective Service provided for two types: I-A-Os and I-Os. Men classified I-A-O were routinely inducted and required to spend two years as noncombatants in the military (usually as medics); I-Os did not enter the military, but performed two years of civilian work approved by Selective Service (often in hospitals). Action patterns utilized by I-A-Os are discussed within the noncombatant category because they did not avert conscription. Frequently, men denied I-O classification applied for and received I-A-O classification.

The draft law, prior to 1967, required religious training and a belief in a supreme being for an I-O classification. In 1967, the supreme being clause was deleted, and in 1970 the religious training clause was dropped. The Selective Service System (1971) demonstrated the results of these deletions—15,888 registrants were classified as conscientious objectors in 1969, whereas 28,188 were so classified in 1970.

Claims for C-O status based on political, philosophical, or personal moral codes were rejected. Many were conscientiously opposed to military service in Southeast Asia, though not morally opposed to war in general. To qualify for C-O status, one's moral opposition to war had to extend beyond any particular military conflict. Whatever the would-be conscientious objector's professed moral grounds, he had to negotiate his case with draft board members. There were three levels of appeal beyond the local draft board: state, presidential, and criminal court. The problematic outcome of negotiation depended in large part on the accounts and "presentations of self" (Goffman 1959) submitted by the potential conscientious objector.

The averters discussed above did not try to change or disrupt the Selective Service System, nor did they try to keep out of the draft at all costs. Some I-Os were opposed to the Selective Service System and desired to see it ended or modified, but their action patterns did not reflect these goals. Some averters who were turned down after applying for one specific exemption or deferment then submitted to induction. Others applied for various alternate deferments within the averter category. Still others resorted to different means of keeping out of the draft, thereby placing themselves in one of the other categories of the typology. For instance, the conscientious objector whose claim for I-O classification was denied could have gone "underground" or emigrated to another country, thus becoming an evader. The potential averter who refused induction after the denial of his claim for exemption became a resister. Averters would not keep out of the draft and out of prison at all costs. Because averters utilized legal means, we must assume that they would not have resorted to actions to escape induction or imprisonment.

Evaders

In contrast to averters, evaders fraudulently or illegally tried to escape the draft. For example, they attempted to get deferments or exemptions with false information on medical records; answered questions incorrectly on various Selective Service forms; committed themseves to mental institutions for 90 days; and falsely claimed mental or emotional problems. Other actions included going "underground" or emigrating to escape induction or prosecution; and stealing or damaging one's file in an attempt to be "forgotten" or lost to the Selective Service System.

Emigrant Evaders

The number of actual draft evaders in Canada is problematic. Under current treaties emigrant evaders are not subject to extradition, and in fact, at the beginning of the Vietnam conflict, many evaders were officially welcomed as emigrants. From 1965 to 1970, more than 46,000 draft-age Americans settled in Canada. Certainly, some of these were not draft evaders. Yet, in the ten years from 1961 to 1970, the number of draft-age U.S. males who emigrated to Canada increased from 1,261 to 5,510. Emigration figures represented only those who asked for and received permission to settle in Canada. Many others settled there illegally (*U.S. News and World Report* 1971). The Chicago Area Draft Resisters (commonly called CADRE in anti-draft circles) claimed that 10,000 men a year emigrated to Canada between 1965 and 1970 (*Christian Century* 1970).

Underground Evaders

Registered men who hid out in ghettos, hippie colonies, communes, and other "away-from-home" places represent this subtype. Though their numbers are unknown, the Central Committee for Conscientious Objectors in Philadelphia estimated them to be in the thousands, and to constitute a large proportion of the 15,310 Americans listed as "delinquent" by the Selective Service in 1968. Many in the underground have been runaways and "floaters" since their late teens. Some of these have wandered from tenement to tenement in the ghettos where itinerant boarders are common and where no questions are asked (*Saturday Evening Post* 1968).

Evaders did not try to change the system, but rather worked within it illegally to achieve their goals. They simultaneously attempted to stay out of the draft and out of jail at any cost. Some individuals, within and without the Selective Service System, for various reasons directly or indirectly helped evaders. Some doctors wrote fallacious medical reports enabling evaders to receive illegal exemption, and some Selective Service officials allowed them wide behavior and exemption latitudes in order to avoid entangling the system in legal or public "hassles."

Resisters

Resisters, through their action patterns, attempted to change or end the draft by legal or illegal means. Many resisters claimed that they were serving a higher moral law than the Selective Service laws. Resisters included non-cooperators who showed up for induction but refused to step forward when called; those who refused to accept alternative service after receiving I-O status; those who destroyed, mutilated, or returned their draft cards but did not go "underground" or leave the country; and those who refused to register for the draft. Some resisters had previously been denied a conscientious objector classification; others had turned down legitimate deferments and exemptions, but still refused induction. Some refused induction because they objected to military service or conscription, and others believed they were illegally ordered for induction. Refusal of induction denoted an overt form of resistance to the Selective Service System.

Organized demonstrations against the draft have encompassed public draft-card burnings, the mass mailing in of draft cards, sit-ins at draft boards, flag burning, and mass arrests throughout the country. Disruption of the draft was an important goal of many groups and organizations, including activist college instructors and students, clergymen, underground newspapers, and antiwar groups such as Students for a Democratic Society, Clergy and Laymen Against the War, the Resistance, and Women's Strike for Peace. According to CADRE, between 50,000 and 100,000 men simply did not register between October 31, 1967 and October 31, 1969. Destruction of draft files in several cities during this period hampered hundreds of draft boards for periods of six months to a year (*Christian Century* 1970). Most draft law prosecutions after 1971 were for the following violations: non-registration, public destruction of draft cards and draft board files, and refusal of military duty or civilian alternative service (Tatum 1970).

Incarcerated Resisters

Prison authorities viewed inmate resisters as a unique collectivity. As a group, they were more intelligent, more independent, less fearful, and less alienated than conventional inmates. Though some made "satisfactory institutional adjustment," others who were aware of outside support rebelled against prison regulations and routines, protesting against Jim Crow practices, mail and other censorships, free prison labor, and curtailed freedom of speech. Some engaged in overt agitation, civil disobedience, and work strikes (Gaylin 1970).

While resisters tried to keep out of the draft at all costs, they would not do anything to avoid incarceration. Many were willing to go to jail, or would risk it, while attempting to disrupt the Selective Service System or set a favorable precedent in court. Many refused to cooperate with the system, yet did not go "underground" or leave the country, thereby rendering themselves vulnerable to prosecution and prison terms.

Noncombatants

Though exact figures are not available, military and church officials estimate that there were about 5,000 I-A-Os in uniform in 1970. One-third or more of these were thought to be Seventh Day Adventists. Members of various other religious sects and men with non-religious, ethical proscriptions against bearing arms made up the remainder. Many I-A-Os who initially entered the military as regular draftees successfully applied for transfer to noncombatant status. More than 2,500 men from 1964 to 1970 (approximately 75 a month during 1970) effected this change. Only about 6 to 8 percent of all medics who served in Vietnam were noncombatants. The regulations did not prevent noncombatants from serving in Vietnam, and I-A-O medics were among the first draftees sent there (Tatum 1970). Noncombatants accepted induction but objected to bearing arms. They did not try to change the system and legally carried out their objections within it.

GOAL OF THE OFFENDER

Tax evaders and objectors to military conscription aimed to avoid compliance with certain government laws, rules, and regulations. Objectors to military taxation appealed to a moral law higher than existing secular tax laws in support of refusals to pay income tax. Objectors to property taxation avowedly subscribed to a principle of equitable taxation not provided by existing tax laws, and they desired to change current tax laws. Two sub-types (resisters and noncombatants) among objectors to military conscription professed moral reasons for their actions. A sizeable number of evaders purported to act on the basis of personal, economic, and educational considerations. Offenders in these groups were otherwise law-abiding, non-deviant, respectable citizens who supported the existing political and economic system.

LEGAL STATUS OF THE OFFENSE

All tax evaders broke local, state, or federal tax laws. Among objectors to military service, evaders and resisters violated rules, regulations, or laws of the Selective Service System. Some averters and noncombatants violated Selective Service laws and regulations, though others did not. Though all objectors to military conscription transgressed the established norm prescribing that all citizens should be willing and eager to accept general military conscription as a patriotic duty, some did not violate statute laws. The legal status of most objectors to military conscription was problematic, because the category of objection depended upon many fluctuating variables within the criminal labeling process: the objector's choice of action patterns; changes in draft laws and Selective Service procedures; the informal rules and ad hoc decisions of local draft boards; the outcomes resulting from various negotiating processes (with doctors, lawyers, draft counselors, draft boards, the Selective Service appeals system, and court personnel); and the draft process stage at which the objector was studied. On the other hand, once finally labeled, objectors were quick to differentiate themselves from other "less noble" objector categories.

The I-Os considered I-A-Os to be "cop outs;" and resisters defined I-Os and I-A-Os as "cop outs." All of these groups reviled evaders (undergrounders and refugees in Canada) as lacking in courage and "thinking only of themselves instead of the issues." Many emigrant evaders viewed other objectors as fools in an unworthy, sinking ship. The resisters who followed Gandhi's teachings advocated a nonviolent program: fill the halls with sincere, educated, nonviolent war resisters who peacefully turn in their draft cards—until troubled public opinion forces the government to change its policies (*Saturday Evening Post* 1968; Clausen 1967; Emerick 1972).

NATURE OF THE OFFENSE

Tax evaders and objectors to military conscription participated in overt, nonviolent offenses—with the exception of conscription resisters, some of whom resorted to violence against property. All tax evaders were members of formal organizations whose aims and ideologies supported their evasions. All objectors to military conscription had access to and the support of several anti-conscription organizations as well as draft counselors. Many if not most evaders, resisters, and noncombatants were members of formal organizations which opposed military conscription during the Vietnam conflict. All tax evaders and draft resisters, evaders, and noncombatants participated in collusion with the supporting formal organizations to which they belonged. Draft averters engaged in collusion with doctors, draft lawyers, and draft counselors who helped them avoid conscription.

Group support for tax evaders comes from pacifist religious organizations and militant taxpayer protest groups. These evaders have received some support from the government and the public, but almost no support from the corporate structure. Group support for draft averters' actions was frequently found in various kinds of peace, antiwar, and draft-help groups. Irving Louis Horowitz (1970) classified some 150 organizations and anti-Vietnam protest groups, and 75 to 100 of these as specifically antidraft. The organizations supported averters as well as other types of objectors. The increased number of averters, coupled with the complex and ever changing draft-law regulations, fostered and supported a large number of draft counselors and draft lawyers. According to the *National Draft Counseling Directory* (1971), all but four states had draft counselors. Many organizations published books and memos about the draft and military, helped groups form new counseling services, trained draft and military counselors, and aided counselors and lawyers with difficult cases. Draft lawyers claimed that they did not counsel clients to evade or resist the draft, but rather advised them how to legally avoid conscription. Many claimed they could legally keep anyone out of military service (*Time* 1969). Many religious organizations offered counseling services to averters, supplied official denominational statements on war and military service to averters, and helped conscientious objectors find alternative service jobs. Averters received little support from the government and the corporate structure, although some segments of the public were sympathetic with their efforts to avoid conscription.

Draft evaders received group support from memberships that also supported averters. Some individuals for various reasons directly or indirectly helped evaders. Some doctors wrote fallacious medical reports enabling them to receive illegal exemptions. Some Selective Service officials allowed them wide behavior and exemption latitudes in order to avoid entangling the system in legal or public "hassles." Evaders received virtually no government, corporate, or public support, with the exception of a few peers, doctors, and Selective Service personnel.

Draft resisters found group support from the same sources as did averters, and additional support from the more militant anti-conscription groups. Leaflets from international organizations addressed to American servicemen listed twelve organizations that promised assistance to deserters and draft resisters (*Nation* 1969). Resisters received support from peers but not from the government, the corporate structure, or the public. Noncombatants whose stance stemmed from church doctrine received group support. Positions based on ethical reasons devoid of religious or church doctrine received weak support. Noncombatant support (governmental, corporate, public) was generally weak because noncombatants entered the armed services when called.

Societal reaction to tax evaders has been mixed. The reactions to persons refusing to pay military taxes has been strong; for example, the IRS levied against objectors' salaries and personal property items (such as automobiles). On the other hand, societal reaction to property tax objectors has been weak. These tax evaders have rarely been indicted or prosecuted for their failure to pay property taxes. This will probably change should large groups of taxpayers refuse to pay taxes without changes in state laws permitting them to do so. The focus of debate in California has been the 1978 initiative amendment to the state constitution compelling a cutback of roughly 60 percent in property taxes—about $7 billion of local government money.* The initiative had the allure of simplicity: no property tax shall exceed 1 percent of the property's full cash value; full cash value means the assessed sum that appeared in the public records in 1975-76; local government taxes after this year may not rise above 2 percent of the base point each year, no matter what the inflation rate. Should other states adopt such measures, a real battle will be at hand because tax monies must come from somewhere to pay for a host of services citizens have become accustomed to receiving, and many other required services that they don't usually think about, such as prisons, mental institutions, schools, and hospitals. The corporate sector (where the wealth really is) is of course the logical target for the tax burden. But then we don't tax wealth, but rather income and property (primarily private homes), and surely the corporate sector will refuse to pick up the slack should ordinary taxpayers succeed in diminishing their property taxes (Leary 1978).

Societal reaction to the draft averters' action patterns was usually neutral because these problematic adaptations did not violate criminal norms. The requested classifications were generally granted if the supporting claims and accounts appeared legitimate. At the "worst," the would-be averter was inducted. Alternately, he could have resorted to other pattern adaptations. Societal reaction to evaders was negative, because they engaged in illegal action patterns. Evaders, if caught and prosecuted, could receive a maximum of five years in prison and a fine of $10,000. The degree of punishment frequently depended upon the evader's racial or ethnic group, his lawyer, his judge, and the region of the United States in which he was tried (Gaylin 1970). Societal reaction toward resisters was negative or mixed, but the growing unpopularity of the Vietnam conflict attenuated negative reactions. Sanctions ranged from court acquittal to fines, probation, or prison sentences. The maximum penalty was the same as that for evaders. Societal reaction to noncombatants' actions was mixed, varying from mildly negative to neutral responses. No requests for I-A-O status were denied.

---

*Proposition Thirteen became law in California on June 6, 1978 whereby a reduction of between and 35 and 60 percent was made in homeowners' and corporate property taxes. Much has been published and promulgated about the reduction in homeowners' property taxes. Little has been said about the more awesome reduction in corporate property taxes. Obviously the middle and lower classes will continue to meet the tax burden for public services in California. What's more, public services will be reduced. But then, the capitalist class doesn't really have to worry about public services, and meanwhile, it receives a reduction in taxes.

BIBLIOGRAPHY

Adams, Walter. 1973. "The Antitrust Alternative." In *Corporate Power in America*, eds. R. Nader and M. Green. New York: Grossman.

Adler, Renata. 1977. "Reflections on Political Scandal." *New York Review of Books* 24 (December 8):20–33.

Agee, Phillip. 1975. *Inside the Company: CIA Diary*. New York: Stonehill Publishing Company.

Alexander, Herbert. 1976. *Financing the 1972 Election*. Princeton, N.J.: Citizen's Research Foundation.

Altman, Lawrence K. 1978. "The Drugs in Developing Countries Now Cause Worry." New York *Times*, March 12: E7.

Anderson, Charles H. 1974. *The Political Economy of Social Class*. Englewood Cliffs, N.J.: Prentice-Hall.

Anderson, Jack (United Features Syndicate, Inc.) 1976a. "Political Payoffs Are Documented." March 22.

———. 1976b. "The Power of the Multinationals." March 23.

———. 1976c. "Government Ignoring Health Standards." July 27.

———. 1976d. "Dictatorships Receive U.S. Backing." October 11.

———. 1976e. "A Citizens Committee Is Needed To Crack Down on Congressmen Who Cheat." *Parade*, November 21: 4–5.

———. 1977 "Muckraker Runs Strange Risks." September 9.

———. 1978a. "Products Banned Here Sold Abroad." March 1.

———. 1978b. "Chilling World of Hoover's FBI." April 17.

———. 1978c. "Equal Justice Written, But Not Practiced." May 7.

Anderson, Jack, and George Clifford. 1974. *The Anderson Papers*. New York: Ballantine.

Anderson, Jack, and Les Whitten (United Features Syndicate, Inc.) 1976a. "Poisoned Fields." January 23.

———. 1976b. "Passing the Buck on Migrant Labor." April 22.

——. 1976c. "Adjournment Cans Renegotiation Unit." October 14.

——. 1977a. "CIA Gave Money to Israel, Too." July 9.

——. 1977b. "Revelry Road to Federal Contracts." October 18.

——. 1977c. "Tycoons Fighting Consumer Bill." October 31.

Antar, Elias. 1978. "Sadat Blasts Israelis." *Clarion-Ledger* (Jackson, Mississippi), January 22: 1, 14.

Atlanta Constitution. 1975. "NSA Chief Reveals Eavesdropping." October 30: i5A.

Auchincloss, Kenneth. 1970. "The Ravaged Environment." *Newsweek*, January 26: 30–45.

Aug, Stephen. 1976. "Report Cites ICC Small-Trucker Bias." *Commercial Appeal* (Memphis, Tennessee), February 3: 16.

Bailey, Kenneth D. 1973. "Constructing Monolithic and Polythetic Typologies by the Heuristic Method." *Sociological Quarterly* 14 (Summer): 291–308.

Baker, George. 1975. "Milk, Fruit Feel the Stirrings of Antitrust." *New York Times*, October 5: F7.

Baraheni, Reza. 1976. "Terror in Iran." *New York Review of Books* 23 (October 28): 21–25.

Barber, Richard J. 1971. "The New Partnership: Big Government and Big Business." In *The Triple Revolution Emerging*, eds. R. Perrucci and M. Pilisuk. Boston: Little, Brown.

Barker, Thomas and Julian B. Roebuck. 1973. *An Empirical Typology of Police Corruption.* Springfield: Charles S. Thomas.

Barnet, Richard and Ronald E. Muller. 1974. *Global Reach.* New York: Simon and Schuster.

Bernstein, Marver. 1955. *Regulating Business by Independent Commission.* Princeton, New Jersey: Princeton University Press.

Birmingham News. 1975. "Firm Denied Donations, CIA Funds Linked." July 9: 37.

——. 1978. "Passman Is Indicted in Park Payoff Probe." April 1: 1, 3.

Birns, Lawrence. 1973. "The Death of Chile." *New York Review of Books* 20 (November 1): 32–33.

Blackstock, Paul. 1964. *The Strategy of Subversion*. Chicago: Quadrangle.

Blair, John. 1977. *The Control of Oil*. New York: Pantheon.

Bonsal, Phillip. 1971. *Cuba, Castro, and the United States*. Pittsburgh: University of Pittsburgh Press.

Borrosage, Robert. 1975. "Secrecy vs. the Constitution." *Society* 12 (March/April): 71–75.

Brodeur, Paul. 1974. *Expendable Americans*. New York: Viking Press.

Brody, Jane. "Chemicals: Health is the New Priority." *New York Times*, January 9: NES 39.

Brown, William J. 1977. "The Myth of Capital-Gains Taxes." *New York Times*, August 14: F12.

Burnham, David. 1970. "Graft Here Said to Run Into Millions." *New York Times Magazine* 119: 1–18.

———. 1972. "14 City Policemen Got CIA Training." *New York Times*, December 17: 23.

———. 1978. "Dispute Arises Over Agency's Plan to Identify and Curb Carcinogens. New York *Times*, March 5: 1, 46.

Burt, Richard. 1978. "U.S. Planning To Cut Arms Sales in 1978." *New York Times*, January 1: 11.

Cavan, Ruth. 1964. "Underworld, Conventional, and Ideological Crime." *Journal of Criminal Law, Criminology, and Police Science* 55: 235–40.

Chambliss, William J. 1969. *Crime and the Legal Process*. New York: McGraw Hill.

———. 1971. "Vice, Corruption, Bureaucracy and Power." *Wisconsin Law Review* (December): 1150–73.

———. 1974. "The State, the Law and the Definition of Behavior as Criminal or Deviant." In *Handbook of Criminology*, ed. D. Glaser. Chicago: Rand McNally.

———. 1975. "The Political Economy of Crime: A Comparative Study of Nigeria and the United States." In *Criminal Law in Action*, ed. W. Chambliss. Santa Barbara: Hamilton.

———. 1976. "Vice, Corruption, Bureaucracy, and Power." In *Whose Law? What Order?* eds. W. Chambliss and M. Mankoff. New York: Wiley.

Chattanooga News-Free Press. 1977. "6-Year Battle Expected on Telephone Competition." January 12: B7.

Chattanooga Times. 1977. "FCC Declines to Split Up A.T. and T., Western Electric." February 24: 24.

Chomsky, Noam. 1975. "Introduction." In *Cointelpro: The FBI's Secret War on Freedom*, ed. C. Perkins. New York: Monad Press.

Christian Century. 1970. "Draft Resistance Mounting." June 10: 719.

———. 1974. "A Step Forward for War Tax Objectors." April 3: 371–73.

Clarion-Ledger (Jackson, Mississippi) (Associated Press) 1975a. "CIA Reportedly Opened, Read Mail of Ameicans." September 25: 8.

———. 1975b. "CIA Illegally Opened Letters to USSR." October 22: 18.

———. 1975c. "Wisconsin University Activists of 60s Infiltrated by Policemen." December 8: 2.

———. 1975d. "110 Socialists Listed in FBI Danger Index." December 18: 8.

———. 1976a. "Agency's Inaction on Pesticides Told." February 12: C1.

———. 1976b. "4 Agencies Discriminate on Loans, Suit Claims." April 28: 4.

———. 1976c. "EPA Admits Inadequate Readiness." May 5: 4.

———. 1976d. "Memo: FBI Aided '69 Chicago Panther Raid." May 7: 6.

———. 1976e. "Panel: U.S. Still Discriminating." May 12: C5.

———. 1976f. "Panel: Mortgage Bias Laws Unenforced." June 1: 5.

———. 1976g. "Great Lakes Making Slow Recovery From Abuses." June 26: 23.

———. 1976h. "Panel Probe Urged of FBI Role in Black Party Chief's Death." November 27: 34.

———. 1976i. "Black Panthers Sue FBI, CIA, IRS." December 2: 2.

———. 1977a. "Investigators Say Texaco Withholding Natural Gas Production." February 23: A1, 20.

———. 1977b. "Panel: Gulf Broke Law, Withheld Gas." February 24: A1, 24.

———. 1977c. "Records Show Chicago Police Spied on Iranian Students." March 10: 6.

——. 1977d. "Chemical Fumes Blamed For Illnesses Along Ohio." April 1: 10.

——. 1977e. "Files Show FBI Wiretapping, Possible Burglary of Lawyers." August 25: 9.

——. 1977f. "CIA Reveals Bizarre Experiment." August 26: 9.

——. 1977g. "FBI Paid Informers for Socialist Data." September 21: 5.

——. 1977h. "Hanna Indicted for Bribe." October 15: 1 and 14.

——. 1977i. "Political Vice Lawyers in Great Demand." October 19.

——. 1977j. "ABA Helped FBI In Guild Action." October 24: 10A.

——. 1977k. "Bribery Made Criminal Act." November 2: 4.

——. 1977l. "Cointelpro." November 22: 6.

——. 1977m. "FBI's 'Dirty Tricks' Tactics Made Public." November 23: 1, 18.

——. 1977n. "FBI Planted Slanted KKK Newspaper Stories." November 23: 7.

——. 1977o. "Carter Nominee Refuses to Disclose Oil Clients." December 1.

——. 1978a. "Justice Department Details Abuses by Hoover, Others." January 11: 1, 16.

——. 1978b. "Carter To Limit Arms Sales To Some Countries." February 2: 2.

——. 1978c. "Study of Low-Level Radiation Causing Quite a Stir." February 20: 6.

——. 1978d. "Senator Wants Inquiry of Shipworker's Health." February 20: 7.

——. 1978e. "The Kepone War." February 28: 4B.

——. 1978f. "Congressman Admits Guilt in $200,000 Fraud Scheme." March 18: 5.

——. 1978g. "High Court Ruling Opens Way for Kent State Retrial." March 21: 8.

——. 1978h. "Former Head of FBI Indicted." April 11: 1, 2.

——. 1978i. "Mideast Arms Package Submitted to Congress." April 29: 1, 18.

——. 1978j. "Power of Presidency a Spy Trial Issue." April 30: A2.

——. 1978k. "Plea Bargaining Possibilities Explored by Passman Attorneys." May 7: A10.

——. 1978l. "Oil and Gas Lawyer OK'd for Energy Post." May 10: 4.

Clinard, Marshall B., and Richard Quinney. 1973. *Criminal Behavior Systems: A Typology*. New York: Holt, Rinehart, and Winston.

Clausen, Oliver. 1967. "Boys Without a Country." *New York Times Magazine*, May 21: 25–34.

Cockburn, Alexander. 1974. "Sweet Mysteries of Watergate." *New York Review of Books* 21 (November 28): 8–16.

Cockburn, Alexander and James Ridgeway. 1977. "Carter's Powerless Energy Policy." *New York Review of Books* 24 (March 26): 31–36.

Coleman, James. 1978. "Power and the Structure of Society." In *Corporate and Government Deviance*, eds. M. Ermann and R. Lundman. New York: Oxford University Press.

Columbia Law Review. 1973. "The Espionage Statutes and Publication of Defense Information." 73 (May).

Commager, Henry S. 1972. "The Case for Amnesty." *New York Review of Books* 18 (April 6): 23–25.

——. 1976. "Is 'Intelligence' Constitutional?" *New York Review of Books* 23 (September 30): 32–37.

Commercial Appeal (Memphis, Tennessee) (United Press International) 1975a. "Spy Plan Used, Church Says." September 24: 8.

——. 1975b. "Senate Panel Discloses 238 Burglaries In Checking on Groups." September 26: 1.

——. 1975c. "Move to Trim Pollution Laws Blasted by Environmentalists." September 28: 13.

——. 1976a. "FBI Stalked Women's Drive 2 Years, Documents Show." March 12: 28.

——. 1976b. "First Federal Officers Indicted for Wiretap." March 12: 28.

——. 1976c. "FBI Documents Reveal 92 Burglaries in 60s of Socialist's Offices." March 29: 1.

——. 1976d. "FBI Agent Says Break-Ins Authorized." July 29: 12.

———. 1977. "Illegal Donations Cost Gulf a $229,500 Fine." November 12: 22.

Conot, Robert. 1974. "A Little Bit of Crud." *New York Times Book Review*, September 22: 4–5.

Commission to Investigate Alleged Police Corruption. 1971. *Interim Report on Investigative Phase* (July 1). New York.

Cook, Fred J. 1966. *The Corrupted Land: The Social Morality of Modern America*. New York: MacMillan.

Crewdson, John. 1976. "FBI Said to Yield Stolen Record." *New York Times*, August 1: 1, 33.

Crider, Bill. 1975. "Offshore Drilling Art Born Off Louisiana Coast." *Clarion-Ledger* (Jackson, Mississippi), October 12: H7.

Cummings, John and Drew Fetherston. 1976. "Army Germ Warfare Tests on U.S. Cities Tied to Death, Diseases." *Des Moines Register*, December 22: 1, 2.

D'Amato, A. H., H. Gould, and L. Woods. 1969. "War Crimes and Vietnam: The 'Nuremburg Defense' and the Military Service Resister." *California Law Review* 57 (November): 1055–110.

Davis, Angela. 1971. "Political Prisoners, Prisons, and Black Liberation." In *If They Come In the Morning*, eds. A. Davis et al. New York: Signet.

Denzin, Norman K. 1977. "Notes on the Crimogenic Hypothesis: A Case Study of the American Liquor Industry." *American Sociological Review* 42 (December): 905–20.

Domhoff, G. William. 1970. *The Higher Circles*. New York: Random House.

———. 1974. *The Bohemian Grove and Other Retreats*. New York: Harper and Row.

———. 1978. *Who Really Rules?* New Brunswick, New Jersey: Transaction Books.

Douglas, Jack D. and John M. Johnson. 1977. *Official Deviance: Readings in Malfeasance, Misfeasance, and Other Forms of Corruption*. Philadelphia: J. B. Lippincott Company.

Dudar, Helen. 1977. "The Price of Blowing the Whistle." *New York Times Magazine*, October 30: 41–54.

Ehrlich, Paul and Anne H. Ehrlich. 1972. *Population/Resources/Environment: Issues in Human Ecology.* 2d ed. San Francisco: W. H. Freeman and Company.

Emerick, Kenneth. 1972. *War Resisters Canada.* Knox, Pennsylvania: Pennsylvania Free Press.

Engler, Robert. 1967. *The Politics of Oil: A Study of Private Power and Democratic Directions.* Chicago: University of Chicago Press.

———. 1977. *The Brotherhood of Oil: Energy Policy and the Public Interest.* Chicago: University of Chicago Press.

Engquist, Virginia and Frances S. Coles. 1970. "'Political' Criminals in America: O'Hare (1923); Contine and Rainer (1950)." *Issues in Criminology* 5 (Summer): 209-20.

Ermann, M. David and Richard J. Lundman. 1978. *Corporate and Government Deviance: Problems of Organizational Behavior in Contemporary Society.* New York: Oxford University Press.

Falk, Richard. 1975. "CIA Covert Intervention and International Law" *Society* 12 (March/April): 39-44.

Fensterwald, Bernard, Jr. 1977. *Assassination of JFK: By Coincidence or Conspiracy?* New York: Kensington Publishing Corporation.

Ferdinand, Theodore N. 1966. *Typologies of Delinquency.* New York: Random House.

Ferrari, Robert. 1919. "Political Crime and Criminal Evidence." *Minnesota Law Review* 3: 365.

Fitzgerald, Ernest. 1973. "The Pentagon as the Enemy of Capitalism." *World*, February 27: 18-21.

Foner, Eric. 1977. "Get a Lawyer." *New York Review of Books* 24 (April 24): 37-39.

Franklin, Ben A. 1967. "Protesters Defying Deadline Seized in Capital." *New York Times*, October 23: 1, 32.

———. 1970. "Federal Computers Amass Files on Suspect Citizens." *New York Times*, October 23: 1, 32.

Galliher, John F. and James L. McCartney. 1977. *Criminology: Power, Crime and Criminal Law.* Homewood, Illinois: Dorsey.

Gardiner, John A. 1970. *The Politics of Corruption.* New York: Russell Sage Foundation.

Gaylin, Willard. 1970. *In the Service of Their Country*. New York: Random House.

Gerassi, John. 1968. *North Vietnam: A Documentary History*. Indianapolis: Bobbs-Merrill.

Gerstenzang, James. 1978. "Carter Blasts Russia: Says USSR Shipping Arms." *Clarion-Ledger* (Jackson, Mississippi), January 13: 1, 16.

Goeller, David. 1978. "Agnew Case Kept Secret From Nixon." *Clarion-Ledger* (Jackson, Mississippi), March 4: 1, 22.

Goffman, Erving. 1959. *The Presentation of Self in Everyday Life*. Garden City, New York: Doubleday Anchor.

Goldfarb, Ronald. 1974. *Jails: The Ultimate Ghetto of the Criminal Justice System*. Garden City, New York: Anchor.

Gordon, David M. 1975. "Recession is Capitalism as Usual." *New York Times Magazine*, April 27: 18–19.

——. 1976. "Class and the Economics of Crime." In *Whose Law? What Order?* eds. W. Chambliss and M. Mankoff. New York: Wiley.

Green, Mark J. 1972. *The Closed Enterprise System: Ralph Nader's Study Group Report on Antitrust Enforcement*. New York: Grossman.

Green, Mark J., James Fallows, Bruce Rosenthal, and David Zwick. 1972. *Who Runs Congress?* New York: Bantam.

Green, Mark J., Bruce Rosenthal, David R. Zwick, James M. Fallows, and Lynn Darling. 1975. *Who Runs Congress?* New York: Bantam.

Gwirtzman, Milton S. 1975. "Is Bribery Defensible?" *New York Times Magazine*, October 5: 19, 100–10.

Hager, Barry M. 1977. "Business Roundtable Lobby Winning Victories in Congress." *Clarion-Ledger* (Jackson, Mississippi), September 30: 13A.

Halloran, Richard. 1977a. "Korean Probe and Why It Dragged On." *New York Times*, June 12: 4.

——. 1977b. "Influencing Policymakers Was Always the Aim." *New York Times*, December 4: E5.

Hancock, Kelly and Don G. Gibbons. 1975. "The Future of Crime in American Society." Unpublished manuscript, Department of Sociology, Portland State University.

Hempel, Carl C. 1952. "Typological Methods in the Natural and the Social Sciences." *Proceedings of the American Philosophical Association, Eastern Division*, part I. Philadelphia: University of Pennsylvania Press.

Henderson, William and Larry C. Ledebur. 1970. *Economic Disparity: Problems and Strategies for the Black American*. New York: Free Press.

Henry, Diane. 1978. "Illegal Wiretapping Ascribed to Police by New Haven Panel." *New York Times*, January 29: 23.

Hersh, Seymour. 1974. "Huge CIA Operation Reported in U.S. Against Anti-war Forces, Other Dissidents in Nixon Years." *New York Times*, December 22: 1 and 26.

Hershey, Robert D. 1977. "Payoffs: Are they Stopped or Just Better Hidden?" *New York Times*, January 9: NES 23.

Hicks, Nancy. 1976. "Study Links Deaths in 5–Year Period to Jobless Stress." *Commercial Appeal* (Memphis, Tennessee), October 31: A5.

Hill, Gladwin. 1977. "Pollution: Cost Becomes a Factor." *New York Times*, January 9: NES 39.

Hoenig, Gary. 1977. "Four Years for Gov. Mandel." *New York Times*. October 9: E6.

Horrock, Nicholas. 1975. "IRS Is Now Collecting Much More than Taxes." *New York Times*, April 20: E4.

——. 1976. "Car Burnings and Assaults on Radicals Linked to FBI Agents in Last 5 Years." *New York Times*, July 11: 20.

——. 1977. "Files on CIA Drug-Testing Work Said to List 'Prominent' Doctors." *New York Times*, July 17: 48.

——. 1978. "'Agents' in Academia Are Recruiting Spies." *New York Times*, January 1: E3.

Horowitz, Irving Louis. 1970. *The Struggle is the Message*. Berkeley: Glendessary Press.

Hovey, Harold A. 1966. *United States Military Assistance*. New York: Praeger.

Inciardi, James A. 1975. *Careers in Crime*. Chicago: Rand-McNally.

Ingraham, B. and Kazuhiko Tokoro. 1969. "Political Crime in the United States and Japan." *Issues in Criminology* 4 (Spring): 145–70.

Jabs, Cynthia. 1976. "Timberland Rules Tighten." New York *Times*, February 8: F4.

Jackson, Brooks. 1978. "Watergate Prosecutors Dropped Justice Probe." *Clarion-Ledger* (Jackson, Mississippi), January 22: 3.

Jackson, Robert. 1976. "IRS Said to Have Violated Law." Jackson *Daily News* (Jackson, Mississippi), June 30: 10.

Jackson Daily News (Jackson, Mississippi) (Associated Press) 1976a. "NSA Said 'Eavesdropping.'" May 12: 11.

———. 1976b. "NRC Doesn't Regulate Nuclear Power." October 27: 3.

———. 1976c. "Nader Group Says IRS Soft on Audits." November 15: 14.

Jacobsen, Michael. 1974. *Nutrition Scoreboard: Your Guide to Better Eating.* Washington: Center for Science in the Public Interest.

Jensen, Michael C. 1976a. "Business Builds Its Political War Chest—Legally." *New York Times*, May 28: F2.

———. 1976b. "G.E.'s Campaign Chest." *New York Times*, May 16: F1 and F5.

———. 1976c. "Where the Corporate Money Goes." *New York Times*, May 16: F5.

———. 1978. "Tobacco, A Potent Lobby." *New York Times*, February 19: section 3, 1-4.

Johnston, Richard L. 1964. "Butenko and Ivanov Guilty in Spy Case." *New York Times*, December 3: 1, 8.

Jones, William H. 1975. "U.S. Aided Lockheed Dealings." *Washington Post*, September 12: 1, 4.

Kaiser, Robert G. 1978. "Arms Sales Policy Tests Strength of 'Israeli Lobby.'" *Clarion-Ledger* (Jackson, Mississippi), March 10: E1.

Kandel, Jonathan. 1978. "European Arms Exports Growing." *New York Times*, April 2: 1, 4.

Karber, Phillip A. 1971. "Urban Terrorism: Baseline Data and a Conceptual Framework." *Social Science Quarterly* 52 (December): 521-40.

Karmen, Andrew. 1974. "Agents Provocateurs in the Contemporary U.S. Leftist Movement." In *The Criminologist: Crime and the Criminal*, ed. C. Reasons. Pacific Palisades, California: Goodyear.

Kempster, Norman. 1978. "Carter Imposes List of Restrictions on CIA." *Clarion-Ledger* (Jackson, Mississippi), January 25: 1, 10.

Kessler, Ronald. 1978. "GSA, FBI Seeking Corruption." *Clarion-Ledger* (Jackson, Mississippi), March 5: A15.

Kirchheimer, Otto. 1961. *Political Justice: The Use of Legal Procedure for Political Ends*. Princeton: Princeton University Press.

Kissinger, Henry A. 1975. Statement Before the International Relations Committee on Security Assistance. November 6.

Kohlmeier, Louis. 1976. "Price-Fixing in the Professions." *New York Times*, April 18: F3.

Kolko, Gabriel. 1962. *Wealth and Power in America*. New York: Praeger.

———. 1963. *The Triumph of Conservatism*. London: The Free Press.

———. 1969. *The Roots of American Foreign Policy*. Boston: Beacon.

Kraft, Joseph. 1975. "Cloudy Oil Issue Covers the Gulf." *Commercial Appeal* (Memphis, Tennessee), October 4.

Ladner, George. 1976. "Senate Report Says FBI Still 'Breaking In.'" *Jackson Daily News* (Jackson, Mississippi), May 12: 9.

Lampman, Robert. 1962. *The Share of Top Wealth-Holders in National Wealth*. Princeton, N.J.: Princeton University Press.

Leary, Mary. 1978. "California Vote Signals Growing Taxpayer Revolt." *Clarion-Ledger* (Jackson, Mississippi), May 24: 5B.

Leinsdorf, David and Donald Etra. 1973. *Citibank: Ralph Nader's Study Group Report on First National City Bank*. New York: Grossman.

Lieberman, Jethro. 1972. *How the Government Breaks the Law*. New York: Stein and Day.

Lieuwen, Edwin. 1967. *Arms and Politics in Latin America*. New York: Praeger.

Lindblom, Charles E. 1977. *Politics and Markets: the World's Political-Economic Systems*. New York: Basic Books.

Lindsay, Mike. 1977. "After the B–1, a New Scramble for Arms Deals." *New York Times*, September 4: F6–7.

London *Times*. 1966. "Undisclosed Number of Patton Tanks Sent to Israel." February 7: 9.

Los Angeles *Times*. 1975. "FBI Admits it Opened Mail in 8 Cities in Illegal Program Parallel to that of CIA." October 2: 1.

Lubash, Arnold H. 1976. "316 Used by FBI In Informer Role." New York *Times*, September 5: 24.

Lundberg, Ferdinand. 1968. *The Rich and The Super Rich*. New York: Bantam.

McArdle, Catherine. 1964. *The Role of Military Assistance in the Problem of Arms Control: The Middle East, Latin America, and Africa*. Cambridge, Massachusetts: Center for International Studies.

McCarthy, Eugene. 1967. "Arms and the Man Who Sells Them." *Atlantic Monthly*, October: 82–86.

McCarthy, Mary. 1974. "Watergate." *New York Review of Books* 21 (April 4): 6–8.

McKee, Michael and Ian Robertson. 1975. *Social Problems*. Kingsport, Tennessee: Kingsport Press.

McKinney, John C. 1966. *Constructive Typology and Social Theory*. New York: Appleton-Century-Crofts.

Marchetti, Victor and John D. Marks. 1974. *The CIA and the Cult of Intelligence*. New York: Dell.

Marcuse, Herbert. 1969. *Essay on Liberation*. Boston: Beacon.

Marro, Anthony. 1976. "FBI Black Bag Jobs." *The New Republic* 175 (July 17): 13–14.

———. 1977. "Helms, Ex–CIA Chief Pleads No Contest To 2 Misdemeanors." *New York Times*, November 1: 1.

Marx, Gary. 1977. "Civil Disorder and Agents of Social Control." In *Official Deviance: Readings in Malfeasance, Misfeasance, and Other Forms of Corruption*, eds. J. Douglas and J. Johnson. Philadelphia: J. B. Lippincott. Company.

Meadows, Donnella H., et al. 1972. *The Limits to Growth*. New York: Signet.

Merton, Robert and Robert Nisbet. 1971. *Contemporary Social Problems*. New York: Harcourt Brace Jovanovich.

Messick, Hank. 1968. *Syndicate in the Sun*. New York: MacMillan.

Meyer, Karl and Tad Szulc. 1962. *The Cuban Invasion*. New York: Praeger.

Mills, C. Wright. 1967. *The Power Elite*. New York: Oxford University Press.

Minor, W. William. 1975. "Political Crime, Political Justice, and Political Prisoners." *Criminology* 12 (February): 385-98.

Mintz, Morton. 1976. "Regulations Fail to Prevent Serious Drug Abuse." *Clarion-Ledger* (Jackson, Mississippi), July 4: A10.

Mintz, Morton and Jerry Cohen. 1971. *America, Inc.* New York: Dial.

Molotch, Harvey. 1973. "Oil in Santa Barbara and Power in America." In *Deviance, Conflict, and Criminality*, ed. S. Denisoff and C. McCaghy. New York: Rand McNally.

Moran, Richard. 1977. "Awaiting the Crown's Pleasure: The Case of Daniel M'Naughton." *Criminology* 15 (1): 7-26.

Morris, Roger. 1975. "The Aftermath of CIA Intervention." *Society* 12 (March/April): 76-80.

Mouledoux, Joseph C. 1975. "Political Crime and the Negro Revolution." In *Criminal Behavior Systems: A Typology*, eds. M. Clinard and R. Quinney. New York: Holt, Rinehart, and Winston.

Nation. 1969. "To American Servicemen in Europe." 205 (November 13): 487-91.

National Committee for the Defense of Joanne Cheismard and Clark Squire. 1972. "Break de Chains." Pamphlet. New York City.

Niederhoffer, Arthur. 1969. *Behind the Shield: The Police in Urban Society*. Garden City, New York: Anchor Books.

Newsweek. 1970. "Rx for Draft Dodgers." 76 (August 3): 42-43.

———. 1971. "Cops on the Take." 78 (November 1): 48-53.

New York Times. 1960. "Soviet U.N. Aide and Artist Held Here As Spies Seeking Air Photos of Chicago." October 28: 1-2.

———. 1963a. "U.S. Exchanges 2 Russian Spies For 2 Americans." October 12: 1, 6.

———. 1963b. "Jersey Engineer and Russian Arrested in Spy Case Involving Air Force Data." October 30: 1, 5.

———. 1964a. "U.S. Drops Trial of 2 in Spy Case; Cites 'Security.'" October 3: 1.

——. 1964b. "2 Accused As Spies Deported By U.S." October 16: 3.

——. 1964c. "Butenko and Ivanov Guilty in Spy Case." December 3: 1, 8.

——. 1964d. "Butenko and Ivanov Given Long Terms." December 19: 1, 13.

——. 1966a. "Israelis Will Buy U.S. Jet Bombers." May 20: 1, 10.

——. 1966b. "The Starfighter Affair: West German Factions Use a Warplane As a Political Weapon." August 30: 7.

——. 1966c. "Retired Colonel Pleads Guilty in Soviet Agent Plot." December 17: 14.

——. 1966d. "U.S. Giving Jordan Arms to Bolster Her Against Israel." December 27: 1, 5.

——. 1967a. "Ex-Officer Given 15-Year Term For Supplying Secrets to Soviets." March 2: 16.

——. 1967b. "Baker Convicted On 7 of 9 Counts; Plans to Appeal." January 30: 18.

——. 1968. "Defense Department Bars Role in Paris Air Show During 1969." February 8: 6.

——. 1969. "Teachers Ranks Swollen by Men Avoiding Draft." January 7: E2.

——. 1970. "Health Cost of Environmental Misuse Estimated at $35 Billion a Year." October 7: 33.

——. 1971a. "Black Separatists Raided in Jackson, Miss.; 3 Lawmen Wounded." August 19: 27.

——. 1971b. "Oil Companies Agree to Pay Beach Front Owners For Oil Slick." November 26: 41.

——. 1974a. "Granddaughter of Hearst Abducted by 3." February 6: 1, 44.

——. 1974b. "Atlanta Constitution Editor Kidnapped; 'Revolutionary Army' Seeks $700,000." February 22: 1.

——. 1974c. "$9 Million Ends Suit On Oil Spill." July 24: 44.

——. 1975a. "Geological Survey Is Scored by GAO On Aides' Holdings." March 5: 18.

——. 1975b. "The Dark Side of the IRS." October 5: E2.

———. 1975c. "FPC is Accused of Laxity on Gas." October 20: 53, 56.

———. 1976a. "Excerpts From Senate's Intelligence Report." April 29: 31-33.

———. 1976b. "The World's Political Jails." October 3: E2.

———. 1977a. "Alarm Sounds and CIA Wakes Up in Nightmare Alley." August 7: section 4, 1.

———. 1977b. "New Intelligence on Intelligence Agency Abuses." August 14: E3.

———. 1977c. "U.S. Fines Gulf Oil for Free Trips." November 23: section D, 1.

———. 1977d. "CIA Documents Reveal Presence of Agents on 'Problem' Campuses." December 18: 68.

———. 1977e. "The CIA's 3-Decade Effort To Mold the World's Views." December 25: 1, 12.

———. 1978a. "Judge Orders U.S. to Pay and Apologize to Lamont For Opening His Letters." February 19: 32.

———. 1978b. "Detroit Stunned by Recall Blitz." March 12: section 3, 1.

———. 1978c. "Hancho Kim is Guilty in Bribe Plot." April 9: 1, 23.

New York Times Magazine. 1971. "Murphy Among the Meat Eaters." December 19: 44.

———. 1976. "The Trial of the CIA." September 12:

Ostrow, Ronald J. 1978. "ITT Executives Indicted." *Clarion-Ledger* (Jackson, Mississippi), March 21: 1 and 12A.

Packard, Vance. 1964. *The Naked Society.* New York: McKay.

Packer, Herbert. 1962. "Offenses Against the State." *Annals of the American Academy of Political and Social Science* 339: 77-89.

Patman Committee. 1972. "Investments and Major Interlocks Between Major Banks and Major Corporations." In *American Society, Inc.* ed. M. Zeitlin. Chicago: Markham.

Petras, James and Morris Morley. 1975. *The United States and Chile.* New York: Monthly Review Press.

Powers, Thomas. 1972. "The Government is Watching." *Atlantic* 230 (October): 51-63.

President's Commission on Law Enforcement and Administration of Justice. 1967. *Task Force: The Police*. Washington, D.C.: Government Printing Office.

Proxmire, William. 1978. "The Foreign Payoff Law Is a Necessity." *New York Times*, March 5: F16.

Quinney, Richard. 1974. *Critique of Legal Order*. Boston: Little, Brown and Company.

———. 1975. *Criminology*. Boston: Little, Brown and Company.

———. 1977. *Class, State and Crime*. New York: David McKay Company, Inc.

Quinney, Richard and John Wildeman. 1977. *The Problem of Crime*. New York: Harper and Row.

Rattner, Stephen. 1977. "Public Overcharges Laid to Oil Concerns." *New York Times*, April 29: 1, D10.

Raymond, Jack. 1963. "Four Seized by FBI as Soviet Spies; One on U.N. Staff." *New York Times*, July 3: 1, 5.

Reasons, Charles E. 1974. *The Criminologist: Crime and the Criminal*. Pacific Palisades, California: Goodyear.

Reichley, James. 1973. "Getting at the Roots of Watergate." *Fortune* 88 (1): 90-93, 170-74.

Reinhold, Robert. 1971. "Ellsberg Yields, Is Indicted; Says He Gave Data to Press." *New York Times*, June 29: 1 and 8.

Reiss, Albert J., Jr. 1968. "The Study of Deviant Behavior: Where the Action Is." In *Approaches to Deviance*, ed. James K. Skipper, Mark Lefton, and Charles H. McCaghy. New York: Appleton.

———. 1972. *The Police and the Public*. New Haven: Yale University Press.

Reiss, Albert J. Jr., and Donald J. Black. 1967. "Interrogation and the Criminal Process." *Annals of the American Academy of Political and Social Science* 374: 47-54.

Richards, Bill. 1975. "LSD Used in U.S. Interrogation." *Washington Post*, September 13: 2.

Rienow, Robert and Leona Train Rienow. 1969. *Moment in the Sun*. New York: Ballantine.

Ripley, Anthony. 1973. "Evidence Shows Gifts to Agnew." New York *Times,* October 11: 1.

Roebuck, Julian. 1976. Review of *A Time to Die* by Tom Wicker. *Journal of Criminal Law and Criminology* 67 (1): 127–28.

Roebuck, Julian and Thomas Barker. 1974. "A Typology of Police Corruption." *Social Problems* 24 (3): 423–37.

Roebuck, Julian and Rodney N. Friery. 1975. "A Typology of Objectors to Military Conscription." Unpublished manuscript. Department of Sociology, Mississippi State University.

Roebuck, Julian and Wolfgang Frese. 1976. *The Rendezvous: A Case Study of An After-Hours Club.* New York: The Free Press.

Ross, Thomas. 1975. "Spying in the United States." *Society* 12 (March/April): 64–70.

Rothschild, Emma. 1977a. "The Arms Boom and How to Stop It." *New York Review of Books* 23 (January 20): 24–29.

——. 1977b. "Carter and Arms: No Sale." *New York Review of Books* 24 (September 15): 10–14.

Royko, Mike. 1971. *Boss.* New York: Signet.

Sage, Wayne. 1974. "Crime and the Clockwork Lemon." *Human Behavior.* September 16–28.

St. Louis *Post-Dispatch.* 1976. "FBI Role in Black Gang Warfare." January 5: 1.

Sale, Kirkpatrick. 1973. "The World Behind Watergate." *New York Review of Books* 20 (May 3): 9–15.

——. 1975a. "The Political Underground Is Small, and Often Violent." *New York Times,* October 5: E3.

——. 1975b. "Laying the Dust." *New York Review of Books* 22 (December 11): 5–9.

Sampson, Anthony T. 1973. *The Sovereign State of ITT.* New York: Stein and Day.

——. 1975. *The Seven Sisters.* New York: Viking Press.

——. 1977. *The Arms Bazaar.* New York: Viking Press.

Saturday Evening Post. 1968. "Hell No, We Won't Go." 241 (January 27): 21–26.

Schafer, Stephen. 1971. "The Concept of the Political Criminal." *Journal of Criminal Law, Criminology, and Police Science* 62: 380–87.

———. 1974. *The Political Criminal*. New York: Free Press.

Schlissel, Lillian, ed. 1969. *Conscience in America*. New York: E.P. Dutton and Company.

Schorr, Daniel. 1977. "The Assassins." *New York Review of Books* 24 (October 13): 14–21.

Schroeder, T. 1919. "Political Crime Defined." *Michigan Law Review*, 30: 18.

Schurtzen, Leslie, ed. 1971. *National Draft Counseling Directory*. Chicago: Youth Counseling Foundation.

Securities and Exchange Commission. 1975. *Report of the Special Committee of the Board of Directors of Gulf Oil Corporation*. December 30.

Seeman, Melvin. 1975. "Alienation Studies." In *Annual Review of Sociology*, ed. A. Inkeles, J. Coleman, and N. Smelser. Palo Alto: Annual Reviews, Inc.

Selective Service System. 1970. *Semiannual Report of the Director of Selective Service*. Washington, D.C.: Government Printing Office.

———. 1971. *Semiannual Report of the Director of Selective Service*. Washington, D.C.: Government Printing Office.

Shearer, Lloyd. 1976. "Advisory Committees." *Parade*, May 2: 6.

———. 1977. "On the FBI Front." *Parade*, November 27: 4.

Sherrill, Robert. 1972. *Why They Call It Politics*. New York: Harcourt Brace Jovanovich.

Stark, Rodney. 1969. *Police Riots*. Belmont, CA: Wadsworth.

Stern, Philip M. 1972. "Uncle Sam's Welfare Program For the Rich." *The New York Times Magazine*, pp. 28, 60, 61, 64, 66, 71.

Stockholm International Peace Research Institute. 1977. *World Armaments and Disarmaments Yearbook*. Cambridge, Mass.: MIT Press.

Stockwell, John. 1977. *In Search of Enemies: A CIA Study*. New York: W. W. Norton & Co.

Stoddard, Ellwyn. 1968. "The Informal Code of Police Deviancy: A Group Approach to 'Blue Coat' Crime." *Journal of Criminal Law, Criminology, and Police Science*, 59: 201–13.

Stone, I. F. 1969. "Nixon and the Arms Race: The Bomber Boondoggle." *New York Review of Books* 11 (January 2): 6–10.

———. 1976. "The Schorr Case: The Real Dangers." *New York Review of Books* 23 (April 1): 6–11.

Suttler, David. 1970. *IV-F: A Guide to Draft Exemption*. New York: Grove Press.

Swartz, Joel. 1975. "Silent Killers at Work." *Crime and Social Justice* 3 (Spring-Summer): 15–20.

Sweezy, Paul. 1973. "Galbraith's Utopia." *New York Review of Books* 20 (November 15): 3–6.

Sykes, Gresham M. 1972. "The Future of Criminality." *American Behavioral Scientist* 15 (February): 409–19.

———. 1974. "The Rise of Critical Criminology." *Journal of Criminal Law and Criminology* 65 (June): 206–14.

———. 1978. *Criminology*. Chicago: Harcourt Brace Jovanovich.

Symbionese Liberation Army. 1973. "Declare War." *Berkeley Barb*, August 21: 3.

Tanzer, Michael. 1969. *The Political Economy of International Oil and the Underdeveloped Countries*. Boston: Beacon.

Tatum, Arlo, ed. 1970. *Handbook for Conscientious Objectors*. Philadelphia: Larchwood Press.

Taylor, Telford. 1970. *Nuremburg and Vietnam: An American Tragedy*. Chicago: Quadrangle Books.

Teodori, Massimo. 1969. *The New Left: A Documentary History*. Indianapolis: Bobbs-Merrill.

Thayer, George. 1969. *The War Business*. New York: Simon and Schuster.

Thomas, Jo. 1977. "Extent of University Work for CIA Is Hard to Pin Down." *New York Times*, October 9: 78.

———. 1978. "Audit Shows Agency Hid Its Consultants." *New York Times*, March 12: 17.

Thurow, Lester C. 1976. "Tax Wealth, Not Income." *New York Times Magazine* (April 11): 32–33, 102–07.

Tieded, Saralee. 1978. "Money Can't Replace Life for Asbestos Plant Workers." *Clarion-Ledger* (Jackson, Mississippi), February 20: 7.

Time. 1969. "Helping to Avoid the Draft." 94 (October 10): 57–58.

——. 1975. "A Fateful Trial Closes A Sorry Chapter." January 13: 9–16.

Tully, Andrew. 1962. *CIA, The Inside Story*. New York: William Morrow.

Tulsky, Fredric. 1978. "Demonstrators in Tupelo Vow to Boycott Business." *Clarion-Ledger* (Jackson, Mississippi), March 19: 1, 16A.

Turk, Austin T. 1975. *Political Criminality and Political Policing*. New York: MSS Modular Publishers.

Turner, Jonathan and Charles E. Starnes. 1976. *Inequality: Privilege and Poverty in America*. Pacific Palisades, California: Goodyear.

Tybor, Joseph. 1978a. "FBI Kept Files on 27,000 Chicagoans." *Clarion-Ledger* (Jackson, Mississippi), January 21: 1, 4.

——. 1978b. "FBI Has More Spies Than Number It Admitted." *Clarion-Ledger* (Jackson, Mississippi), May 7: 1.

U.S. Department of Defense. 1976. *Foreign Military Sales Agreements* (November).

U.S. Department of Labor. 1972. *Report to the President on Occupational Health*. (May).

——. 1975. *Foreign Defense Sales and Grants, Fiscal Year 1974–1975; Labor and Material Requirements*. Bureau of Labor Statistics.

U.S. Department of State. 1977. *Report to Congress on Arms Transfer Policy* (June).

U.S. District Court for the District of Columbia. 1975. *Securities and Exchange Commission* v. *Gulf Oil Corporation et al.*, Civil Action No. 75–0324, March 11.

U.S. House of Representatives. 1971. Advisory Committees. *Hearings before the Subcommittee on Intergovernmental Relations, Committee on Government Operations*, Part 2.

——. 1974a. *Access to Records*. Washington, D.C.: Government Printing Office.

———. 1974b. *Terrorism*. Washington, D.C.: Government Printing Office.

———. 1975. *Impeachment of Richard M. Nixon, President of the United States*. New York: Bantam.

U.S. News and World Report. 1971. "Millions Who Avoided the Draft." 70 (March 1): 33.

———. 1977. "Nations Taxpayers Are Getting Angry—And Getting Organized." (April 25).

U.S. Senate. 1962. *Final Report, Senate Small Business Committee*. Senate Report 25. Washington, D.C.

———. 1967. *Arms Sales to Near East and South Asian Countries*. Hearings before the Subcommittee on Near Eastern and South Asian Affairs of the Committee on Foreign Relations, March 14–June 22.

———. 1973a. *Hearings Before the Select Committee on Nutrition and Human Needs*. Washington, D.C.: Government Printing Office.

———. 1973b. *Disclosure of Corporate Ownership*. Committee on Government Operations, Subcommittees on Intergovernmental Relations, and Budgeting, Management, and Expenditures. 93rd. Congress, Washington, D.C. pp. 129–33.

———. 1973c. *Preliminary FTC Staff Report, Investigation of the Petroleum Industry*. Permanent Subcommittee on Investigations, Committee on Common Government Operations, 93rd Congress, 1st Session, Washington, D.C.

———. 1974a. *The Senate Watergate Report*. Vol. 1. Pinebrook, N.J.: Dell.

———. 1974b. *Military Surveillance*. Hearings of the Subcommittee on Constitutional Rights of the Committee on the Judiciary. April 9 and 10. Washington, D.C.

———. 1974c. *Hearings on Multinational Petroleum Corporations and Foreign Policy*. Committee on Foreign Relations, Subcommittee on Multinational Corporations. Washington, D.C.

———. 1974d. *U.S. Policy Toward Cuba*. Hearings before the Subcommittee on Western Hemisphere Affairs of the Committee on Foreign Relations. 93rd Congress, 1st Session, Washington, D.C.

———. 1975. *Report on Multinational Corporations and U.S. Foreign Policy*. Senate Foreign Relations Committee, Subcommittee on Multinational Corporations. 93rd Congress, 2nd Session, Washington, D.C. Part 9.

———. 1976. *Intelligence Activities and the Rights of Americans*, Part II. Select Committee to Study Governmental Operations with Respect to Intelligence Activities. Report 94-755, April 26: 1-20.

University of Michigan Survey Research Center. 1960. *1960 Survey of Consumer Finances*. Ann Arbor: Survey Research Center.

Vanderbilt Law Review. 1971. "Warrantless Wiretapping of Suspected Domestic Dissident Group's Conversation Violates Fourth Amendment." 24: 1289-95.

Vanik, Charles. 1976. "Corporate Tax Study, 1976." *Congressional Record*. Proceedings and Debates of the 94th Congress, 2nd Session, Vol. 122, No. 151, Part III, October 1: H12327-J12331.

Vidal, Gore. 1972. "Homage to Daniel Shays." *New York Review of Books* 29 (August 10): 8-12.

Vidich, Arthur J. 1977. "Political Legitimacy in Bureaucratic Society: An Analysis of Watergate." In *Official Deviance: Readings in Malfeasance, Misfeasance, and Other Forms of Corruption*, eds. J. Douglas and J. Johnson. Philadelphia: J.B. Lippincott.

Viorst, Milton. 1976. "FBI Mayhem." *New York Review of Books* 23 (March 18): 21-28.

Vold, George. 1958. *Theoretical Criminology*. New York: Oxford University Press.

Von Hoffman, Nicholas. 1976. "Unasked Questions." *New York Review of Books* 23 (June 10): 3-7.

Wald, Patricia. 1967. "Poverty and Criminal Justice." In *The President's Commission on Law Enforcement and Administration of Justice*. Washington, D.C.: Government Printing Office.

Waldman, Michael. 1973. "The Revolutionary as Criminal in 19th Century France: A Study of the Communards and 'Deportes.'" *Science and Society* 37 (1): 31-55.

Walker, Daniel. 1969. *Rights in Conflict*. Washington, D.C.: Government Printing Office.

Wall, Robert. 1972. "Special Agent for the FBI." *New York Review of Books* 18 (January 27): 12-18.

Wall Street Journal. 1972. "Santa Barbara Fines 4 Oil Firms $500 Each For Polluting Waters." January 12: 8.

Washington Post. 1968. "Government Aide Solicited Support From Oil Industry for Promotion." December 11: A15.

Wehr, Elizabeth. 1974. "Administration In Drug War With Hostile Drug Industry." *Clarion-Ledger* (Jackson, Mississippi), April 23: F4.

Wehrwein, Austin C. 1961. "Soviet Spy Suspect Freed By U.S. to Better Relations." *New York Times*, March 25: 1 and 6.

Weissman, Stephen R. 1975. "Senate Details, Deplores CIA's Murder Plots." *New York Times*, November 23f: 1.

Westley, William A. 1970. *Violence and the Police: A Sociological Study of Law, Custom and Morality*. Cambridge, Massachusetts: MIT Press.

Wheeler, Stanton. 1976. "Trends and Problems in the Sociological Study of Crime." *Social Problems* 23: 525-34.

Wicker, Tom. 1975. *A Time to Die*. New York: Quadrangle Press and The New York Times Book Co.

——. 1977. "Hanging On To the Tail of a Bear." *New York Times*, February 22: 31.

Wilson, James Q. 1970. *Varieties of Police Behavior*. New York: Antheneum.

Winfrey, Carey. 1978. "Again, the Ethics of Medical Research." *New York Times*, March 5: E31.

Wise, David. 1975. "Cloak and Dagger Operations: An Overview." *Society* 12 (March/April): 26-32.

——. 1976. "The Campaign to Destroy Martin Luther King." *New York Review of Books* 23 (November 11): 38-42.

——. 1977. *The American Police State*. New York: Random House.

Wise, David and Thomas Ross. 1964. *The Invisible Government*. New York: Random House.

NAME INDEX

227

SUBJECT INDEX

race, 70, 90, 92; foreign
military sales, 73, 77, 78;
hard-sale of arms, 22; Starfighters, 74, 89; U.S. arms
companies, 58
Army, 40, 41, 60, 62, 76, 108,
109, 115, 193; Counter-
Intelligence Analysis Division,
115; counter-intelligence operations, 110; intelligence,
109, 118; surveillance program, 109
Arosemena regime, 83
artificial colorings and flavorings, 48
artificial foods, 48
asbestos, 44, 45, 49, 65
Ashland Oil, 56, 88
assassination, 82, 94, 96, 132
Atomic Energy Commission,
47, 149, 180
Attica, 126, 128, 130, 131
Attica Brothers Legal Defense,
131
attorney general, 113, 118
auto recall, 149-50

bacterial experiments, 41, 62,
64, 68
banks, 10, 55, 66, 88, 142,
143, 155, 160, 178
Batista regime, 81
Bay of Pigs, 74, 83, 139
Bechtel Corporation, 56
behavioral engineering, 40
behavioral experiments, 38, 40,
62, 64, 68
Belgium, 74
Berlin Democratic Club, 109-10
Bertrand Russell International
War Crimes Tribunal, 71
black extremists, 97
Black Liberation Army, 94, 95,
96, 98-99
blacklisting, 109

Black Muslims, 29, 35
Black Nationalist movements,
35
Black Panthers, 29, 33, 35, 94,
95, 99, 114
Blackstone Rangers, 33
Black Studies program, 108
blind memo, 30
bombing and arson attacks, 94,
95, 96, 97
boycotting offenses, 136
brainwashing, 38
Brazil, 50, 83, 85
bribery, 8, 22, 70, 86-87, 88-
90, 100, 102-04, 171, 176,
177, 178, 179, 183
British Petroleum Oil Company,
79, 80
bureaucratic corruption, 181
Bureau of Indian Affairs, 188
Bureau of Land Management,
164
Bureau of Mines, 146, 155
Burma, 74
burnings, 95
Business Council, 11
Business Roundtable, 12, 53, 66
Byhalia, Mississippi, 133
bystanders, 126

California, 190, 200
Cambodia, 27, 126-27, 134
campaign contributions, 11, 24,
63, 66, 68, 102, 178, 179
campus disturbances, 97, 132,
133-34; Kent State University,
36, 126-28, 130, 131
Canada, 195
capital gains, 178
capitalist: agents, 7, 16, 17,
22, 138, 139, 142; class, 1,
8-11, 13-16, 66, 68, 98, 138,
185; control, 14; economic
system, 25; goals, 15; ideology,
42, 90; society, 62; system, 16,

criminal conspiracy, 165;
disorderly conduct, 135, 136;
disturbing the peace, 135;
forgery, 99; kidnapping, 99;
murder, 99, 130, 131; perjury, 92, 93, 139, 177, 182;
possession of weapons, 135,
136; robbery, 97, 99; sodomy,
131; theft, 96, 99, 183; vandalism, 99, 132, 135, 136
corporations, 14, 115; corporate
agents, 7, 14, 21, 43, 63, 66,
68-69, 70, 77, 86, 90-91,
118, 138, 182, 183, 185;
corporate monopoly, 152;
corporate officials, 11; corporate polluters, 49; corporate pollution, 49; corporate power, 15; corporate
profit, 91; corporate stock,
10, 155; corporate structure,
53, 62, 67, 86, 92, 184-86,
199; corporate surveillance
activities, 118; corporate
survival, 90; corporate tax
rate, 157-58; corporate team
agents, 164, 182, 184; corporate teams, 68, 69, 92
correctional officers, 128
corruption of authority, 169
Council of Economic Advisors,
51
Council on Economic Development, 11
Council on Foreign Relations, 11
counter-inaugural demonstration
(Washington), 135
counter-intelligence operations,
35, 62
covert propaganda, 22
credit bureaus, 115
credit reports, 116
criminal labeling process, 198
criminal law, 14, 182-83
criminal justice system, 13

criminal statutes, 181
critical criminology, 1
cross burnings, 95
crude oil, 46, 63, 90, 152-53,
154, 156-57, 158
CS gas, 71
Cuba, 74, 81
Customs Bureau, 55

dairy price supports, 166
data banks, 115
Days of Rage, 97
DDT, 45-46
deduction of tangible drilling
costs, 158
Defense Department procurement
officers, 52
Defense Intelligence Agency, 24,
115
Defense Security Assistance
Agency (DSSA), 73
Democratic National Committee
Headquarters, 24
Democratic National Convention
(1968), 6, 35, 36, 108, 126,
134, 135
demonstrations, 25; antibusing,
3, antiwar, 6, 8, 30, 61,
126, 134, 135; civil rights, 3;
mass, 132, 134-35, 137;
political, 135
demonstrators, 6, 35, 126
Department of Agriculture, 146,
185, 186
Department of Defense, 46, 56,
57, 72-73, 76, 77, 87, 89,
106, 150, 185
Department of Health, Education
and Welfare, 43, 54, 97,
115, 188
Department of Interior, 46, 155,
160, 162, 162-64; leasing
policy, 162, 163
Department of Labor, 27, 43,
59, 147

destruction of the environment, 68, 70
detergents, 49
developing countries, 76, 77
dirty money, 171, 172, 173, 175
dirty tricks, 23, 25, 61, 63
disloyal behavior, 99
disloyal opposition, 31
dissenters, 6, 23, 30, 38, 62, 107, 108
District of Columbia police, 115
divestiture of oil, 90
domestic agents, 123
domestic economy, 59, 66
domestic espionage, 119, 124
domestic intelligence operations, 8, 67, 111
domestic security, 25, 113
domestic security investigations, 113
domestic spies, 123-24
domestic surveillance, 64, 82, 110, 113
Dominican Republic, 83
Dow Chemical, 85
draft counselors, 198, 199
draft-law regulations, 192, 199
drug companies, 50, 148, 185
drug experiments, 62, 64, 68
due process of law, 130, 167
dummy invoices, 88

economic imperialism, 81
economic rewards, 16
economic structure, 7, 157
Ecuador, 83, 85, 91
Egypt, 78
E. I. Dupont Company, 145
embargo, 79, 161
empirical world, 18, 20
employment maintenance, 90
employment rate, 63
enemies list, 27, 62
Energy Research and Development Administration, 144

England, 5, 78
entrapment, 8, 35, 64
Environmental Protection Agency, 65, 144-45, 146
Environmental Protection and Quality Act, 65
Equal Employment Opportunity Commission, 27
espionage, 21, 23, 118-21, 123-24
Esso, 81-82
establishment, 94, 95
ethics committee, 178; House Ethics Committee, 177; Senate Ethics Committee, 177
Ethiopia, 79
ethnic groups, 108
European nations, 58
eutrophication, 45
evaders, 191, 195, 196, 200
executive order prohibiting federal employees from receiving favors (1965), 66
Export-Import Bank of Washington, D.C., 76
expropriation, 83, 84, 94, 96, 98
extortion, 28, 97
Exxon, 23, 88, 155, 157

factory representatives, 150
failure to register as a foreign agent, 103
fall money, 171
false arrest, 130
false consciousness, 183, 184
favorable balance of payments, 78
FBI, 24, 29-34, 35-36, 62, 63, 67, 95, 105-06, 111-13, 114, 121, 122, 139, 141, 142, 165, 178, 179, 181
federal antiriot act (1968), 99
Federal Communications Commission, 143, 178
federal contracts, 179-80

government documents, 18
government team agents, 69,
    92, 182, 184
Grange, 141
group health programs, 151
Grumman Aerospace Corpora-
    tion, 60
Guatemala, 83
guerrilla war, 23, 38, 95
Gulf Oil, 23, 55, 56, 66, 81,
    88, 157, 161, 163
Guyana, 83

Haiphong harbor, 25
harassment, 100
harboring deserters from the
    armed forces, 99
Hartford Life Insurance Com-
    pany, 50
Health and Safety Office of the
    Bureau of Mines, 146
herbicidal chemicals, 71
hexachlora cyclopentadiene, 45
Holmesberg State Prison
    (Philadelphia), 41
House Interstate and Foreign
    Commerce Committee, 54
Hughes Tool Company, 55
Huston Plan, 23, 24-25, 61, 63,
    106, 107
hydrocarbons, 145

ideology, 2, 3, 4, 5, 13, 14, 18,
    30, 31, 62, 95, 109, 117, 132
income, 9, 10
income tax, 157, 183, 187-88
independent oil companies, 154
India, 76
India-Pakistan War (1965), 76
individual tax rates, 157
Indonesia, 74, 79, 83, 85, 89
industrial growth, 62
industrial proletariat, 16
Industrial Workers of the World,
    4

inmates, 128
Insecticide, Fungicide and Ro-
    denticide Act (1947), 146-47
insurrectionaries, 130
intelligence, 121; agents, 82;
    community, 64; division (Jus-
    tice Department), 115; files,
    114; gathering, 31, 70, 105-
    06, 114
interactional settings, 7
interest groups, 13
interlocking bureaucracy, 179
interlocking directorates, 155,
    160
interlocking social circles, 14
Internal Revenue agents, 141
Internal Revenue Code, 189
Internal Revenue Service, 33,
    35, 55, 56, 62, 64, 67, 114,
    148-49, 165, 166, 188, 189;
    audits, 27
international law, 8, 17, 91, 182
International Logistics Negotia-
    tions Section of the Interna-
    tional Security Affairs Division
    of the Defense Department,
    73, 76
International Petroleum Com-
    pany, 81
International Telephone and Tele-
    graph, 23, 24, 50-52, 55, 66,
    83-84, 85, 86, 87, 92; Hart-
    ford merges, 50-51, 66
Interstate Commerce Commis-
    sion, 140-41, 145-46, 186
Iran, 75, 78, 79, 80, 83, 85,
    87, 89, 100, 102-03
Iranian government, 79, 80, 87
Iranian oil, 79-80
Iranian Students Association, 114
Iraq, 80
Iraq National Oil Company, 80
Israel, 75, 78
Italian Christian Democratic
    party, 88

Italian Social Democratic party, 88

Italy, 85, 88

Jackson State University, 126
Japan, 89
John Birch Society, 94, 108
Johns-Manville plant, 44
Joint Economic Committee of Congress, 60
Jordan, 75, 85
junk foods, 48
juristic persons, 7
Justice Department, 51, 52, 92, 104, 113, 141–42, 151, 152, 158, 177, 178, 181; Internal Security Division, 115

Kennedy administration, 30
Kepone, 42, 147–48
kickbacks, 87, 88, 100, 103, 170, 177, 179
Korea, 101
Korean CIA, 101
Korean studies, 101
Ku Klux Klan, 31, 34, 94–95

labeling, 2
labor disputes, 97
laissez-faire philosophy, 140
land leases, 162
Laos, 27
Latin American countries, 80–81, 82, 83, 84
law and order men, 173
laws prohibiting desecration of the American flag, 99
Lawyers Guild, 112
Lawyers' Military Defense Committee, 110
League of Women Voters, 108
left-wing: organizations, 30–31, 35, 82, 83, 94, 95, 98; regimes, 91
libel laws, 63

Library of Congress, 142
Libyan oil, 156
Life Sciences Corporation, 42, 147
Limits to Growth, The, 42
lobbying, 22, 28, 50, 51–53, 54, 62, 65, 68, 100, 145, 152, 185, 186; corporate lobbyists, 62, 65, 66; foreign lobbyists, 102
Lockheed (Aircraft Co.), 56, 57, 60, 74, 86, 87, 89, 185
loitering and trespassing, 135
looting, 99, 132

magnesium, 48
mail: covers, 24, 113; fraud, 102, 103, 179, 183; surveillance, 106
managerial agents, 15
managerial class, 15
Manila, 74
manipulation, 22, 23, 28, 48, 66, 82, 87, 94
manufacture of evidence, 8
Marshall and Isley Bank Stock Corporation, 178
Massachusetts congressional delegation, 60
mass media, 14, 67, 85, 135
McDonnell Douglas Corporation, 89
means of production, 11
medical associations, 151, 152
Mercurio, 84
mercury pesticides, 45
Middle East, 75, 78, 79, 80, 88, 153, 156
middlemen, 86, 87, 89
military conscription, 187, 190, 191
military-industrial complex, 56–57, 58–59, 63, 66, 68, 72, 73, 76, 78, 90, 92, 103, 134
military taxes, 188, 189

Vietnam Veterans Against
the War, 36, 110
Vietnam war, 16, 23, 25, 34,
70, 77, 90, 91, 92, 122, 123,
124, 134, 135, 136, 190, 191
Vinnell Corporation, 76
violence, 25, 29, 98
Virgin Islands, 83

war: crimes, 16; resisters,
5; War Powers Act, 137
Watergate complexus, 182;
break-in, 24, 166; cover-
up, 139, 166; hearings, 6;
scandal, 18, 67, 118, 139,
165, 182, 183, 184; Special
Prosecution Force, 164-66,
182-83; Special Prosecutor,
183; Special Prosecutor's
Office, 182, 184; tapes, 66
wealth, 9, 10
Weather Underground, 3, 17,
94-95, 96, 97, 99
welfare mothers' organization,
109, 114

Western Electric, 143
Western Enterprise, 74
Western Oil and Gas Association, 163
white-collar crime, 104, 141,
142, 184
white-collar workers, 15-16
white extremists, 97
White House, 24, 25, 26, 27,
66, 84, 106, 107, 117, 163,
166
wiretapping laws, 117
wiretappings, 24, 25, 27, 30,
67, 105, 106, 109, 111, 112,
114, 117, 166
Women's Liberation Movement,
112
Women's Strike for Peace, 196
working class, 11, 13, 63
World Council of Churches, 110
World War II, 72

Young Socialist Alliance, 111

Zaire, 83, 85

ABOUT THE AUTHORS

JULIAN B. ROEBUCK, Ph.D., is Professor of Sociology in the Department of Sociology at Mississippi State University. He has contributed several books, monographs, and articles to the fields of criminology and deviant behavior.

STANLEY C. WEEBER, M.A., has contributed several articles and papers to the fields of criminology and deviant behavior. He was awarded first place in the International Student Research Paper Forum at the American Society of Criminology Meetings in 1975 for his paper, "Political Crime."

RELATED TITLES
Published by
Praeger Special Studies

DECISIONS FOR SALE: Corruption and Reform in
Land-Use and Building Regulation

> John A. Gardiner
> Theodore R. Lyman

INTERNATIONAL TERRORISM: National, Regional and
Global Perspectives

> edited by
> Yonah Alexander

*PUBLIC LAW AND PUBLIC POLICY

> edited by
> John A. Gardiner

*Also available in paperback.